Photography in the Digital Age

Volume I
The Art of Image Capture

by
Hugh J. Lawton

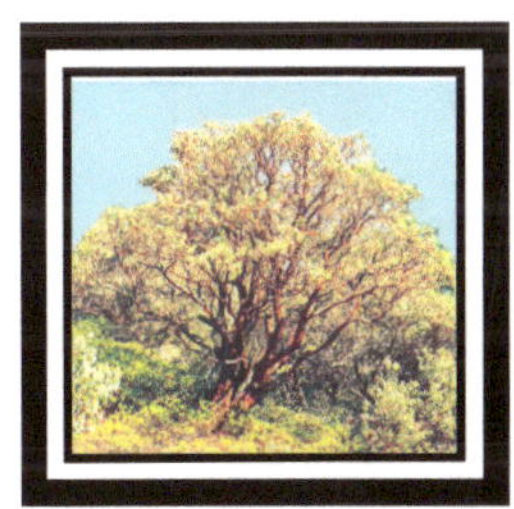

Published by Manzanita Press

Dedication

This work is dedicated to the three most important women in my life:

For My Dear Mother
Eloise Eileen Lawton
Who Gave Me the Gift of Photography

And

For My Beloved
Michelle Kitman Yan
Who Stayed By Me Through Good Times and Bad

And

For My Cherished Daughter
Katherine Alexis Lessin
Who Gave Me the Gift of Joy

Photography in the Digital Age
Volume I – The Art of Image Capture

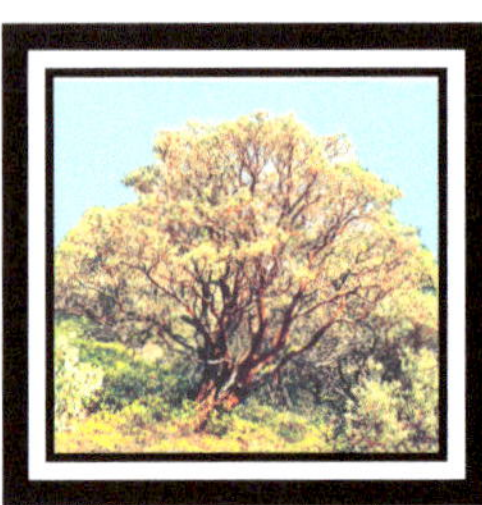

Manzanita Press
Post Office Box 520
Morton, Washington 98564
U.S.A

Unattributed quotations are by Hugh J. Lawton

Library of Congress Cataloging-in-Publication Data:
Lawton, Hugh J.
Photography in the Digital Age – Volume I The Art of Image Capture
by Hugh J. Lawton

Edited by Kris Ashley
Cover Design by Veronica Dabis
Indexing by Angela Howard
p. cm.

Edition ISBNs:

Softcover 978-0-9907474-0-6

eBook 978-0-9907474-3-7

Library of Congress Control Number: 2014918720

First Edition 2015
Includes bibliographical references and index.

Table of Contents

Acknowledgements

Since the birth of photography in the middle of the nineteenth century, there have been a legion of excellent photographers who have contributed outstanding work to the evolution of this art form. Although the countless contributors to the art of photography are too numerous to name, pioneers such as Paul Strand, Edward Weston, Dorthea Lange, and Eliot Porter are some of the legendary giants that inspired this volume.

In addition, this volume could not have come to life without the extraordinary editorial contributions from Kris Ashley of Belvedere Editing, the wonderful graphic design contributions from Veronica Dabis of Veronica Van Gogh graphic design, and the great indexing work done by Angela Howard.

Foreword

In 1839, Sir John Herschel, credited with creating the first glass negative, coined the word photography, which translates to "drawing with light." The fascination with capturing and preserving "slices" and seconds of light's presence, and the many ways to manipulate and eventually print the resonance of that light, has evolved significantly over the nearly two centuries that have passed since Thomas Wedgwood's early experiments with shadow image photograms and Louis Daguerre's famous daguerreotypes. Indeed, what originally formed from a history of fine tuning a balance of chemistry and optics has further evolved into our modern technological age of binary capture, a modern age in which everyone from professionals, hobbyists, and those who simply just want to preserve a moment, can aim a device (whether it be a manual camera, a DSLR, or even a smartphone), choose a composition, and then click a shutter and slice a sliver of those memories. Over this span of time, a veritable cornucopia of techniques, styles, subjects, and tools have surfaced and evolved along with the process, and now, as we settle comfortably into the 21st century, the modern photography enthusiast can choose to explore techniques of the past, take advantage of modern innovations, or blend the two as he or she wishes. Indeed, one can find a myriad of tools and processes to craft an individual vision— from the daguerreotype to images printed on thin sheets of metal, from long exposures to infrared to HDR, from landscape and portrait photography to architectural and commercial photography, from wide angle lenses to prime lenses to zoom lenses to tilt shift lenses, from neutral density filters to a variety of color filters or their software rendering equivalents, from black and white film to digital RAW files, from the zone system to histograms, from sepia tone to cyanotypes to digitized tonal processing, from the pinhole camera to 35mm to medium format and large format cameras to DSLRs, point and shoots and smartphones. One can also choose between the various possibilities of the traditional darkroom and its chemical alchemies for producing prints or embrace the digital darkroom with Photoshop and other software and with the latest, ever improving ink technologies and printers.

Interestingly, however, those who embrace the modern possibilities of printing and processing in the digital world of photography, no matter how computerized or software-ized, still utilize many of the basic principles developed and written by those many visionaries who have experimented and failed and succeeded in an ever evolving field-- such as, for example, Ansel Adams and his zone system. And while Adams' methods and understandings are still every bit as relevant in today's digitalized world, the time has come for a detailed, hands on, informative book that addresses the multitude of new tools, methods and possibilities that this digital revolution offers the modern artist. After all, regardless of which tools and methods one uses, every photographer still harnesses and draws with that light and its inevitable shadows, the goal remaining the same even as the tools and digital possibilities offer a myriad of new avenues to explore. With an eye always on the past and a respectful and thorough knowledge for how photography has evolved into our modern digital age, Hugh J. Lawton provides an insightful understanding of modern digital photography and how not only to capture that light but also to better understand the process and its many techniques so that you can then harness that light and create your own "drawings of light."

Nathan Wirth,
a slice of silence photography - www.nlwirth.com

Nathan Wirth, who was born and raised in San Francisco, is a self taught photographer that uses a variety of techniques— including long exposure and infrared— to express his unending wonder of the fundamental fact of existence by attempting to focus on the silence that we can sometimes perceive in between the incessant waves of sound that often dominate our perceptions of the world.

Preface

In 1980, Ansel Adams, with his editor Robert Baker, authored a series of three books on photography entitled *The Camera, The Negative,* and *The Print.* These three books stand as the definitive works for the traditional art of emulsion and chemical-based photography. However, Adams was insightful enough to understand the impact that electronics would have on the art of photography. In the introduction to his second volume, *The Negative,* Adams discusses the imminent "electronic revolution".

Since the publication of Adams' books, that electronic revolution has indeed changed the face of photography in a profound manner, but until now, there was no comprehensive series of books which explored all of the aspects of the art of photography in the context of the electronic revolution. Photography in the Digital Age is a series of three volumes that address the shift to this new technology, and explore the integration of traditional photographic techniques with digital photography.

The three volumes are as follows:

Volume I – The Art of Image Capture

Volume II – The Image Master File

Volume III – Images for Print, Licensing, and Internet

In a world of change, the learners shall inherit the earth,
while the learned shall find themselves perfectly suited
for a world that no longer exists.

-- Eric Hoffer

Introduction

Symbol Creation

A photographic image is a cultural symbol. Since the publication of Charles Darwin's *On the Origin of Species*, biologists and anthropologists have been trying to determine the key differences between humans and their fellow members of the animal kingdom. Prior to the 1960s, anthropologists firmly believed that it was man's ability to make tools that distinguished humans from the rest of the primates. However, when Jane Goodall began her chimpanzee studies in July of 1960 at Gombe in Tanzania, she discovered that chimpanzees also make tools, and the "man the tool maker" theory went out the window.

There does seem to be one aspect of human behavior that is unique to the human species – the creation of abstract symbols. A symbol is defined by Merriam Webster as an object, picture, written word, sound, or particular mark that represents something else by association, resemblance, or convention. While it is true that animals such as gibbons and even elephants use sounds to communicate elementary ideas, the creation of abstract symbols in writing and visual images is a uniquely human attribute.

The human propensity for symbol creation has evolved in response to the pressures of natural selection; our human ancestors developed their symbol creation capabilities while trying to solve specific adaptive problems. As a result of those evolutionary pressures, the human mind has developed a predisposition toward certain specific archetypes, methods of perception, and patterns of thought creation. These symbols and patterns are imbedded in the genetic structure of the human biology, and they have contributed to the survival and advancement of the human species.

In the analysis of symbol creation, it is useful to consider the three primary modes of human thinking – logical thinking, associative thinking, and narrative thinking. Logical thinking involves the conscious rational aspects of the human brain. Although early forms of logical thinking can be found in both China and India, the beginnings of formal rational thinking can be traced back to Aristotle in Greece. Aristotle developed a system of logic that was based on logical definitions, axioms, and tools that can be used to construct logical thought patterns.

Logic is traditionally divided into inductive and deductive reasoning. Inductive reasoning involves the derivation of general conclusions based on specific examples. Deductive reasoning involves the derivation of conclusions based on definitions, axioms, and logical tools such as the syllogism. The definitions and axioms used in deductive logic are very simple. For example, an object cannot exist and not exist at the same time. "A = not A" is not possible. Syllogisms try to deduce truth by using basic rules of logic.

For example:

All men are mortal,
Socrates is a man,
Therefore, Socrates is mortal

Conscious logical thought processes are the basis for analytical thinking and the scientific method. New symbols and mental constructs are created through the formal logic processes. The world of logical thinking is the world of scientific time and space.

Associative thinking involves either the conscious or subconscious combination of existing symbols in order to create new symbols. Associative thinking can take place in the dream state where symbols from the subconscious mind are combined to form new symbols; however, associative thinking can also occur in the conscious state as day dreaming. The world of associative thinking is a state of mind where there is no time and anything is possible. Associative thinking is the basis for creative thought; the creation of art is the result of associative thinking.

Finally, narrative thinking is the human process of storytelling. Narrative thinking is the source for a broad range of arts that are directly related to storytelling. All three of these types of thought patterns are used in the process of symbol creation. The symbols that make up stories can be derived from real life experiences, the story-teller's imagination, or a combination of both. New symbols are created alongside the vestiges of previously created symbols.

The chapters in this volume will explore all of the creative, rational, and narrative dimensions of photo image capture; however, the initial chapters will attempt to put the digital revolution into a historical context, placing the reader into the fast-flowing river of innovation that has completely reinvented photography over the last twenty years.

The digital revolution has become the great equalizer for the art of photography. Digital photo media has completely changed the face of photography to the point where all photographers are beginners. Professional and amateur photographers alike have had to relearn the photographic tools and techniques from this new approach. Because of its ease of use, the new digital photo media has made photography accessible to millions of new users. But how did photography get to this place in history?

The Digital Revolution

The first two chapters of this volume address key technical innovations that have driven the digital revolution, as well as the creative concept of visualization in art. Chapter one, on the history of modern digital photography, discusses the technological innovations that have contributed to the digital revolution in photography. Chapter two, on visualization, discusses the creative process that occurs when an image crystallizes in the mind of the artist.

Fiat Lux – Let There Be Light

Chapters three and four introduce the reader to the primary subject matter of photography – light. Light is an enigma in nature that has been the topic of discussion for both philosophers and scientists. Chapter three traces both the mythological and scientific interpretations for the dual nature of light. Chapter four adopts a practical scientific approach to the understanding of light as it applies to the art of image capture, including a detailed discussion of color spaces, an understanding of which is critical in order to approach the topics in chapters five and six.

The Science of Image Capture

Chapter five extends the study of light to a detailed examination of the standard exposure model. The standard exposure model has been developed as a teaching tool that is used to explain image capture. The standard exposure model includes the following components:

- Incident Light
- Reflected Light
- The Subject
- The Camera
- The Capture Media
- The Exposure Axis
- The Image Frame
- The Photographer's Eye

Chapters five and six also contain information regarding the scientific techniques and procedures involved in image capture, namely, the Zone System and light filtration. The Zone System and the extension of the Zone System into light filtration make up the rational scientific aspects of image capture. For the Zone System and light filtration, logic and the scientific method are the conceptual frameworks needed to understand the application of these standard procedures.

Ansel Adams and Fred Archer defined the Zone System in 1939-40; it was derived from the sensitometry and densitometry work that was done by Ferdinand Hurter and Vero Charles Driffield in the latter part of the nineteenth century. Also, the Adams/Archer version of the Zone System methodology can be traced to a series of articles written by John Davenport for *US Camera* magazine. In 1976, Minor White, Richard Zakia, and Peter Lorenz enhanced the Zone System with a publication entitled *The New Zone System Manual.* More recently, Chris Johnson brought the Zone System into the digital age with his publication *The Practical Zone*

System: For Film and Digital Photography. The steps contained in the Zone System are a set of scientific procedures that photographers use to consistently create perfectly exposed images. The technical aspects of the art of photography have changed a great deal since the invention of the Zone System; however, the application of the Zone System is as relevant in the current digital age as it was then. The Zone System remains the bed rock for the consistent capture of quality images.

Chapter six extends the Zone System workflow into the realm of light filtration. The chapter uses the exposure model to explain the various ways that reflected light can be modified in the process of image capture. The Zone System is integrated with the discussion of light filtration so that the reader can obtain a comprehensive understanding of light filtration within the Zone System.

The Art of Image Capture

Chapters seven and eight discuss the creative combinations of the components of image capture for both natural light and studio photography. Chapter seven uses the standard exposure model to review natural light photography. The chapter also contains a survey of typical natural light subjects, and it discusses the methods used to effectively capture a natural light image.

Chapter eight contains an elementary review of the components of artificial light photography. The chapter provides an inventory of the components of artificial light photography as well as some suggestions on how to effectively combine these components in order to capture high quality studio images.

These two chapters focus on the application of scientific techniques defined in chapters five and six in order to achieve the photographer's creative goals, but they also approach image capture from an associative/artistic perspective.

The Narrative

Every picture tells a story, and the final chapter in this volume assembles all of the scientific and creative components of image capture to successfully complete a photo narrative. Chapter nine combines all of the rational and creative components from the earlier chapters into an overall framework of image capture. The framework consists of the following three conceptual workflows:

- The Visual Language
- The Visual Style
- The Composition Process

The goal of the final chapter is to effectively combine all of the aspects of image capture so that the reader can successfully capture images that will communicate a meaningful photo narrative. A photograph can never be an exact replication of reality, rather it is the individual photographer's *interpretation* of reality. Analog and digital photographic media are not capable of the exact reproduction of the real world, and it is the photographer's responsibility to use all of the scientific and creative tools at their disposal to achieve the capture of their visualized version of an image. If this volume provides the photographer with the tools necessary to effectively communicate their photo narrative, then it is a success.

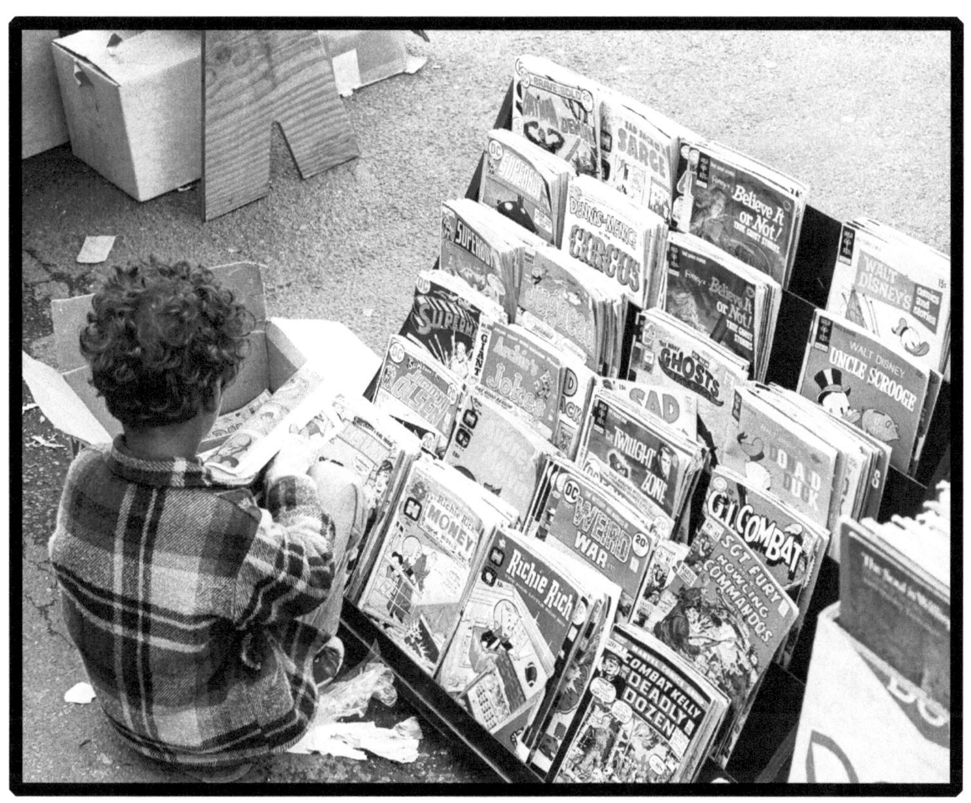

Figure I.1 -- Komics Kid
Manzanita Photography

It isn't all over; everything has not been invented;
the human adventure is just beginning.

-- Gene Roddenberry

Chapter One

The Dawn of the Digital Age

The digital revolution has had a significant impact on all of human society, but the impact that the digital revolution has had on the art of photography has been almost unbelievable. Over the last twenty years, the face of photography has been completely reinvented. Many traditional photographers have refused to believe that the complete redefinition of photography was sustainable; however, the pace of change in photography has continued to accelerate. It is difficult to imagine that the changes that have occurred over the last twenty years could possibly reverse course.

Innovations in the photo media have spurred a renewed interest in photography that has not been seen since the days of George Eastman's Brownie camera, and like Eastman's Brownie revolution, the digital revolution can be traced to simplification and innovation within key categories of technology:

- Innovation in computer technology
- Transformations in image capture technology
- The development of computer-based photo-editing software
- The development of Ink-based photo printing

Listed below are some of the key events that have driven the modernization for the above areas of technology. At the end of each section, an attempt is made to project future developments for each of the categories.

Innovation in Computer Technology

The first programmable computing machines were developed in the 1940s after the end of World War II. These first computers used gas tubes as switches, which caused the machines to generate an excessive amount of heat. With the invention of the transistor in 1947 and the development of solid state electronics in 1959, large-scale computers moved from the realm of science fiction to science fact. In 1965, Intel co-founder Gordon E. Moore **(Figure 1.1)** stumbled upon a trend in computing power and transistor density. Mr. Moore correctly determined that the number of components in integrated circuits had doubled every year since the invention of the integrated circuit in 1959; based on this, he predicted that computer power would double every year until approximately 2020. This axiom became known as *Moore's Law.* Moore slightly altered his prediction in 1975 to a doubling of the computing power every two years. Over the last thirty years, Moore's Law has proven to be very accurate, and it seems that it will continue to be accurate in the near future.

1946 —

The first large-scale programmable computer is unveiled at the University of Pennsylvania. The computer was named ENIAC which stood for Electronic Numerical Integrator and Computer. This first computer was designed by physicist John Mauchley and electrical engineer J. Presper Eckert.

1947 —

William Shockley, John Bardeen, and Walter Brattain **(Figure 1.2)** succeed in building the first practical point transistor at Bell Labs in Murray Hill, New Jersey. The transistor could function as both an amplifier and an on-off switch. The amplification property of the transistor would be used in electronic devices such as the transistor radio. The switching properties of the transistor would be used in representing the binary ones and zeroes that drive all modern computers.

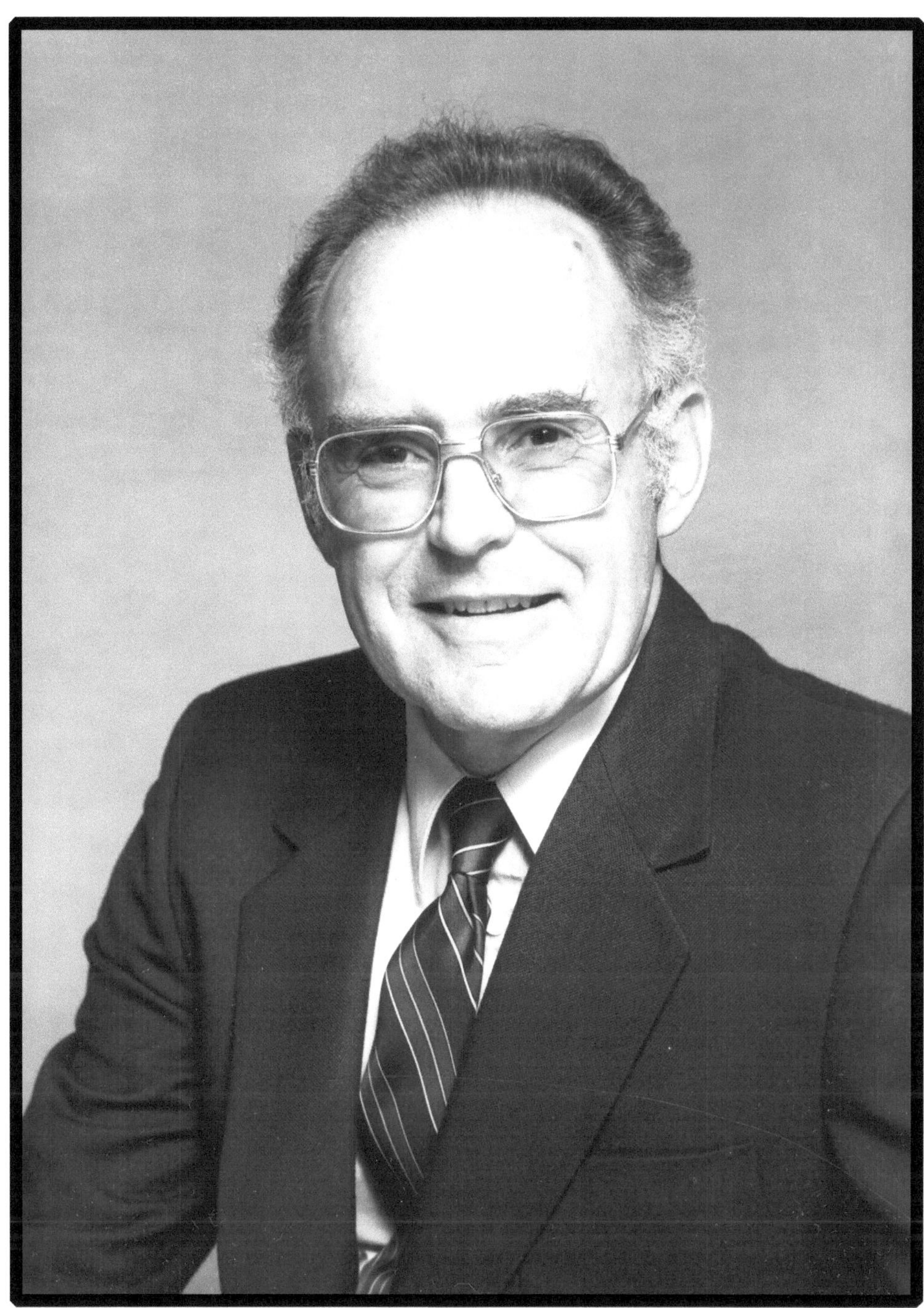

Figure 1.1
Gordon Moore

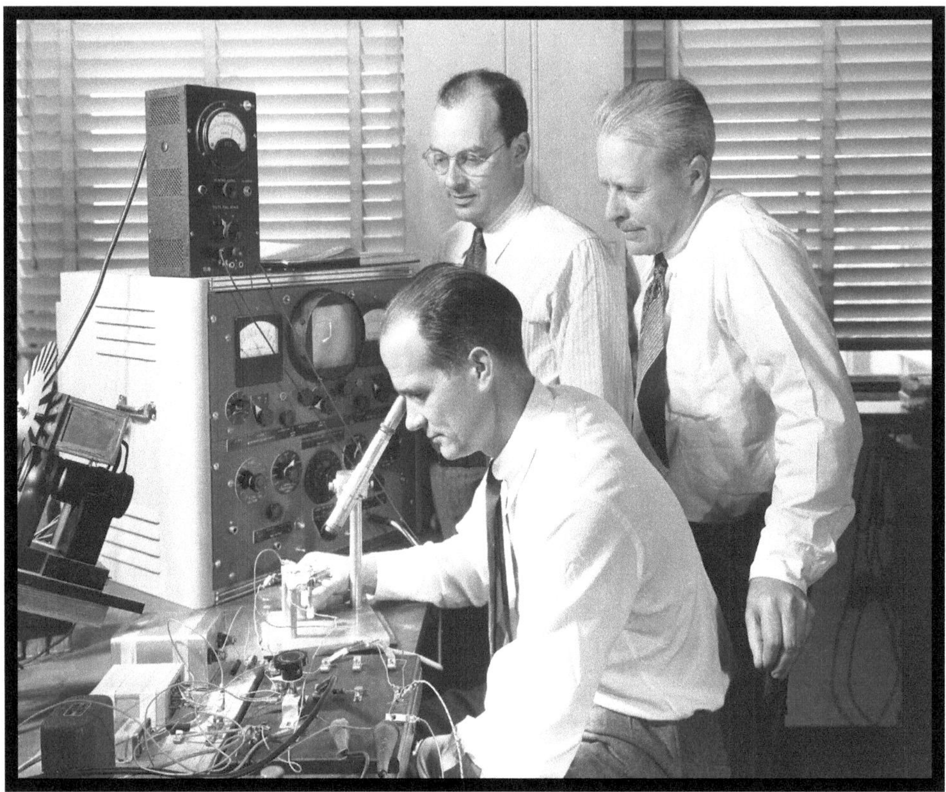

Figure 1.2
William Shockley (foreground),
John Bardeen (background left),
Walter Brattain (background right)

As stated by Walter Isaacson in his book *The Innovators*: "The transistor, as the device was soon named, became to digital age, what the steam engine was to the Industrial Revolution" (Walter Isaacson, *The Innovators*, P. 131). Shockley, Bardeen, and Brattain would win the 1956 Nobel Prize in physics for their invention. The invention of the transistor marks the beginning of the age of solid state electronics.

1959 —

CalComp Corporation begins selling the first computer graphics device known as the *digital plotter*. The CalComp digital plotter was the first device to translate mathematical data from a computer into visual images, maps, architectural renderings, and engineering mockups.

Texas Instruments scientist Jack Kilby **(Figure 1.3)** invents the first integrated circuit by etching a miniature electronic circuit onto a substrate of germanium. Kilby filed a patent request for his "solid circuit", and Texas Instruments immediately began the manufacture of the circuit. These scientific breakthroughs marked the dawn of the "chip technology" that would drive the digital age. Kilby received the 2000 Nobel Prize in physics for his invention.

Fairchild Semiconductor engineers Robert Noyce, Gordon Moore, and Jean Hoerni **(Figure 1.4)** developed a silicon etched circuit similar to the Texas Instruments device using what they called "the planar process". Noyce and Moore would go on to found the chip manufacturing company Intel.

1969 —

Intel scientists Marcian "Ted" Hoff and Stanley Mazor developed the architectural design and instruction set for the first silicon based programmable microchip. The device was named the Intel 4004. This architectural design was implemented by Intel engineer Federico Foggin using a silicon gate design methodology.

1977 —

Apple Computer Company announces its personal computer called the Apple II at the West Coast Computer Faire in San Francisco. The Apple II was driven by a 1 MHz Motorola processor with a maximum of 48 Kb (48 thousand bytes or kilobytes) of random access memory.

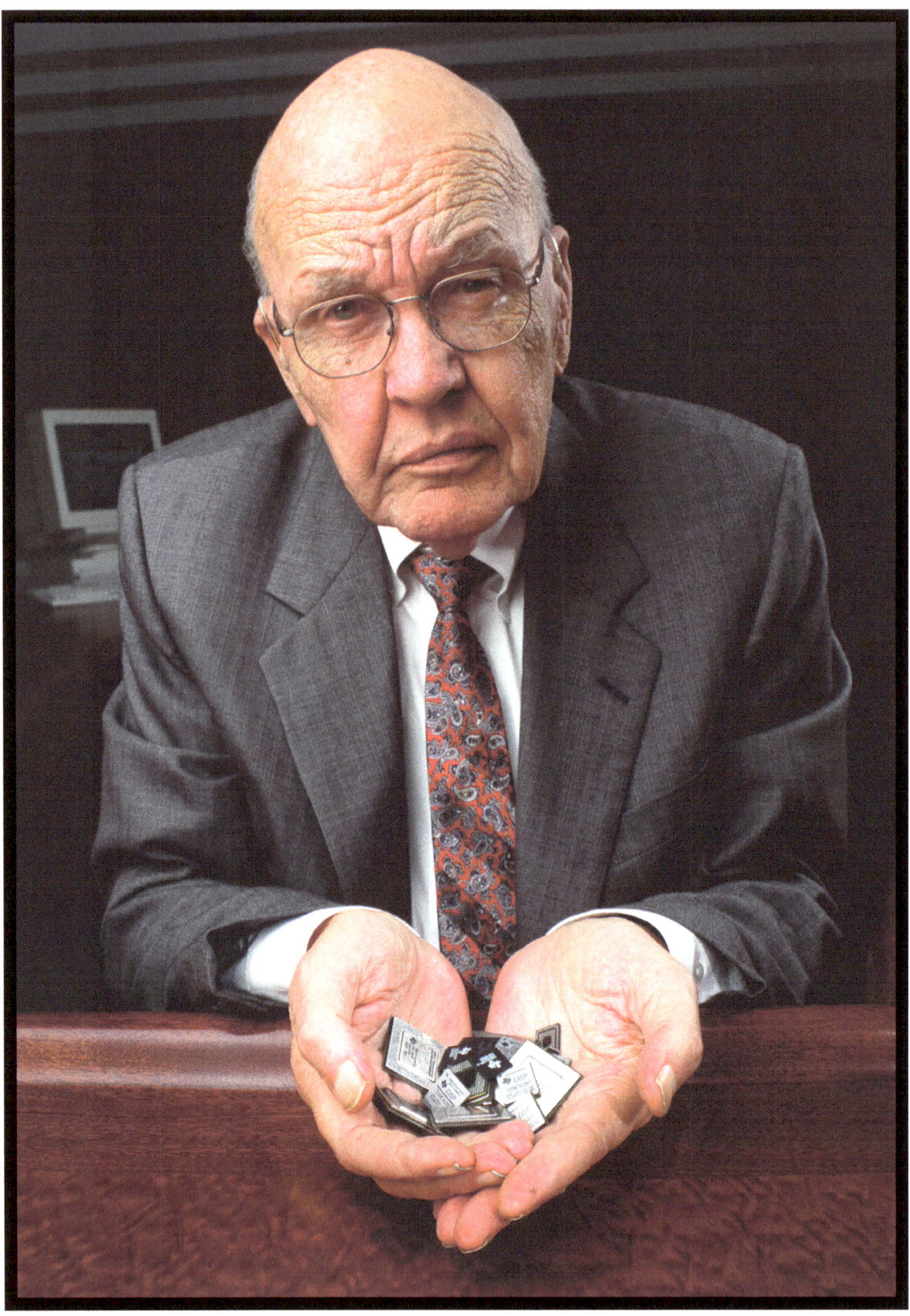

Figure 1.3
Jack Kilby

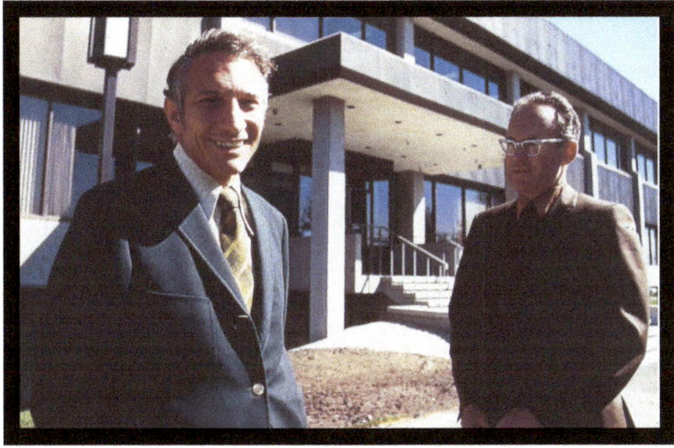

Figure 1.4
Robert Noyce (left)
Gordon Moore (right)

1981 —

International Business Machines begins selling its personal computer. The IBM 5150 contained a 4.7 MHz Intel processor and up to 640 Kb (640 thousand bytes) of random access memory.

1984 —

Apple Corporation begins selling the Macintosh line of personal computers. The first Macintosh computers were driven by a Motorola 6809E processor and 64 Kb of random access memory. The first Macintoshes came with a nine inch 256 X 256 pixel display and they were the first personal computers to support a sophisticated GUI (Graphic User Interface) which was controlled by a mouse.

1989 —

Disney color engineer David Coons **(Figure 1.5)** uses his custom computer software to scan, edit, and print a photograph of musician Joni Mitchell. The final print was printed on an IRIS inkjet printer. The Joni Mitchell photograph was part of a collection of photographs that were given to Coons by pop singer Graham Nash.

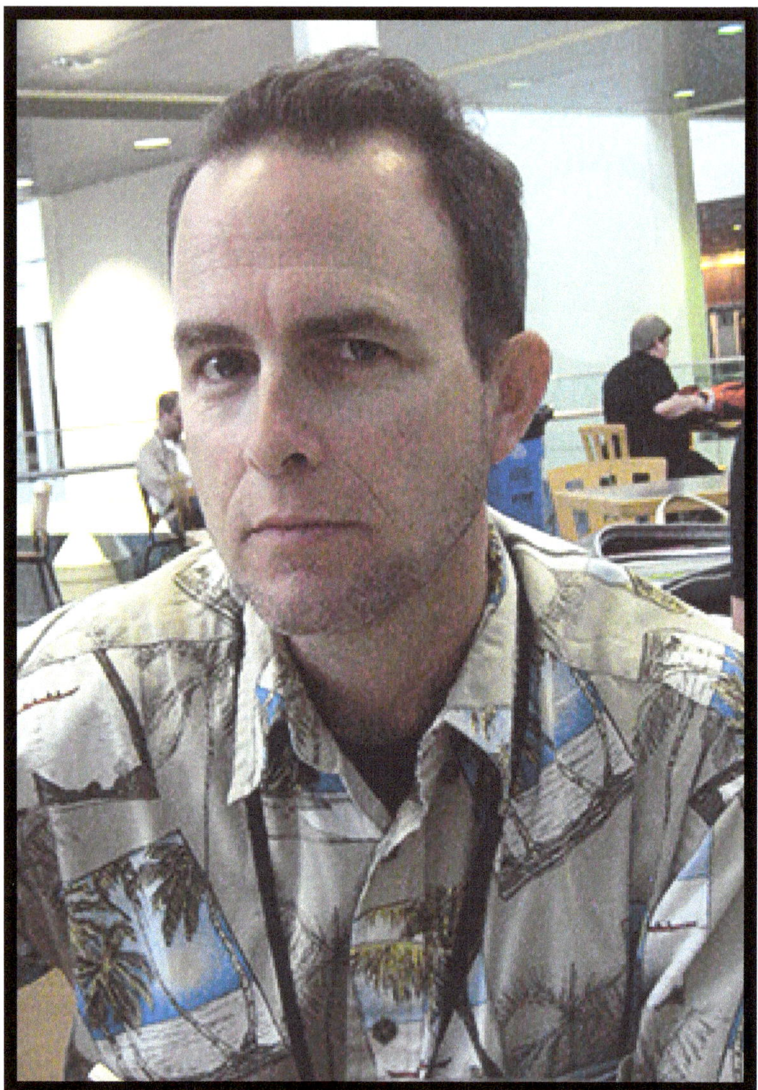

Figure 1.5
David Coons

The Future –

The computing power of modern computers continues to follow Moore's Law. In addition, innovations in disk storage, monitor display, and telecommunications continue to move at a blistering pace.

The latest high power computers exploit a technique known as *parallel processing*. Parallel processing involves the use of multiple CPU (Central Processing Unit) chips to simultaneously accomplish computing tasks, which greatly increases the overall compute power of the unit.

Electronic Image Capture

Electronic image capture is dependent upon innovations in the charged couple device (CCD) and the CMOS Active Pixel Sensors (CMOS/APS). These two pieces of integrated circuitry are the driving force behind both scanners and digital cameras.

1969 —

George E. Smith **(Figure 1.6)** and Willard Boyle **(Figure 1.7)** of Bell Labs invent the first Charge Coupled Device (CCD). The CCD is an image sensor consisting of an integrated circuit containing an array of linked or coupled light sensitive capacitors. The CCD is the corner stone upon which digital photography was built.

1975 —

Steve Sasson of the Eastman Kodak Company captures the first digital image using a Fairchild Industries CCD chip. The black and white image took twenty-three seconds to capture, and it was recorded on magnetic cassette tape.

1981 —

The Sony Corporation demonstrates an early version of the Sony Mavica (Magnetic Video Camera) digital camera. The Sony camera had the capability to record up to fifty single frames on a 2" X 2" video floppy disk.

1988 —

The Fuji Film Holdings Company of Japan releases the first camera to capture and store images as a digital electronic file – The Fuji DS-1P. The camera used a 16 Mb (16 million bytes) internal memory card to store the images captured by the camera.

The ability to store and transmit electronic images is greatly enhanced by the development of the JPEG (Joint Photographic Experts Group) and MPEG (Moving Picture Experts Group) file compression standards. The JPEG and MPEG groups are established by the International Organization of Standardization (ISO/CCITT/IEC) in order to define standards for audio and video file compression and transmission.

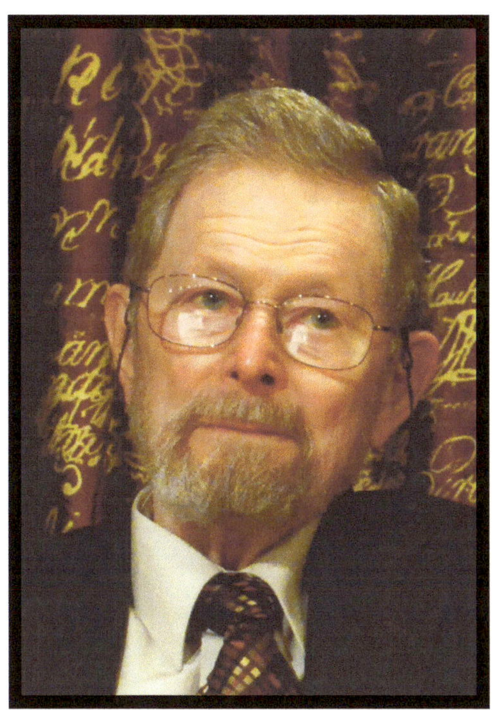

Figure 1.6
George E. Smith (left)

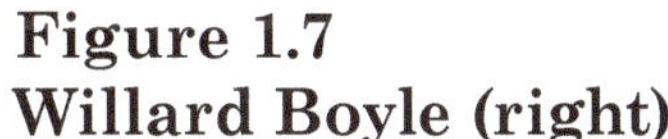

Figure 1.7
Willard Boyle (right)

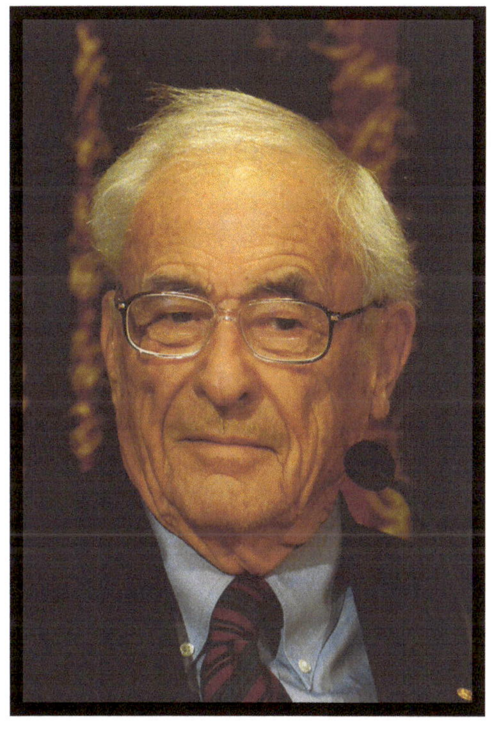

1991 —

The Eastman Kodak Company begins selling the DCS-100 single lens reflex digital camera. The camera used a 1.3 megapixel CCD sensor that was fitted into a Nikon F3 camera body. The original DCS-100 sold for $13,000.

1992 —

The Eastman Kodak Company begins selling a system for digitizing and storing electronic images on a compact disk (CD). The low-cost system used a proprietary encoding algorithm to store up to 100 digital images on a CD. However, the system did not gain wide popularity due to the rapid drop in the cost of high-quality scanners, thus making it possible to scan and store images without the use of Kodak's proprietary software.

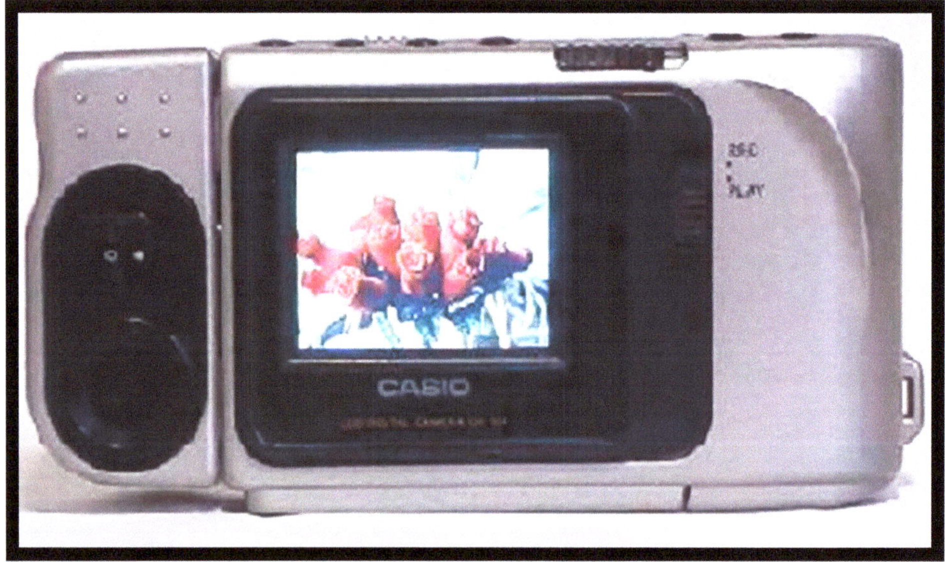

Figure 1.8
Casio QV-10

1995 —

The Casio Computer Company begins selling the Casio QV-10 **(Figure 1.8)** digital camera, which was the first camera to be equipped with a Liquid Crystal Display (LCD) on the back of the camera.

Key members of the Jet Propulsion Laboratory in Pasadena, California form the Photobit Company, the charter of which was the development of a commercially viable CMOS/APS sensor.

1996 —

The Eastman Kodak Company begins selling the DC-25 digital camera, the first digital camera to use compact flash memory as removable image storage. The memory cards used by the DC-25 could store up to thirty standard resolution (320 X 240 pixel) twenty four bit images. Kodak also supplied their Picture Easy software, which was used to off load the images from the memory card onto a computer.

1999 —

Nikon Corporation releases the first digital single lens reflex (SLR) camera developed by a single manufacturer. The Nikon D1 came with a 2.74 mega pixel sensor, and it cost less than $6,000. The Nikon D1 continued to support the standard Nikon F series lens mount.

2003 —

Canon begins selling the Canon Digital Rebel or 300D single lens reflex digital camera. The 300D came equipped with a six megapixel sensor, and it was the first Canon model to use the Canon EF-S lens mount. At its release, the Canon 300D sold for less than $1000.

2004 —

Swedish camera manufacturer Hasselblad merges with Danish imaging company Imacon. Imacon was a leader in the manufacture of digital photographic image capture equipment.

The Future –

As the number of pixels that can be captured by a digital camera device increases, the need for emulsion-based film and CCD-based scanners will decline significantly. Film will probably survive as a limited specialty market for those photographers who want to continue to use this media. Similarly, glass plate negatives continued to be manufactured and used well into the 1930s even though emulsion-based film became available in 1888. Scanners will continue to be used as a conversion device for existing film, but the manufacture of high end scanners will probably decline.

Listed below are four high end digital capture devices from four leading manufacturers:

1. **Canon EOS 5D** – 22.3 Mega Pixel capture capacity for a 5760 x 3840 pixel frame CMOS/APS sensor.

2. **Nikon D3x** – 24.5 Mega Pixel capture capacity for a 24 x 35.9 mm frame CMOS/APS sensor.

3. **Leica S2P** – 37.5 Mega Pixel capture capacity for a 30 x 45 mm frame CMOS/APS sensor.

Photo Editing Software

As the computing power of the computers increased, so also did the power of the photo editing software. Today, Adobe Photoshop Creative Cloud (CC) can be run on 64 bit operating systems which support a maximum capacity of 32 giga bytes (32 billion bytes) of memory. This latest version of Photoshop also supports sophisticated 3-D and animation features.

1973 —

The first use of computers to create and edit visual images is developed by Richard Shoup at the Xerox research lab in Palo Alto, California. The hardware/software developed by Shoup and other Xerox technicians was called SuperPaint, which became the basis for the explosion of computer graphics, video editing, and computer animation. Shoup would go on to be a major contributor to the success of George Lucas' company Industrial Light and Magic.

1990 —

Version 1.0 of Adobe Photoshop is released for sale. The photo editing computer software was developed by the brothers John Knoll **(Figures 1.9)** and Thomas Knoll **(Figure 1.10).** The initial version of Photoshop was developed for use on the Macintosh line of computers; the Windows version of Photoshop was released in 1992.

2011 —

Beginning in October of 2011, Adobe began offering its Creative Suite of products, including Photoshop, as a subscription-based cloud service.

The Future —

It is hard to imagine photography in the 21st century without a version of Photoshop that keeps pace with the powerful computers that will become available. Photoshop is now an indispensable tool in the photography workflow. The power of Photoshop's photo editing, 3-D, and animation features will probably continue to evolve.

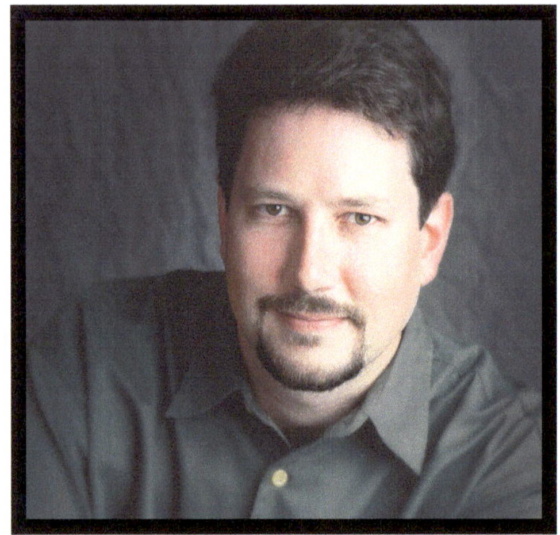

Figure 1.9
John Knoll (left)

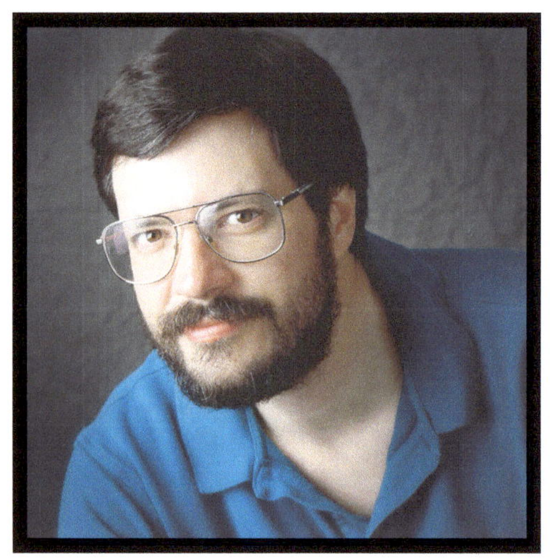

Figure 1.10
Thomas Knoll (right)

Ink-Based Photo Printing

Some of the dye-based IRIS drum printers that were used by Jon Cone and Graham Nash in the early 1980s are still in use, but the developments in the quality of both the printers and inks in use today have been astounding. What seemed like a fantasy to most emulsion-based photo printers just twenty years ago has become a fact of life today. High quality pigment-based ink prints can be made at very low cost on today's ink jet printers, and the projected longevity of these prints has made emulsions based printing a thing of the past.

1967 —

The beginnings of digital printing are featured at the following three prominent exhibitions:

1. **The Machine as Seen at the End of the Mechanical Age** – The Museum of Modern Art , New York,

2. **Some More Beginnings** -- The Brooklyn Museum, New York

3. **Cybernetic Serendipity: The Computer and the Arts** – Institute of Contemporary Arts, London

1971 —

The Los Angeles County Museum of Art features digital printing as part of its exhibition entitled "Art and Technology".

1976 —

International Business Machines begins selling the 6640, the first continuous flow inkjet system.

1977 —

Computer Aided Design and Computer Aided Manufacturing (CAD/CAM) manufacturer Applicon announces the first continuous-flow color inkjet printer.

German manufacturer Siemens launches the first piezoelectric inkjet printer.

1981 —

Canon begins selling its ink-based Bubble Jet printers. These Canon printers used heat to create bubbles of ink in a print head that were ejected from the print head when the bubble expanded.

1982 —

John Warnock and Charles Geschke found Adobe Systems in San Jose, California. Warnock and Geschke along with Doug Brotz, Ed Taft, and Bill Paxton developed a vector graphics computer language for driving laser printers. The computer language was named PostScript. PostScript became the industry standard page description language used in laser printers. In March of 1985, the Apple Laser Writer became the first printer to ship with a factory installed version of PostScript. The Apple Laser Writer printer would be the spark that ignited the desk top publishing revolution of the 1980's.

1984 —

Hewlett-Packard corporation releases the Thinkjet 2225, the first personal thermal inkjet printer. The small desktop Thinkjet used electronic signals to superheat a thin film which resulted in the creation of small ink droplets.

Pioneer digital printer Harry Bowers makes the first digital color print.

1987 —

The IRIS Graphics 3024 inkjet printer is launched at the "Lasers in Graphic" show in Miami, Florida. The high quality drum based IRIS printer was originally intended for the prepress proofing industry. The high quality of IRIS prints was derived from a continuous flow ink technology that had the capacity to break the ink flow into droplets of thirty-two different sizes.

1989 —

Maryanne and John Doe found the printing company Harvest Productions, which was founded for the purpose of developing the fine art of inkjet printing. Harvest Productions would go on to become the largest producer of giclee prints in the world.

1990 —

Jon Cone **(Figure 1.11)** moves his experimental print studio Cone Editions Press from New York to rural Vermont, and he dedicates his new 4200-square-foot studio to the development of digital printmaking. Cone Editions Press would become a center for IRIS printing and other ink-based print technologies.

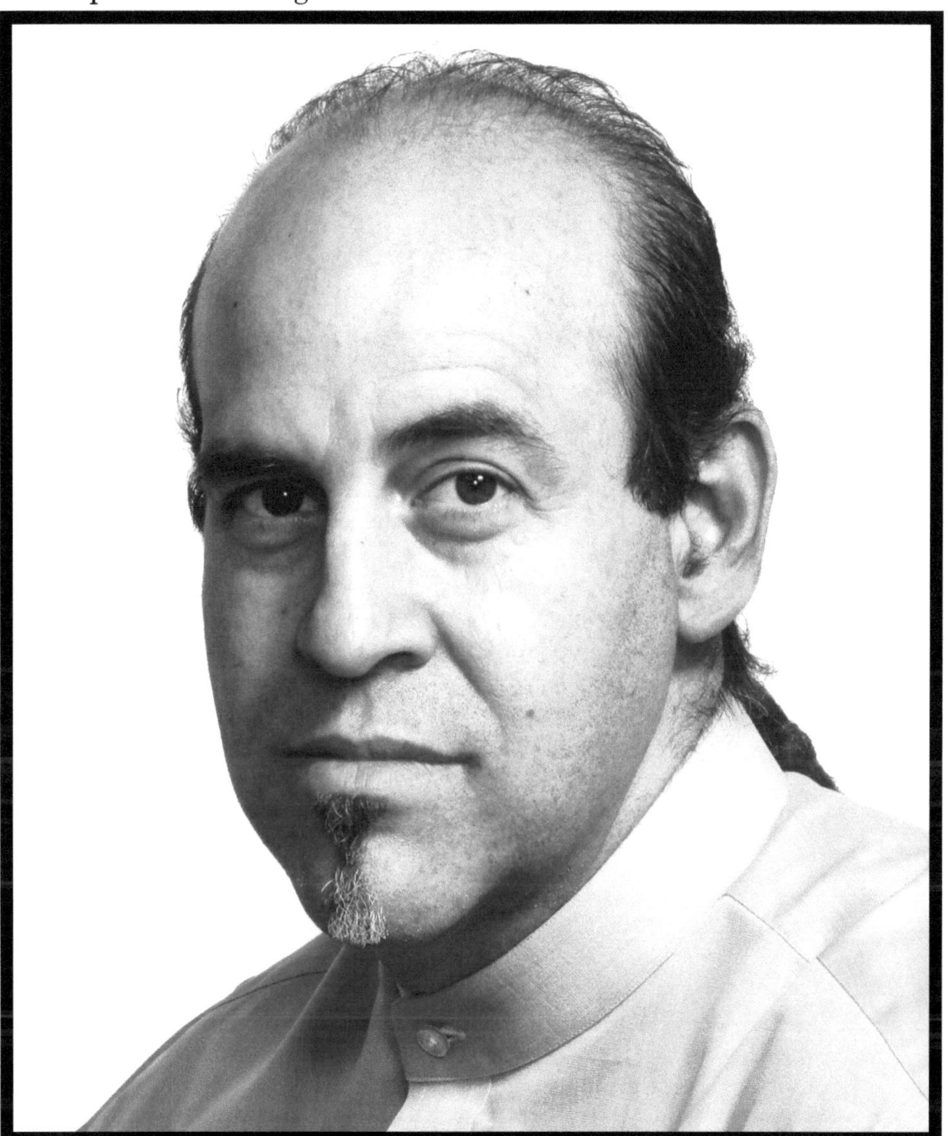

Figure 1.11
Jon Cone

The Simon Lowinsky Gallery in New York presents an exhibition of photographs created by singer Graham Nash. The exhibit was the first fine art show made up entirely of digitally printed work.

Sally Larsen's "Tunnel Point Transformer" becomes the first digital fine art print included in the permanent collection of the Metropolitan Museum of Art in New York City.

1991 —

R. Mac Holbert and Graham Nash **(Figure 1.12)** found Nash Editions as an enterprise dedicated to the development of methods used in the output of Nash's black and white photographs. Nash Editions initially used an IRIS 3047 printer as their primary printing source. Nash Editions employee Jack Duganne coined the term *giclee* which is the French word for spray or spurt of liquid.

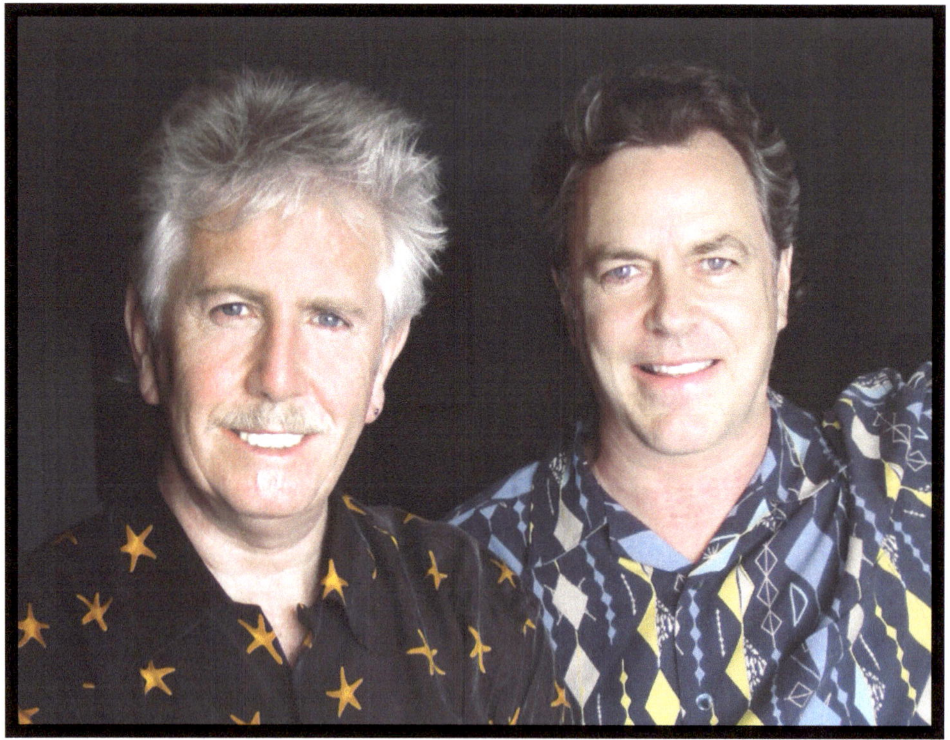

Figure 1.12
Graham Nash (left)
R. Mac Holbert (right)

1994 —

The Epson Company of Japan begins selling the Epson Stylus Color, the first desktop inkjet printer. The 720 dots per inch Stylus Color was the first desk top photo-realistic inkjet printer to become available in the mass market. The original Epson Stylus used four dye-based inks.

Photo technology company Durst began selling the Lambda, a digital laser printing machine, which used digital image files as input to the printing process. It interpreted the digital input file, and then exposed a piece of emulsion-based photographic paper using red, green, and blue lasers. The exposed paper was processed using traditional RA-4 print processing chemistry. The Lambda was the best of both the digital and chemical worlds; it used high quality digital input combined with traditional continuous process chemical printing.

1997 —

The non-profit International Association of Fine Art Digital Printmakers is founded. The goal of IAFADP was to support and encourage the development of digital printing technology. The group also served as a liaison with collectors, museums, and galleries in the development of standards for digital fine art prints.

The National Museum of American Art at the Smithsonian Institution in Washington D. C. presents an exhibition entitled "Digital Atelier: A Printmaking Studio for the 21st Century." The exhibition included the works of digital artists Dorothy Simpson Krause, Bonnie Pierce Lhotka, and Karne Schinenke. The Digital Atelier studio has since spread to locations in Boston, Denver, and Seattle.

1998 —

Jon Cone of Cone Editions Press begins selling the Digital Platinum monochromatic printing system for the IRIS printer. Cone's system combined his ConeTech black and white inks with a software interface for the IRIS Inkjet printer. Cone won the Digital Innovator of 1999 award for his invention.

Dutch manufacturer Mac Dermid Color Span begins selling the Giclee PrintMakers-FA wide format printer. The innovative Mac Dermid dye-based inkjet printer was the first wide format digital printer designed specifically for the fine art market.

American manufacturer Rowland begins selling its HI-Fi Jet wide format inkjet printer. The printer featured six color ink cartridges which used pigment-based inks.

2000 —

Epson Corporation launches its Stylus Pro 2000 desktop inkjet printer, which was the first desktop printer to support pigment-based inks. The printer could make prints up to a maximum size of 19" X 13" and it sold for less than $500.

Jon Cone begins selling his Piezography Black and White ink system for use in Epson inkjet printers. Cone's optical quality monochromatic systems made high quality black and white printing available on the low-cost line of Epson printers.

2002 —

Lexmark begins selling its Z65 color inkjet printer, which supported a resolution of 4800 DPI (Dots Per Inch).

Epson begins selling its new line of color inkjet printers, the Stylus Pro 2100/2200, which supported an ink set of seven pigment-based ink cartridges. In the same year, Epson unveils the Stylus Pro 96, the first two pico-liter ink droplet printer.

Cone Editions Press releases the ConeTech Piezo Tone quad black inkjet inks. Cone touted the new pigment based inks as an improvement in longevity, color stability, and printer performance over his previous ink sets.

2003 —

Hewlett-Packard Corporation began selling the Photosmart 7960 desktop inkjet printer. The H-P Photosmart was unique in its support of eight different ink cartridges although only three of the cartridges could be used at any one time. H-P's inclusion of medium gray and light gray cartridges allowed the Photosmart printer to create excellent monochrome black and white images.

Cone Edition Press expands its line of black and white inks to include pigment-based inks that could be used in Canon inkjet printers.

2004 —

Epson begins selling the Stylus Pro R800, the first 1.5 pico liter ink droplet printer. With the 1.5 pico liter droplet, the R800 supported a print resolution of 5760 X 1440 DPI. The new printer came equipped with new red and blue high gloss inks plus a gloss optimizer cartridge.

2005 —

Epson begins selling its new line of color inkjet printers, the Stylus Pro 4800/7800/9800. The new line of printers came equipped with Epson's new Ultra Chrome K3 pigment-based inks. The new ink set was composed of eight ink cartridges with three shades of black/gray.

The Future –

The quality of both the pigment based inks and their associated printers will continue to expand and improve. The latest Epson inkjet printers support eleven individual ink colors including three shades of black. This improvement in both the quality of the printer technology and ink will continue to be developed.

the voice of beauty speaks softly;
it creeps only into the most fully awakened souls

-- Frederich Nietzsche

Chapter Two

Visualization For Image Capture

In order to understand the notion of *visualization* in photography, some basic definitions are required. Concepts such as aesthetics, beauty, and art need to be examined, and the relationships that link these ideas need to be understood.

Merriam-Webster defines aesthetics as "a branch of philosophy dealing with the nature of beauty, art, and taste, and with the creation and appreciation of art." Merriam-Webster also defines a symbol as "something that stands for or suggests something else by reason of relationship association, convention, or accidental resemblance; especially: a visible sign of something invisible <a lion is a symbol of courage>." Throughout history human beings have demonstrated a distinct proclivity for the creation of a wide range of symbols. Aesthetic art involves the creation of symbols that can be expressed in a particular media – ceramics, sculpture, music, storytelling, painting, or photography. So, what makes an artistic symbol beautiful?

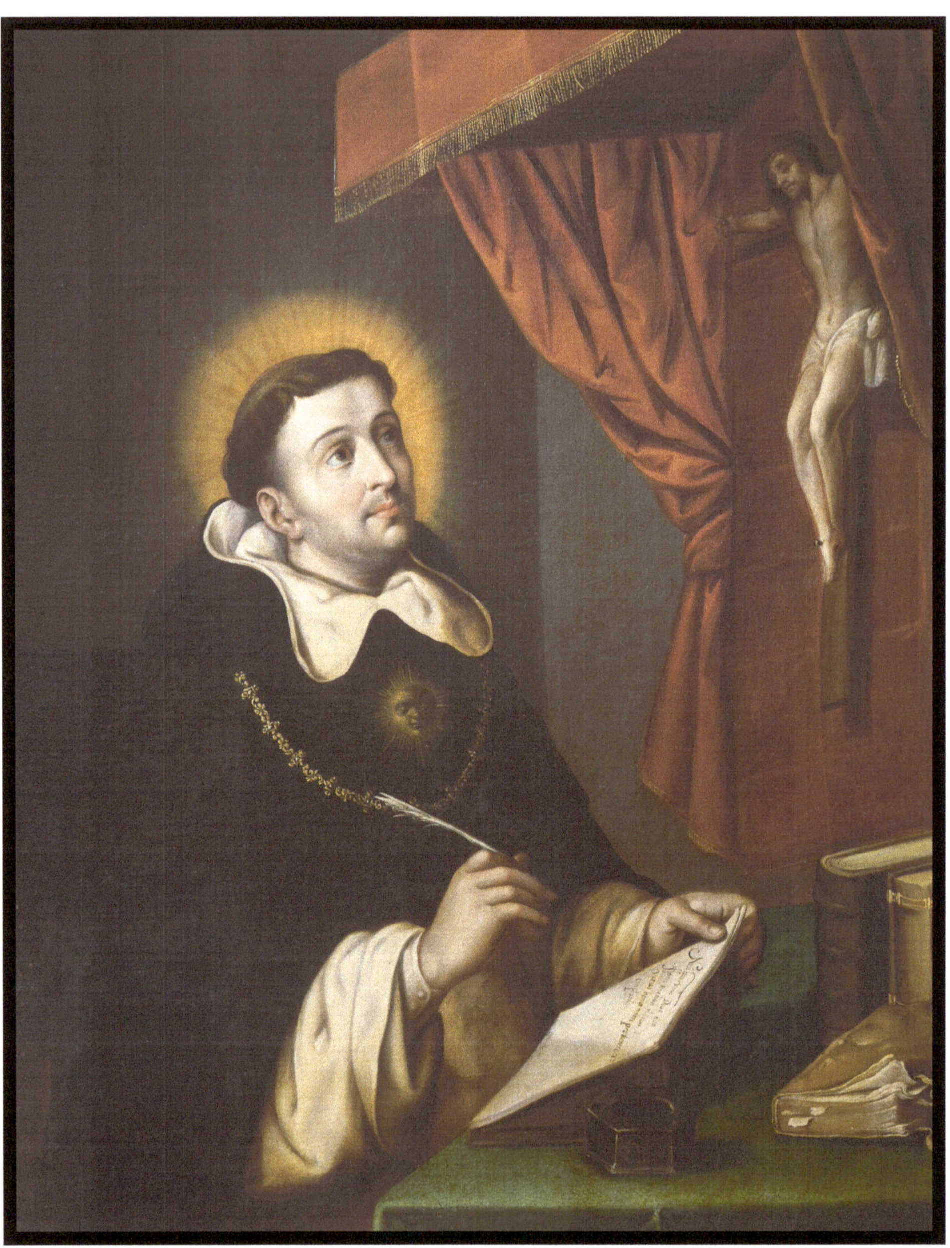

Figure 2.1
Thomas Aquinas

The medieval philosopher Thomas Aquinas (1225 to 1274 CE, **Figure 2.1**) extended Aristotle's definition of beauty by defining three main components of beauty:

- Wholeness
- Harmony
- Clarity

In order for an artistic symbol to be beautiful, it must have wholeness or integrity, proportion or harmony, and clarity or radiance. For the artist, the most important component of beauty is clarity or radiance, because clarity involves the initial formation of the artistic symbol in the mind of the artist. It is the wholeness and harmony of an object or idea that can cause an artistic symbol to be formed in the mind's eye of the artist. For example, good sculptors can imagine a finished statue when they look at a block of marble, and the poet can hear the finished poem in their mind, or a landscape painter can be so struck by a natural scene that he is compelled to transfer the interpreted scene to a canvas. This process of clarity, radiance, or visualization also occurs in the mind of the photographer when he or she chooses to take the time to capture an image. The source of the artistic symbol can be either something from the artist's imagination or some cue from the real world. Once the artistic symbol has been visualized in the mind of the artist, the next steps involve the tools and procedures that the artist uses to translate the visualized image into proper art. Proper art captures the viewer's undivided attention, and consequently it causes the viewer's mind to rise above the fears and desires of everyday life.

For the audience, the quality of proper art is determined by how effectively the artist communicates the wholeness and harmony of their visualization. In his book *Portrait of an Artist as a Young Man*, James Joyce **(see Figure 2.2)** describes the arrest that occurs when viewing proper art: "The tragic emotion, in fact, is the face looking in two ways, toward terror and toward pity, both of which are phases of it. You see I use the word arrest. I mean that the tragic emotion is static. Or rather the dramatic emotion is. The feelings excited by improper art are kinetic, desire and loathing. Desire urges us to possess, to go to something, loathing urges us to abandon, to go from something. The arts which excite them, pornographical or didactic, are therefore improper arts. The esthetic emotion (I used the general term) is therefore static. The mind is

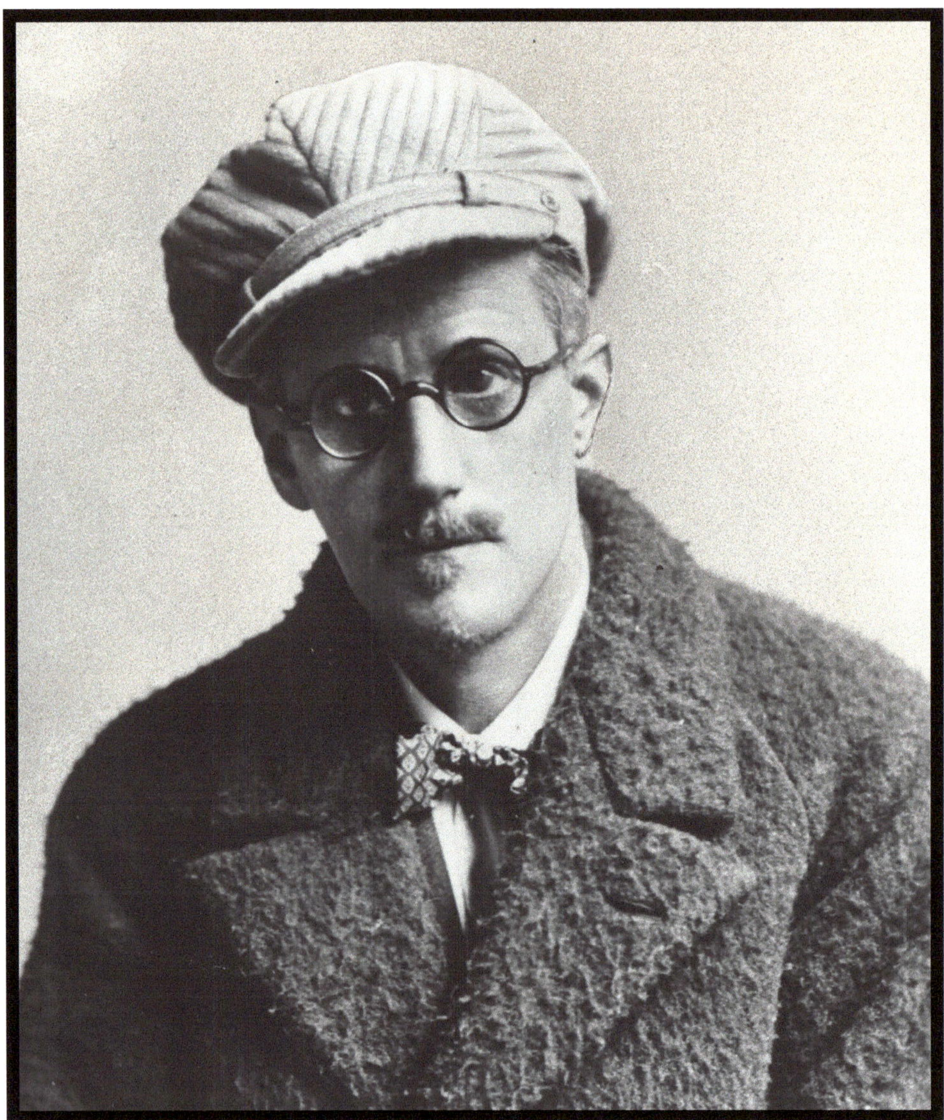

Figure 2.2
James Joyce

arrested and raised above desire and loathing." (James Joyce, Portrait of an Artist as a Young Man, P. 199)

Joyce is describing the same stillness that the Buddha experienced when his meditation led beyond the temptations of fear and desire to an awareness of the transcendent power of the universe. Joyce goes on to describe beauty: "Beauty expressed by the artist cannot awaken in us an emotion which is kinetic or a sensation which is purely physical. It awakens, or ought to awaken, or induces, or ought to induce, an esthetic stasis, and ideal pity or an ideal terror, a stasis called forth, prolonged and at last dissolved by what I call the rhythm of beauty." (Ibid P. 200) The moment of arrest that Joyce is describing occurs when the artist effectively communicates the radiance of the artistic symbol to the audience that is experiencing the aesthetic art.

For the photographer, the first step in the conversion of the visualized image into a final physical image involves the process of image capture. Early photographic capture media like the daguerreotype and wet-plate (collodion) media required immediate processing, which made the end product of image capture readily visible to the photographer. With the advent of dry plate and film media, an air of uncertain tension surrounded the image capture process. This tension came about because dry plate and film media required a secondary development process before the photographer could determine if he had successfully captured the image. If the photographer was attempting to capture a once in a life time event in a remote location, the demands on the photographer to deliver a high-quality result became acute. An extreme example of this phenomena was Robert Capa's photographs from Omaha Beach during the World War II Normandy invasion. Because of errors in film processing, only ten of Capa's 108 images survived the invasion. Due to the uncertainty of the image capture process, film photographers developed tools and techniques such as bracketing, visualization, and the Zone System as aids to the image capture process.

Beginning in the 1930s, Edward Weston **(see Figure 2.3)** and his friend Ansel Adams **(see Figure 2.4)** began teaching the notion of visualization in the creation of their photographs. For Weston, visualization involved the photographer fixing his concept of the final print in his mind before the negative was exposed. For Adams, the notion of visualization was so powerful that he incorporated visualization exercises at the beginning of his three volumes – *The Camera, The Negative*, and *The Print*. Each of the three books contains detailed descriptions of the techniques

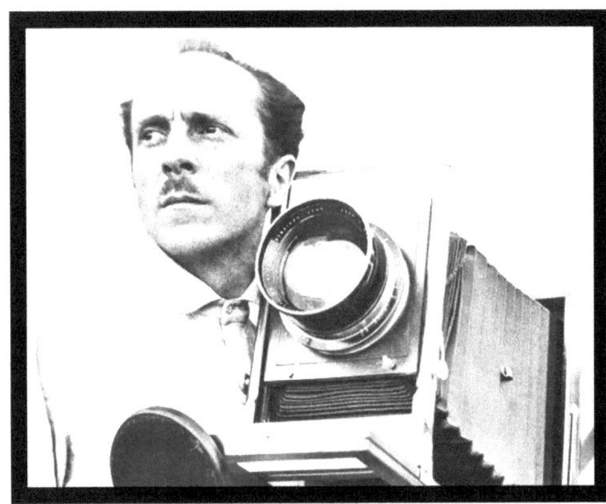

Figure 2.3
Edward Weston (left)

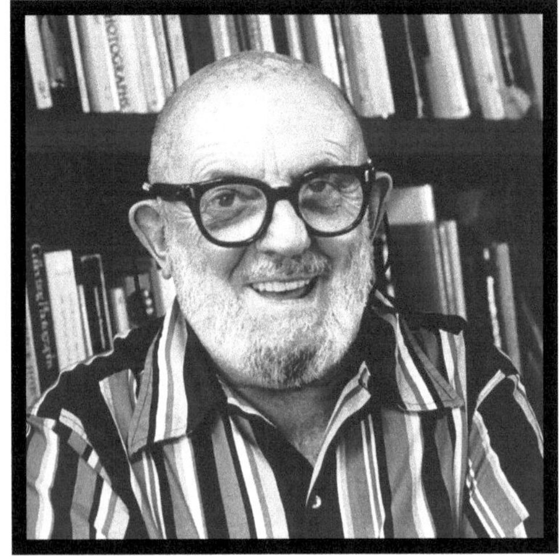

Figure 2.4
Ansel Adams (right)

and procedures necessary for the creation of the end products of each step in the photographic process, and each volume begins with a section on visualization.

Image capture techniques improved in 1949, when Polaroid instant film became available. Medium and large format camera manufacturers developed Polaroid film backs which allowed the photographer to use Polaroid instant film for proofing a photographic scene. Another very powerful image proofing tool became available to the photographer in 1995 when Casio began selling the Casio QV-10, which was the first camera to be equipped with a Liquid Crystal Display on the back of the camera.

With the dawn of the digital age, the simple creation of a perfect negative as the source for an excellent print has greatly expanded. In the digital age, the intermediate step of image capture has been extended to include electronic image capture files as well as negatives and transparencies . The practice of image capture visualization must then take into consideration the creation of a print as well as the creation of electronic image files for both electronic image licensing and for use on the Internet. In the digital age, the input source that is used in creation of the perfect image master file could be a digital camera, a film camera, or a scanner. In all cases, the goal of the image capture visualization step is to capture as much quality information as possible on the input media while thinking ahead to the final products.

The creation of high-quality photographic images is a very complex technical task which requires knowledge of complicated procedures and a wealth of experience. The capture of high-quality photographic images is an intersection of opportunity and preparation. The opportunity to capture photographic images present themselves all the time. The preparation part of the equation involves the photographer's knowledge of the procedures and techniques necessary to turn an opportunity into a high-quality image.

In order to encourage amateur photographers, manufacturers of photography equipment and supplies have always stressed that it was very easy to capture high-quality images. George Eastman's marketing slogan "You Push the Button and We Do the Rest" was the beginning of this trend for over-simplification of the photographic process. In 1981, Ansel Adams wrote in his work *The Negative*: "There is today a severe gulf between the general public's awareness and use of a photograph (which can be described as casual and imprecise for the most part) and the acute precisions of the manufacturers laboratories. There are a few exceptions, but the general trend today is to apply high laboratory standards to produce systems which are sophisticated in themselves, in order that the photographer need not be!" (Ansel Adams, *The Negative*, Introduction P. xii)

In the digital age, this trend toward over-simplification has been extended to an extreme. The art of image capture in the digital age has become deceptively simple. Autofocus lenses, automatic metering, and LCD display screens have relegated the art of image capture to decisions made by a machine. LCD displays are a wonderful proofing tool, but the photographer should spend more time observing and analyzing their subject than they do looking at the LCD display. The art of image capture should always include the following considerations:

1. Always allow a moment for the wholeness and harmony of the subject to form a clear vision in the mind of the photographer.

    - Take time to look at the subject
    - Take time to analyze the subject
    - Stay conscious of the direction and intensity of the incident light
    - Take time to measure the reflected light from the subject
    - Compose the image
    - Use the available proofing tools
    - Bracket the image (this involves taking multiple images at different exposure values.

2. Always try to imagine the end product of the image creation process:
    - The print
    - An electronic image for licensing
    - An electronic image for the Internet

It may seem like this deliberate approach to image capture will be too time-consuming, but with some practice, these procedures will become second nature to the photographer. All of the procedures listed above will be discussed in detail in the following chapters.

A photograph is an artistic symbol, and the creation of a photograph involves the same steps that creators of aesthetic symbols have used throughout human history. The process involves the perception of the wholeness and harmony of the artistic symbol followed by the formation of the visualized image in the mind of the artist. The final steps in the creation of a photograph involve the procedures and techniques necessary to create the final image. For Edward Weston, the final image was a print. In the digital age the final image could be a print, an electronic image for licensing, or an electronic image that could be used on the Internet.

“Light
Light
The visible reminder of the Invisible Light”

-- T. S. Eliot

Chapter Three

Light

Throughout history, human ruminations on the nature of light have been the center of study for both mythology and science. Yet, even in today's era of advanced knowledge, the nature of light remains a mystery for both philosophers and scientists.

The Mythological View

Without light, the universe as we know it would not exist, and without light, life on our planet would certainly not exist. The writings of Moses express this theme with the words *Fiat Lux (Let there be Light)*: "In the Beginning God created the heavens and the earth; the earth was waste and void; darkness covered the abyss and the spirit of God was stirring above the waters. God said "Let there be light" and there was light. God saw the light was good. God separated the light from darkness calling the light Day and the darkness Night. And there was evening and morning the first day." (Genesis 1:3)

The Persian philosopher Zoroaster described the universe as a struggle between the God of Light – Ahura Mazda, and the God of

Darkness – Ahriman (Yasna). In Asian cultures, Joseph Campbell **(Figure 3.1)** relates the myths of light to the notion of reincarnation: "The idea of the reincarnating principle is thus of two orders: first, the reincarnating principle that puts on bodies and puts them off as the Moon puts off its light body: and the other is that principle of sheer light that never dies, the light that is incarnate and immanent in all. Now one of the aims of all of the high-culture religions on the Oriental side of the line is to realize one's own identity with that solar light." (Joseph Campbell, *Myths of Light*, P. 14)

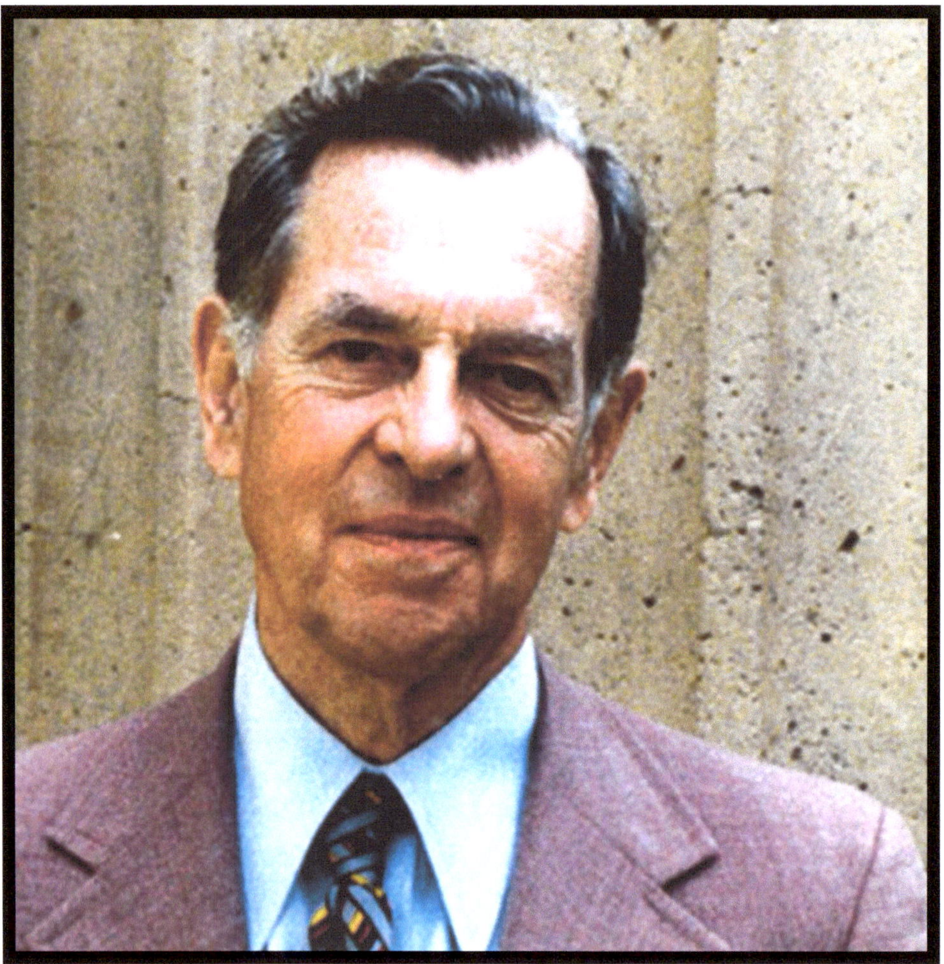

Figure 3.1
Joseph Campbell

Similar interpretations of light existed in the mythologies of the West. In Greek culture, there were gods who were associated with both the constant eternal form of the sun's light and the cyclical waxing and waning light of the moon. Apollo, the god of the sun, represented the constant and eternal aspects of life while Dionysus, the god of wine, represented the energy of life and the cycles of time – birth, life, death, and resurrection. These eternal and cyclical representations of gods in ancient mythology are directly related to the constant and cyclical nature of light that emanates from the sun and the moon.

The Scientific View

In scientific literature, light is defined as electromagnetic radiation with the following three attributes:

1. **Intensity –**
   Intensity or *amplitude* describes the brightness of light. Light intensity can be characterized by the inverse square law, which describes light intensity as a function of the distance from the light source. For example, light at two feet from the source is ½ the intensity of light one foot from the source while light four feet from the source has ¼ the intensity of light at one foot from the source. Light intensity is expressed as candle power and lumens. Candle power or foot candles is the brightness of one candle at one foot from the candle flame source. A lumen is the amount of light that falls on a one square foot surface from one candle one foot from the surface.

2. **Frequency or Wavelength**
   Frequency or *wavelength* describes the wave property of light. As light travels through space it manifests the behavior of a wave, a disturbance that propagates through space and time. Waves are characterized by crests and troughs, and wavelength is the distance from the beginning of one wave pattern to the beginning of the next repeated wave pattern. The visible light spectrum is defined from the wavelengths of approximately 780 nanometers (infra-red light) to approximately 380 nanometers (ultra-violet light) with the colors red, orange, yellow, green, blue, indigo, and violet in between (hence the mnemonic "ROY G. BIV"). Electromagnetic gamma rays and X-rays exist at wavelengths

below ultraviolet and radar and radio waves exist at wavelengths above infrared. The visible wavelengths in the spectrum of light are known as color. The various wave-lengths of light define color as follows:

- RED – 625 to 740 nanometers
- ORANGE – 590 to 625 nanometers
- YELLOW – 565 to 590 nanometers
- GREEN – 500 to 565 nanometers
- CYAN – 485 to 500 nanometers
- BLUE – 440 to 485 nanometers
- VIOLET – 380 to 440 nanometers

One nanometer (nm) is equal to 10^9 meters or one billionth of a meter or one millionth of a millimeter. **(Figure 3.2)**

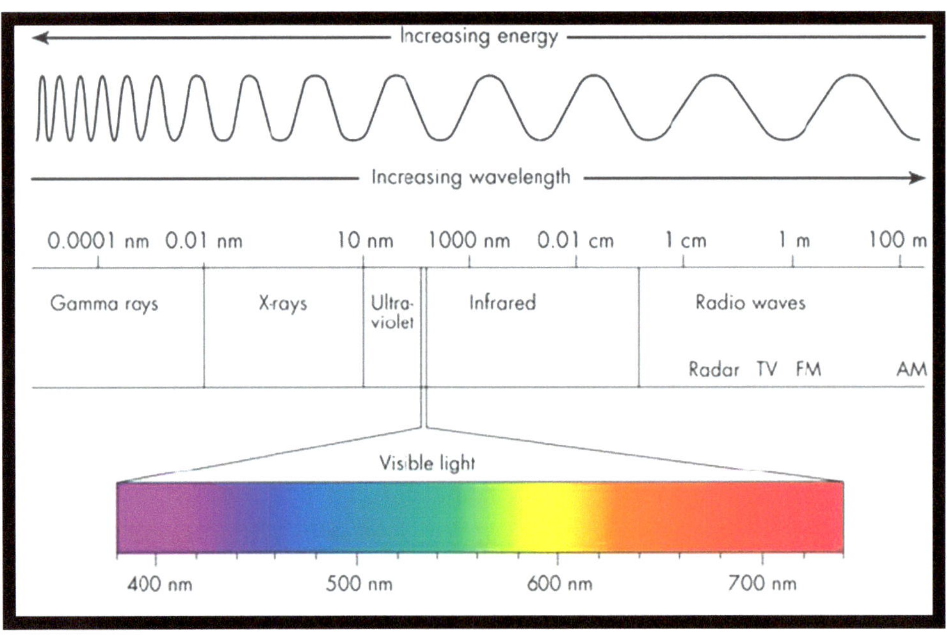

Figure 3.2
The Electromagnetic Spectrum

3. **Polarization**
   Polarization describes an angle of vibration perpendicular to the path traveled by light.

The Journey of Light

Light has a curious dual nature in that it takes on the behaviors of both a particle and a wave. Light behaves as a particle when leaving its source and arriving at its destination, while it manifests the behavior of a wave as it travels on the path from source to destination. Most light sources are thermal like our sun. Thermal or heat-based light sources are referred to by scientists as black body radiators.

Light Sources

Objects that emit light usually do so as a result of the increased temperature of the source object. Thermal based light sources are said to be incandescent. The Kelvin temperature of a theoretical heated black body radiator determines its hue or color temperature. Color temperature is measured in degrees of Kelvin from 1800 K (Red) through 5500 K (White) to 16,000 K (Blue). This range may seem a bit confusing since the color blue is usually thought of as a cold color, but in reality the hottest stars in our universe are blue in color. Listed below are some color temperatures **(Figure 3.3)**:

- 1700 K – Match flame
- 1850 K – Candle
- 2800 K – Incandescent light bulb
- 3350 K – Studio CP light
- 3400 K – Studio lamps
- 4100 K – Moon-light
- 5000 K – Day-light (U. S. Standard)
- 5770 K – Sun temperature
- 6500 K – Day-light (European Standard)
- 9300 K – CRT screen

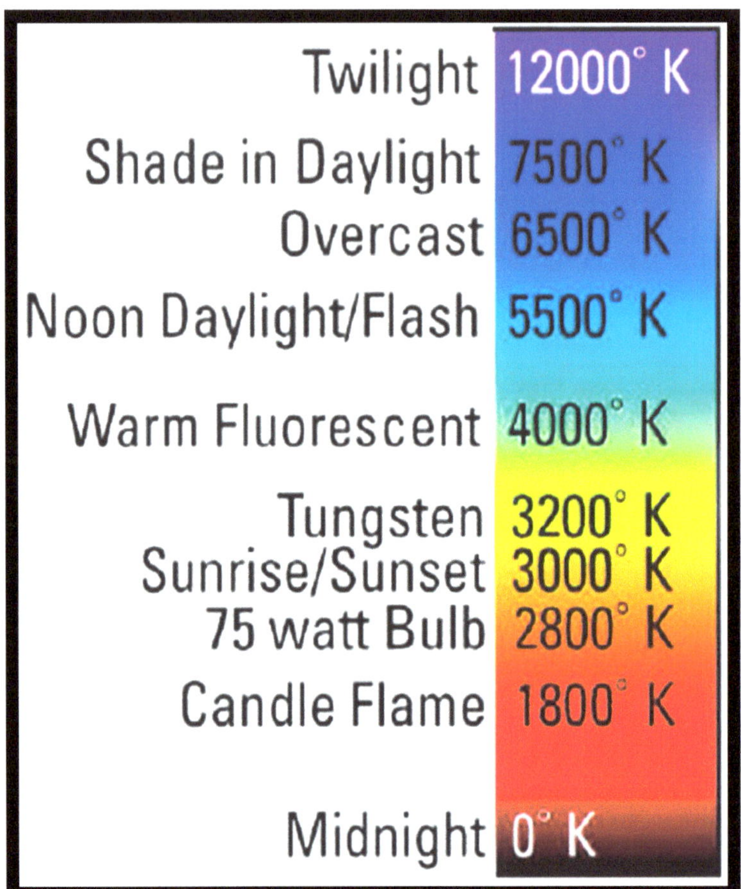

Figure 3.3
Color Temperature

The Journey

As light waves travel through space, they are subject to red shift, diffraction, refraction, and polarization. *Red shift* refers to the spreading of wave length that occurs as waves travel from a source to a destination. As waves travel through space, the wavelength of the light has a tendency to get longer, and the farther that the waves travel, the more the length of the wave increases. This phenomena is known as red shift because the lengthening of the wavelength causes the color of the light to move toward the red portion of the color spectrum. The astronomer Edwin Hubble used the red shift phenomena to measure the distances to objects in outer space.

Diffraction or *interference* refers to the change in light wave patterns that occurs when light waves encounter forces or obstacles on their journey through a space. **(Figure 3.4)** Light wave patterns can be altered by gravity or other electromagnetic forces. The light wave patterns can also be altered when they intersect and overlap other light wave patterns, and they can be modified as they bend around small objects or as they pass through small openings. All of these instances of wave pattern modification are known as diffraction.

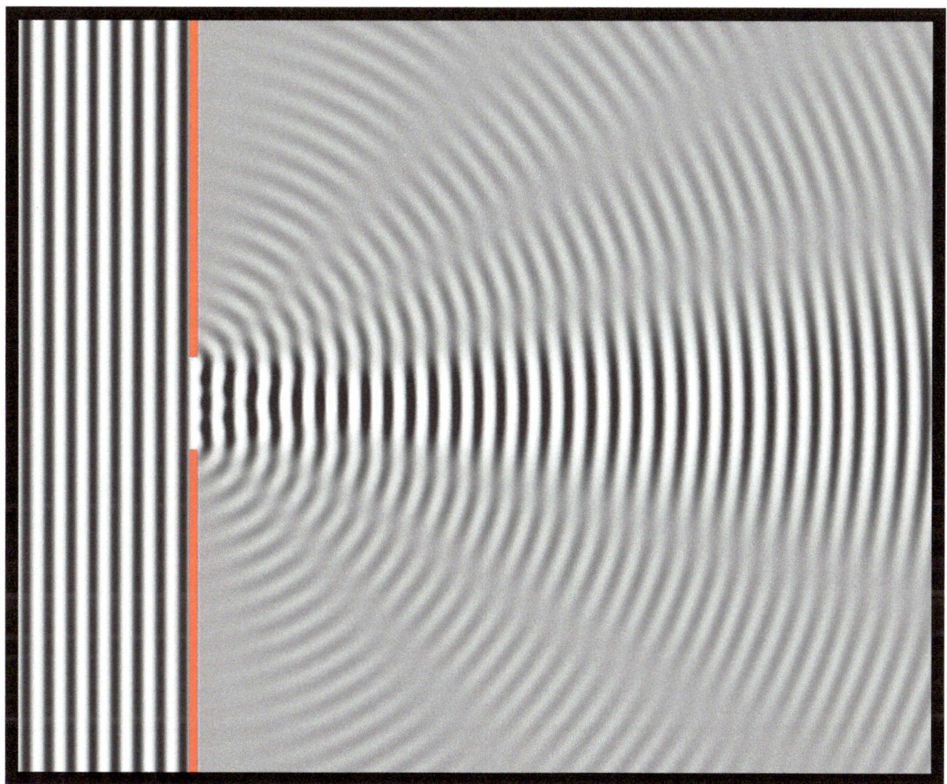

Figure 3.4
Wave Diffraction Patterns

Light waves are capable of traveling through a multitude of media including a vacuum. Light travels at a constant speed of 186,000 miles or 299,792,458 meters per second in a vacuum; however, some media can change the direction and phase velocity of a light wave pattern as the waves pass through the given media. This phenomena is known as *refraction.* The best example of refraction is the appearance of a straw when it is placed in clear water. **(Figure 3.5)**

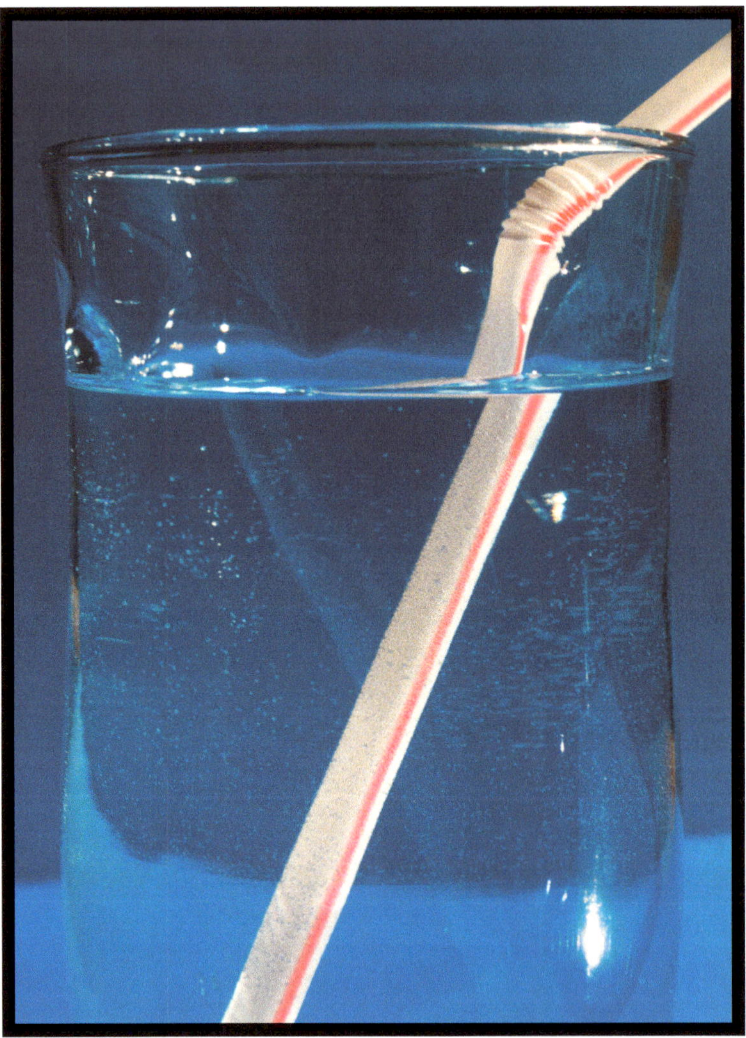

Figure 3.5
Refraction

The straw appears to be bent because the water is causing the light wave pattern to change direction and speed. Refraction is responsible for the creation of rainbows as well as the splitting of white light into its color components as the white light passes through a prism. *Polarization* refers to the oscillation of light waves as they travel through space. Polarization will be discussed in Chapter 6 during the review of polarizing filters.

The Destination

Finally, the light arrives at a destination. The first aspect of arriving light concerns the amount or intensity of light falling on a given object. This quantity is known as *incident light* and it is expressed in units of *Lumens*. Second, the incident light manifests different behavior depending upon the nature of the surface that the arriving light strikes, the arriving light is either reflected, scattered, absorbed, or some combination of these three phenomena.

The basic law of reflection states that the angle of incidence for light in an incoming direction is equal to the angle of reflection for the outgoing reflected light. Examples of this specular light reflection are a mirror, the reflected image on a perfectly still pond, or the reflected image on wet pavement. *Specular highlights* in photography refer to bright light that is reflected from a metal objects like a chrome bumper or the light reflected from the crest of an ocean wave. In contrast to specular reflection, diffuse reflection or scattering is the reflection of light in a multitude of directions. Scattering usually results from light striking a rough or uneven surface.

Lastly, the incident light can be either transmitted through or absorbed by a surface. When light passes through a surface, the surface is known as translucent; examples of translucent surfaces are clear glass and water. A surface can also absorb all, some, or none of the incident light. If the surface absorbs all and reflects none of the incident light, then the surface is called black. If the surface absorbs none and reflects all of the incident light then the surface is called white. A surface can also absorb some wavelengths of light and reflect other wavelengths. The color of a surface is determined by which wavelengths are absorbed and which wavelengths are reflected. For example, if a surface absorbs all wavelengths except red, then the surface is called red. Like-wise, if a surface absorbs all wavelengths except green, then the surface is called green. Consequently, the color of an object is determined by the spectrum of the incident light, the amount of wavelength absorption by the surface, and reflection from the surface of the object. In addition, the reflected light from a surface can appear to be different depending on the type of light source that creates the incident light. This phenomenon is known as metamerism.

A further discussion of the nature of light would take volumes, and this is a book about image capture, of which light is an important but small component. Listed below is a brief history of the modern theory of light so that the reader can pursue further research on this fascinating topic if they so wish.

The Scientific History of Light

Modern research into the theories of light began with the French atomic scientist Pierre Gassendi (1592 – 1655). Gassendi was an avid follower of the Greek philosopher Epicurus who was the inspiration for Gassendi's particle theory of light. Gassendi believed that light was a property of a unique kind of atom (*atom lucificae*) that are identical to heat atoms. (http://plato.stanford.edu/entries/gassendi/)

Gassendi's particle theory was published in his Philosophical Treatise in 1658. British scientist Robert Hooke (1635 -1703) published a wave theory of light in the 1660's, and the debate over the wave/particle duality of light began. From 1670 to 1672, the British scientist Sir Isaac Newton presented a series of lectures on optics. Newton had read Gassendi's work, and he believed that light was composed of particles that he referred to as corpuscles. However, Newton did include a wave attribute of light in order to explain diffraction.

Newton's lectures included experiments with refraction and his famous prism experiments in which he demonstrated the decomposition and recombination of white light into its component colors. In 1671, Newton published his lecture notes at the request of the Royal Society.

Newton's lecture notes entitled *On Color* would later be expanded to become the work entitled *Optics* which was published in 1704. Newton's particle theory of light would dominate science in the 18th Century.

In Holland, the Dutch scientist and clock maker Christian Huygens was also working on a theory of light. In 1678, Huygens developed a wave theory of light, which he published as his *Treatise on Light* in 1690. Other proponents of the wave theory included the Swiss mathematician Leonhard Euler (1707 – 1783) and the French physicist Augustin-Jean Fresnel (1788 - 1827). Euler published his findings in 1746 under the title *Nova Theoria Lucis et Colorum*, and Fresnel presented his wave theory to the French Academie des Sciences in 1817.

In 1810, the German writer and scientist Johann Goethe published his monumental work on light and shadow entitled *The Theory of Color.* Goethe's book contains a remarkably accurate set of experiments that explore light and shadow. *The Theory of Color* made a major contribution to the understanding of how humans perceive light. Goethe's work is still used by many academic art departments as a source for the understanding of color and shadow in art.

In 1845, the British scientist Michael Faraday discovered that the angle of polarization for a light beam could be modified by a magnetic field. This discovery led Faraday to speculate that light is a high frequency electromagnetic vibration. In 1849, the French physicist Hippolyte Fizeau measured the approximate speed of light by using a mirror and cogwheel apparatus. Fizeau reported that light travels at 313,000 kilometers per second. In 1850, Leon Foucault improved Fizeau's light measurements by replacing the cogwheel with Wheatstone's revolving mirror apparatus. Sir Charles Wheatstone was an extremely talented British scientist and inventor who developed a mechanism in the 1830s, which used the a rotating mirror to measure the velocity of an electric current in a wire. Foucault modified Wheatstone's revolving mirror apparatus in order to measure the velocity of light, and his estimated speed of light was published in 1862 as 298,000 kilometers per second.

In 1862, British scientist James Clerk Maxwell **(Figure 3.6)** expanded Michael Faraday's work to discover that light was a self-propagating electromagnetic wave pattern that traveled through space at a constant speed, namely, the speed of light. Maxwell's conclusion that light was an electromagnetic force was published in 1862 under the title *On Physical Lines of Force.* In 1873 Maxwell published a mathematical description of the behavior of electric and magnetic fields known as *Maxwell's Equations.*

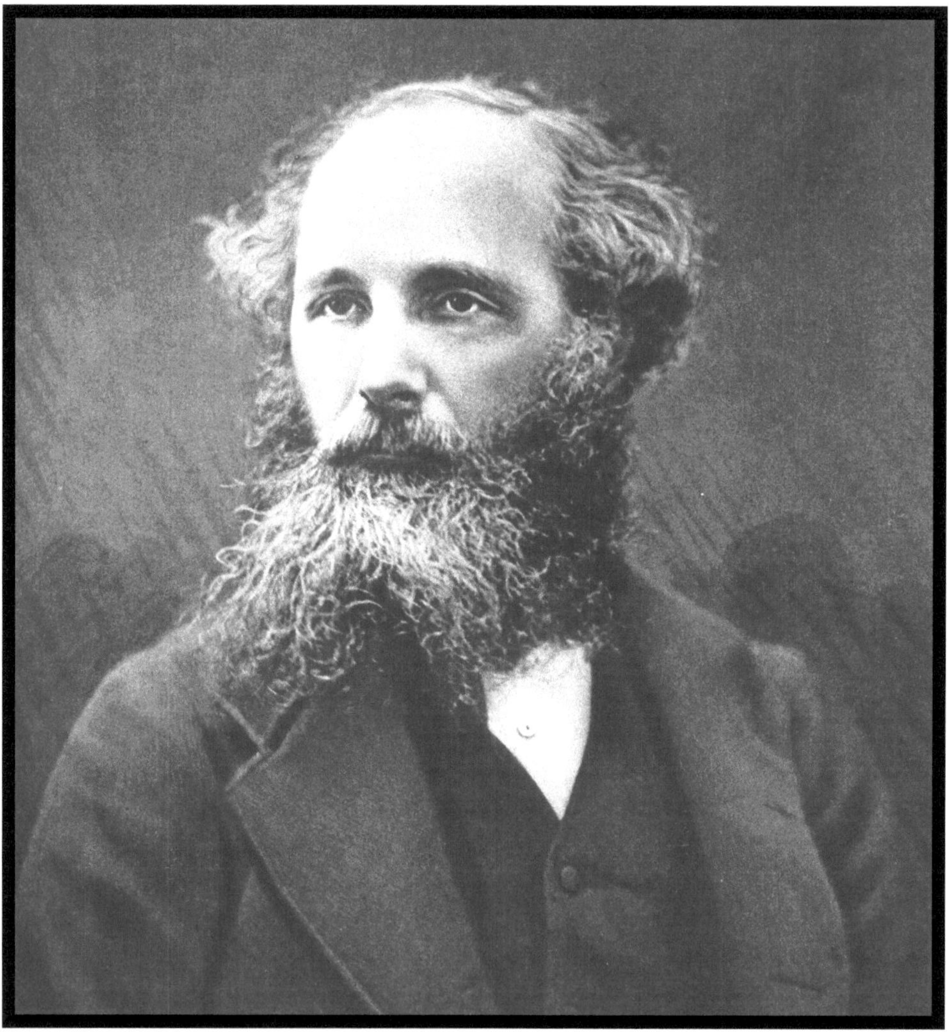

Figure 3.6
James Clerk Maxwell

Early wave theories of light relied on the existence of a medium for the transmission of light waves known as *luminiferous aether.* In 1887, physicists Albert Michelson and Edward Morley performed experiments to measure the speed of light which proved the that the luminiferous aether medium did not exist. These experiments opened the door to the revitalization of the particle theory of light. In 1900, German physicist Max Plank's studies of black body light emission deviated from classical physics by assuming that electromagnetic energy in the form of light was emitted in specific amounts, or *quanta.*

In 1905, Swiss postal worker Albert Einstein expanded upon the works of Isaac Newton, Max Plank, and James Maxwell in a paper which defined Einstein's special theory of relativity, which revised Newton's laws of motion to account for the constant speed of light. Einstein expanded Plank's work to describe light energy as quanta which he called *photons.* Einstein expanded Maxwell's findings to define the equivalence of matter and energy with the constant speed of light as the conversion factor, thus $E = mc^2$.

In 1924, Louis de Broglie proposed a quantum theory which included the wave-like nature of sub atomic particles. In 1929, a group of physicists began the development of Quantum Electrodynamics or QED. QED mathematically describes all phenomena involving electrically charged particles that interact through the exchange of photons. QED includes the interaction between light and matter as well as the interaction between charged particles. The QED theory of photons culminated in the 1940's with Richard Feynman's **(Figure 3.7)** pictorial representations of the QED light phenomena known as Feynman diagrams. Feynman's discoveries were published in 1985 under the title *QED: The Strange Theory of Light and Matter.*

In 1968, a young physicist named Gabriel Veneziano was working at the CERN high energy atom smasher. Veneziano made a connection between his research on the strong nuclear force and a two-hundred-year old formula derived by the Swiss mathematician Leonhard Euler. Veneziano could not explain why Euler's mathematics for the Beta Function worked so well in describing Veneziano's research findings. In 1970, physicists Leonard Susskind, Holger Nielsen, and Yoichiro Namby

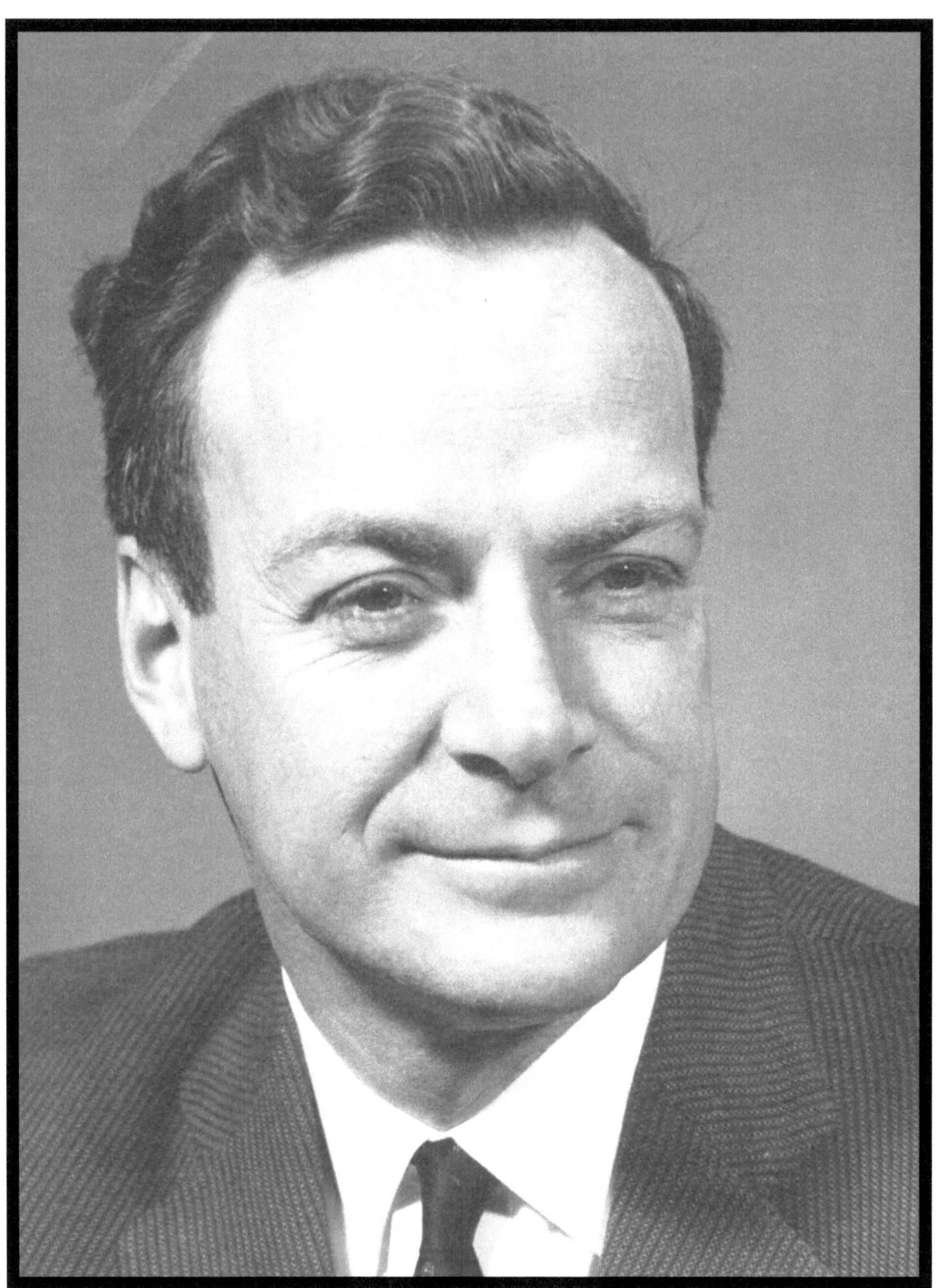

Figure 3.7
Richard Feynman

interpreted Veneziano's findings to define extremely tiny elastic strands that they called *strings.* The birth of string theory was to shed new light on the interpretation of light. Modern theories of light are explored in Brian Greene's two excellent books *The Elegant Universe* and *The Fabric of the Universe* Greene's books put the modern theories of light into the context of string theory and modern universal cosmology.

We can easily forgive a child who is afraid of the dark;
the real tragedy of life is when men are afraid of the light.

-- Plato

Chapter Four

The Capture of Light

Black and White/Color Spaces

Modern photography is concerned with the representation of images in either the black and white medium or the color medium. These two mediums can be expressed by using the grayscale in the case of the black and white medium or color spaces in the case of the color medium.

Grayscale

Understanding the grayscale is crucial to the understanding of black and white photography. Black and white photographic images manifest themselves as black, white, and various shades of gray. **(Figure 4.1)** Black and white photographs are studies of light and shadow with shadows being expressed in black and light expressed in white or shades of gray. For reflected light, the color of the light reflected from a surface is determined by the wavelengths of color that are absorbed by the surface. A black surface absorbs all wavelengths of color and reflects none of the wavelengths of color. On the other hand, white surfaces reflect all of the wavelengths of color and absorb none of the wavelengths of color. For this reason, the residents of California's hot sunny Central

Valley wear white clothing in the summertime and they do not usually purchase black automobiles. Black and white photography represents the various colors reflected from a surface in various shades of gray.

Ansel Adams divided the grayscale into eleven equal parts or zones represented by 0 and the Roman numerals I to X (the Romans did not

Figure 4.1
Grayscale

have a numeral for zero). The Zones span from black or 0% reflectance in Zone 0 to white or 100% reflectance in Zone X. **(Figure 4.2)**

Zone	0	I	II	III	IV	V	VI	VII	VIII	IX	X
Reflectance	100%					18%					0%
Digital Value	0	26	51	77	102	128	153	179	204	230	255

Figure 4.2
Grayscale Zones

Zones I to IX were defined to contain various shades of gray progressing from dark gray in Zone I to middle gray in Zone V to light gray in Zone IX. The gray value in Zone V is also known as middle gray or 18% reflectance. On a geometric scale from black to white, middle gray or 18% reflectance is the middle value. The human eye tends to average viewed surfaces to a value close to middle gray. The understanding of middle gray is the key to understanding the Zone System, which will be explored in Chapter 5.

The Color Wheel

The basic color wheel **(Figure 4.3)** is composed of six primary colors: red, yellow, green, cyan, blue, and magenta.

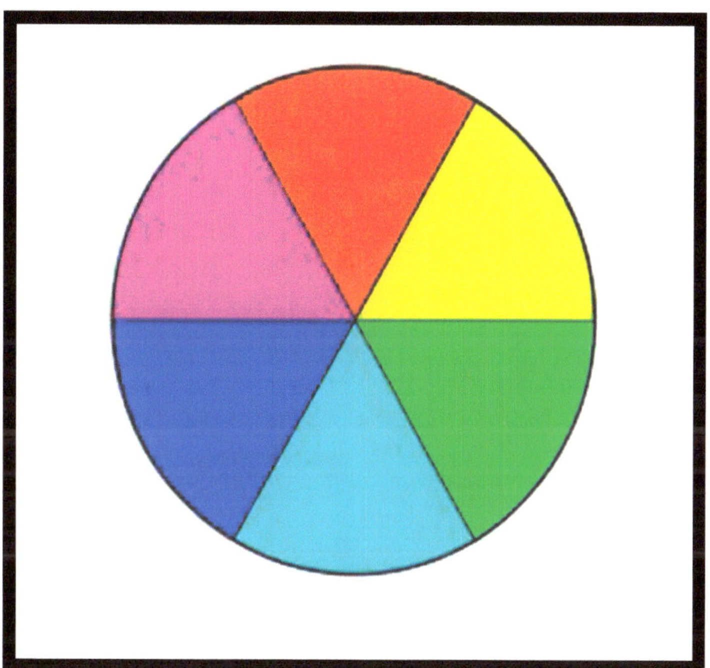

Figure 4.3
Color Wheel

The primary colors that are opposite each other on the color wheel are known as complementary colors. An inverse relationship exists between a given primary color and its complementary color. For example, when the red component in an image increases, then the cyan component decreases. The other interesting aspect of the color wheel is the relationship between a color and its two adjacent colors. The relationship between adjacent colors on the color wheel is as follows:

- Red is equal to one half Magenta and one half Yellow
- Yellow is equal to one half Red and one half Green
- Green is equal to one half Yellow and one half Cyan
- Cyan is equal to one half Green and one half Blue
- Blue is equal to one half Cyan and one half Magenta
- Magenta is equal to one half Blue and one half Red

The adjacent relationship between the components of the color wheel allows for greater flexibility when making color adjustments to an image. For example, in order to increase the red component in an image, either the cyan component can be lowered or the green and blue components can be altered separately since green plus blue is equal to cyan. The independent adjustment of the adjacent component colors provides greater flexibility than the adjustment of the complimentary colors alone.

The HSB Color Space

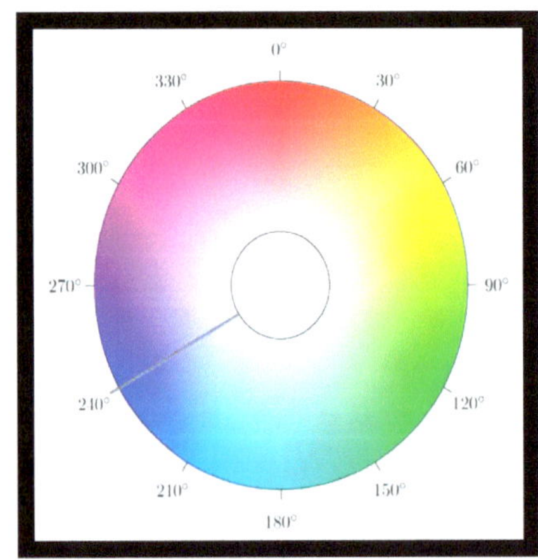

Figure 4.4
HSB Color Model

Another variation on the color wheel is the HSB Color model. **(Figure 4.4)** The HSB color model was defined by Alvey Ray Smith in 1978, and it is used today in support of various computer graphic applications. The HSB color model has three components – *Hue, Saturation,* and *Brightness.* The Hue component of the HSB model is the color itself expressed in increments of sixty degrees around the circumference of a circle.

The HSB model makes the following Hue assignments:

- Red – 0 degrees
- Yellow -- 60 degrees
- Green – 120 degrees
- Cyan – 180 degrees
- Blue – 240 degrees
- Magenta – 300 degrees

Each Hue value corresponds to a section on the color spectrum where the specific color is dominant.

The second component of the HSB model is saturation or *chroma.* Saturation is expressed as a value from 0% to 100%, and saturation represents the purity or intensity of a particular hue. For example, the hue of red (zero degrees on the wheel) with a saturation of 100% would be pure red with no other colors of the spectrum contained in the red hue.

The third component of the HSB model is brightness or value. Brightness is expressed as a value from 0% to 100% with 0% representing black and 100% representing white. The brightness component of the HSB model emulates the rods in human vision. An image with a brightness value of 100 % has no detail and appears as white. As the brightness value is reduced, the image appears to have more detail and depth until the image appears as black at 0%.

Paint, The Human Eye, Projected Light, and Ink

The colors of the visible light spectrum can be organized based on the points of reference that each color space represents. The four points of reference are paint, the human eye, projected light, and ink. The associated color spaces are the traditional painting color space that is used for paint, the lab color space associated with the human eye, the RGB or additive color space associated with projected light, and the CMYK color space associated with ink.

The Paint Color Space

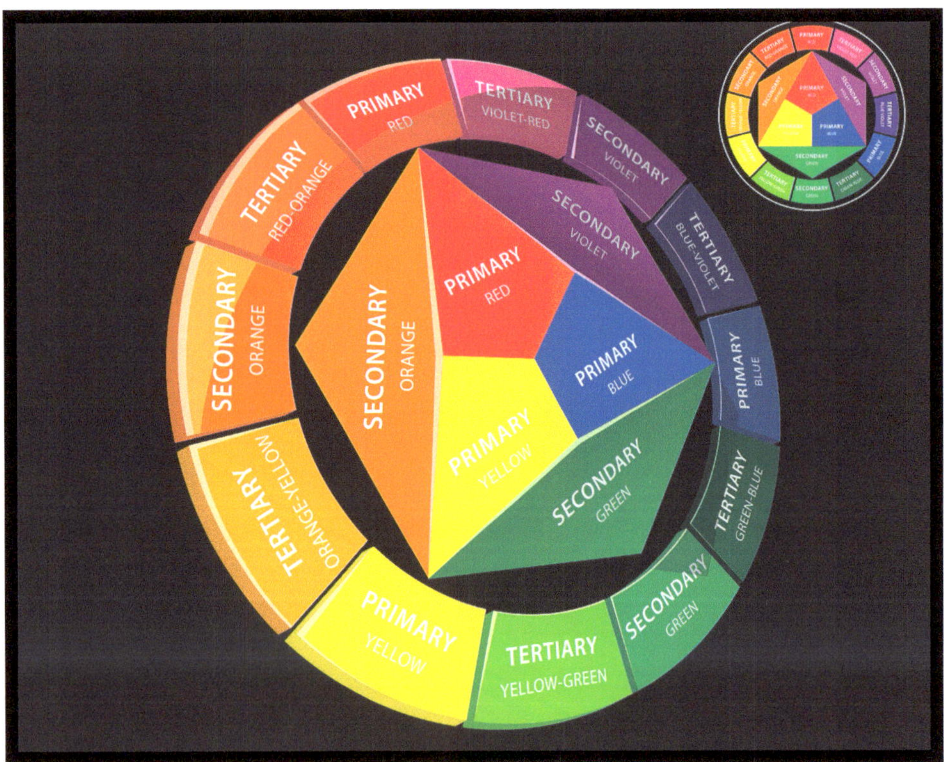

Figure 4.5
Paint Color Space

The traditional paint color space uses red, blue, and yellow as the primary colors with green, orange, and violet as the respective secondary colors that are created by combining two of the primary colors. **(Figure 4.5)**

For example, red and blue are combined to create violet, red and yellow are combined to form orange, and blue and yellow are combined to form green. The painting color space defines six tertiary colors that are created by combining one of the primary colors with one of the secondary colors. The six tertiary colors are red-orange, yellow-green, blue-violet, red-violet, yellow-orange, and blue-green. The three primary, three secondary, and six tertiary colors define the twelve basic hue ranges of the painting color space.

The Human Eye -- Lab Color Space

The retina in the human eye is made up of rods and cones. The rods sense brightness or light intensity while the cones detect color. The retina contains three types of cones with each type of cone being sensitive

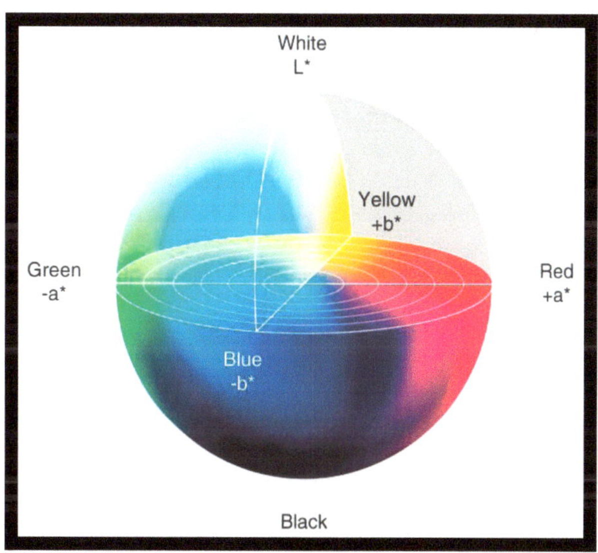

Figure 4.6
Lab Color Space

to certain wavelengths of light. One type of cone is sensitive to red light, one type of cone is sensitive to green light, and one type of cone is sensitive to blue light. Beginning in 1931, the device independent color space known as CIELAB (CIE: International Commission on Illumination) was developed as an attempt to assign a numeric value to every color that is perceived by the human eye. **(Figure 4.6)**

A separate LAB color space was developed by Richard S. Hunter in 1948, and the original CIELAB version was further enhanced in 1976 and is now known as CIE1976 L*A*B*. The LAB color space is defined by three values with the first value 'L' for lightness. The lightness variable has a range of values from 'L'= 0 or black to 'L' = 100 or white. The second variable 'A' represents a range of colors from green to magenta expressed as values from -128 to 127. Negative values of 'A' represent variations of green and positive values of 'A' represent variations of magenta. The third variable 'B' represents a range of colors from blue to yellow using values from -128 to 127. Negative values of 'B' represent variations of blue while positive values of 'B' represent variations of yellow. Adobe Photoshop uses the LAB color space to convert from one color space to a different color space. Because of its device independence, the LAB color space is used as a reference point by the other color spaces.

Projected Light -- The Additive Color Space (RGB)

The RGB or *additive* color space is associated with projected light, such as the light you would see emanating from a traditional cathode ray tube (television or computer monitor). The RGB color space is composed of the three primary colors – red, green, and blue – which correspond to the three types of cones that make up human vision. The RGB color space is also known as additive color because the combination of the three primary colors creates white light. **(Figure 4.7)**

The RGB color space is the most widely used color space in the digital world. Televisions, computer monitors, digital cameras, scanners, lightjet, and inkjet printers all rely on the mixing of RGB colors to produce additive projected color images. The RGB color space is device dependent which means that the expression of the color space is dependent on the gamut of a specific device. Gamut is defined as the range of colors that can be interpreted and expressed by a specific device. For example, the gamut of the human eye is from the wavelengths of approximately 380 nanometers to approximately 780 nanometers, and the gamut of human vision is defined by the LAB color space. Also, each type of film has a specific gamut known as its *spectral sensitivity.* All digital devices -- cameras, monitors, scanners, and printers have a specific gamut which determines how the specific device will interpret and express the RGB color space.

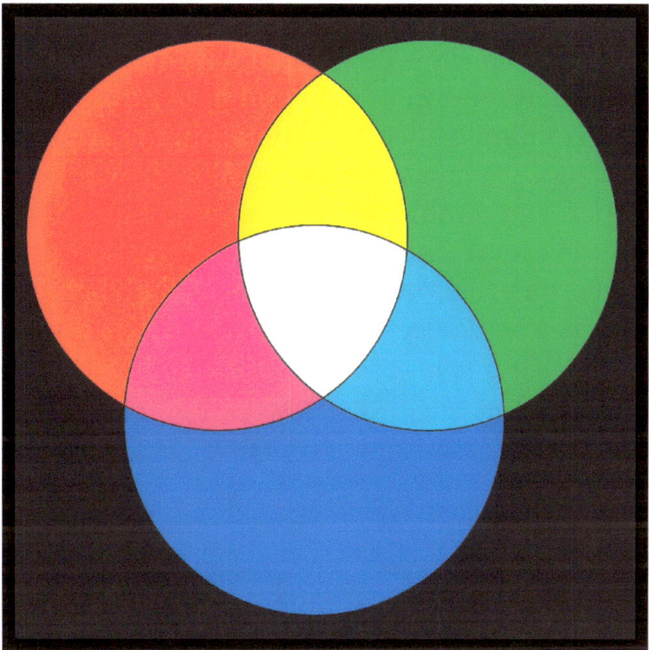

Figure 4.7
RGB Color Space

Ink -- The Subtractive Color Space (CMYK)

The final color space is the CMYK or *subtractive* color space, which is primarily associated with ink and printing. The CMYK color space uses the complementary colors cyan, magenta, and yellow as the components of this color space. Theoretically, the combination of cyan, magenta, and yellow should yield the color black, but because of the impurities of ink, the color that results from the combination of cyan, magenta, and yellow is a brownish-gray color. In order to rectify this problem, a fourth component black has been added to the subtractive color space. Black is represented by the letter 'K' which stands for key tone. **(Figure 4.8)**

The CMYK color space is concerned with light reflected from a printed page. The combination of inks and paper absorb certain parts of the visible spectrum and reflect the remaining portions of the visible spectrum. For example, when we view a yellow flower printed on a white piece of paper, the combination of ink and paper reflects the yellow portion of the visible spectrum contained in the incident light, and it absorbs or subtracts the remaining portions of the visible spectrum. The CMYK color space is also device-dependent, and it is a much smaller color space than the other color spaces. Ink also has the unique capability to reflect different areas of the spectrum based upon the incident light falling on the printed image. This attribute of ink is known as metamerism.

Figure 4.8
CMYK Color Space

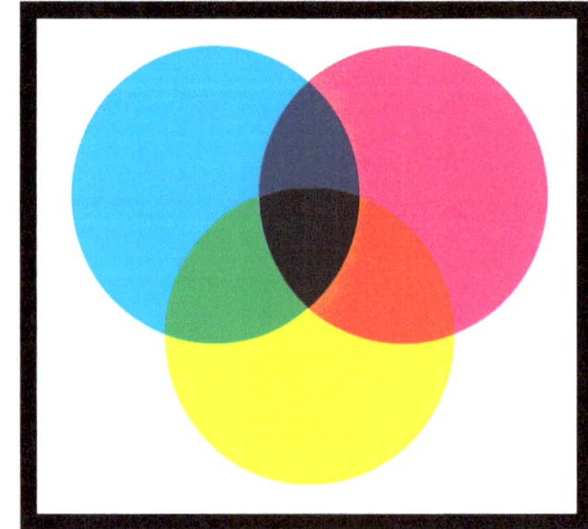

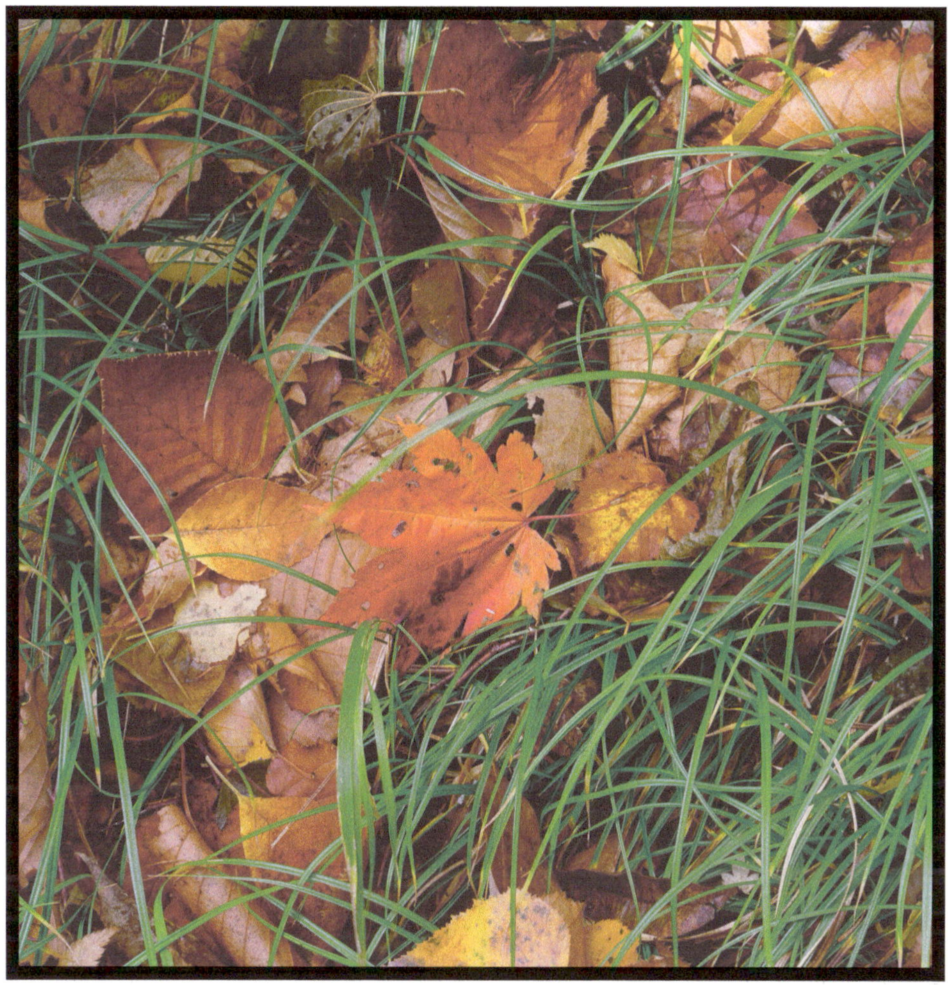

Figure 4.9
Autumn Leaves
Akan National Park
Hokkaiko, Japan

It would be possible to describe everything scientifically,
but it would make no sense; it would be without meaning,
as if you described a Beethoven symphony as a variation in wave pressure.

\- -- Albert Einstein

Chapter Five

Exposure and the Zone System

The Standard Exposure Model

Throughout this volume, certain keywords will be used to describe the image capture process. In order to comprehend this process, a teaching tool known as the **Standard Exposure Model (Figure 5.1)** has been developed.

In order to better understand an exposure, it is useful to decompose the exposure model into key components. For an exposure, the key components are:

- Incident Light
- The Subject
- Reflected Light
- The Exposure Axis
- The Camera
- The Eye of the Photographer

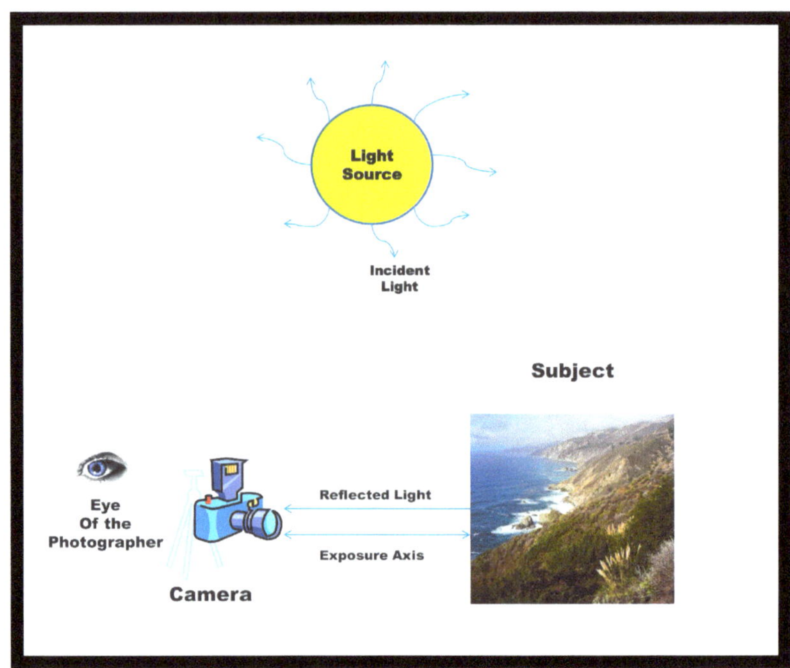

Figure 5.1
The Standard Exposure Model

Incident Light

Incident light is composed of wavelengths of light that emanate from a light source. For natural light photography, the source is the sun; however, incident light can also emanate from the moon, the stars, fire, or lava. For artificial light photography, the light source could be static studio lights or a flash/strobe. Incident light has an intensity, a wavelength or color, and a temperature.

Reflected Light

Reflected light is the wavelengths of light that have bounced off of a surface. Reflected light has intensity, a wavelength or color, and a color temperature. It is the reflected light that is emanating from the subject during the image capture process, and it is the intensity of the reflected light that can be measured by a light meter; it is reflected light that is captured by the capture media.

The Subject

The subject is an object that is captured by the capture media during the image capture process. For different types of photographic images, the subjects will be different. For example in a landscape photograph, the subject would be a natural scene, while in portrait photography, the subject would be an individual. Each subject has a range of tonal values that will be recorded by the camera.

The Exposure Axis

The exposure axis is a straight line that is perpendicular to the capture media, and it extends from the camera to the subject. Reflected light from the subject travels along the exposure axis to the camera lens. As the wavelengths of un-polarized light travel along the exposure axis, the light waves oscillate in all directions. The exposure axis is a critical reference point for the understanding of polarizing filters, as well as an important marker for the understanding of all aspects of image capture.

The Camera

The camera is a light-proof box with a lens that controls both the amount of light and the amount of time that light is allowed to fall on the capture media. In the digital age, cameras come in a wide range of sizes, but traditionally, cameras were grouped into three sizes:

- Small Format (35 mm)
- Medium Format (2 ¼ inches or 55 mm)
- Large Format (4" x 5" or 8" x 10")

An understanding of the role of the camera in the image capture process involves a thorough understanding of the components of the camera – the lens, the capture media, and the image frame.

The Lens

The camera lens is the interpreter of the reflected light emanating from the subject. Lenses are identified by their focal length. Focal length is the necessary distance between the rear element of the lens and the capture media that is required in order to bring subjects at infinity into focus. **(Figure 5.2)** For example, when the focus controls are set to infinity on a 50 mm lens, the rear element of the lens is required to be 50 mm from the capture media in order for distant objects to be in focus. As the subject that needs to be in focus becomes closer to the camera, the rear element of the lens needs to be moved farther away from the capture media in order to achieve correct focus for the subject. Zoom lenses have a variable focal length; for example, an 18 mm to 70 mm zoom lens can have focal lengths in a range from 18 mm to 70 mm.

Lenses have three basic controls: aperture controls, shutter speed controls, and focus controls. The aperture controls determine the size of the opening which allows light to fall on the capture media. The incremental aperture settings are known as f-stops, and the f-stops are expressed as the ratio between the size of the aperture opening and the focal length of the lens. F-stops are written with a lower case f, a slash and a number. For example, a 50 mm lens that is set to f-stop f/16 has an aperture opening of 3.4 mm – 50mm divided by 16 = 3.4mm diameter opening while the f-stop of f/4 would have an aperture opening of 12.5 mm – 50mm divided by 4 = 12.5mm diameter opening .

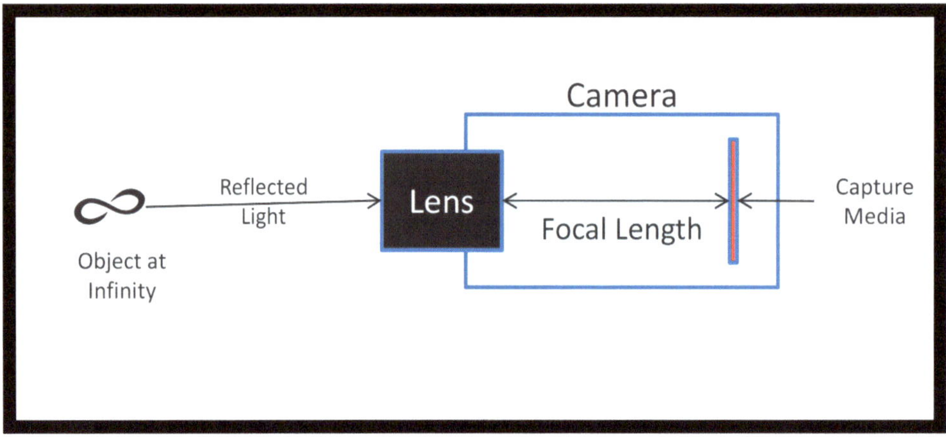

Figure 5.2
Focal Length

What is sometimes confusing is the fact that the smaller the f-stop number becomes, the larger the aperture opening becomes, and each incremental f-stop doubles the aperture opening size, which consequently doubles the amount of light that falls on the capture media. For example, an f-stop of f/4 has an aperture diameter that is twice the size of an f/2.8 f-stop and a f/2 f-stop has an aperture opening that is one-half the size of the f/2.8 f-stop. As the f-stop settings progress from the lowest values to the highest values, the aperture size doubles at each incremental f-stop, with the smallest number f-stop representing the largest aperture for the lens, and the largest f-stop number representing the smallest aperture setting.

The second lens control ring is known as the shutter speed ring. The shutter speed ring controls the amount of time that the capture media is exposed to the reflected light from the subject. When the camera exposure button is pressed, the lens opens its aperture to a specific size for a given length of time. Each incremental setting on the shutter speed ring approximately doubles the amount of time that the aperture remains open.

The third component of the lens is the focus controls, which are used to move the lens elements closer to or farther away from the capture media. Many of the modern digital camera lenses provide an auto focus function which moves the lens elements automatically.

The Capture Media

The final component of the camera is the capture media, which could be film or an array of Charged Couple Device (CCD) or CMOS light sensors. For the capture media, the primary concern is the light sensitivity of either the film or the light sensor array.

Light Sensitivity

Sensitometry is the study of light-sensitive materials, and in photography it extends back to the latter part of the nineteenth century. Beginning in the 1890's, photographers and scientists made serious attempts to standardize the measurement of film emulsion's sensitivity to light.

The measurement of light sensitive photography emulsions was greatly advanced by the work of the scientists Ferdinand Hurter and Charles Driffield. Hurter and Driffield's research defined the light sensitivity of film emulsions as a function of light exposure, as well as the film development methods which included the factors of time and temperature. The findings of Hurter and Driffield were expressed as concepts known as *film density* and the characteristic curve.

Film Density

Density for negative and transparency film refers to the amount of silver that remains on the film after it has been developed. For negative film, the most silver remains on the part of the negative that represents the brightest aspects of the subject, and the least amount of silver remains on the part of the negative that represents the darkest subject properties. When the negative is printed, the most light passes through the least dense portions of the negative, and the least amount of light passes through the most dense portions. The rules of density are reversed for transparency film: the area of the film that has the highest density represent the darkest features of the subject, while the areas of the film that have the least density represent the brightest aspects of the subject.

The Characteristic Curve

Hurter and Driffield also expressed film density as a logarithmic function of *opacity* or the percentage of light that can pass through the negative. This logarithmic function was used to construct the characteristic curve. **(Figure 5.3)** Hurter and Driffield developed the *characteristic curve* which charted the density of a negative against the exposure units for the negative. When the logarithmic value of the density for the negative is mapped against the logarithmic value of the exposure unit, the result is an S-shaped HD curve (for Hurter and Driffield) with three components – the toe, the straight line area, and the shoulder. Each different film emulsion type has a distinctive HD curve which represents the particular emulsion's behavior when it is exposed to light.

Each film manufacturer makes the HD curve for a particular film emulsion type available to the public. The toe area of the HD curve, also called the threshold area of the curve, represents the amount of exposure that is required to trigger a light recording response from the particular emulsion. The toe of the curve is represented by Zones I and II in the Zone System. The threshold areas represents the darkest values for the subject on negative film and the lightest values for the subject on transparency film. The toe is the part of the negative with the least amount of silver remaining after the film is developed, and the most amount of silver for transparency film.

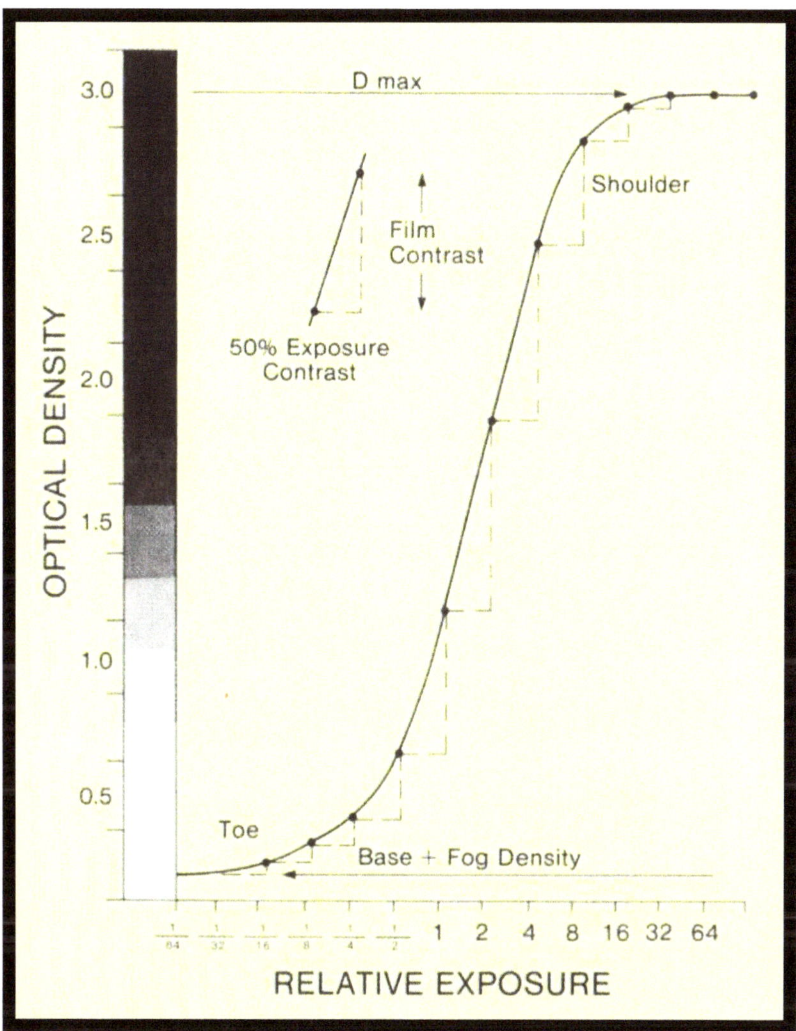

Figure 5.3
The Characteristic Curve

The second part of the HD curve is the straight line section which represents the density values for Zones III to Zone VIII of the Zone System. This range is what is referred to previously as the texture range of the film emulsion. The slope of the straight line section is defined by the ratio of density change to exposure change, and this slope defines the contrast for the particular film or emulsion. The straight line section of the HD curve for a particular film is also referred to as the film's gamma. The final portion of the S-shaped HD curve is called the shoulder, which represents brightest areas of the subject for negative film and the darkest areas of the subject for transparency film. The shoulder of the HD curve is represented by Zone IX of the Zone System, and it is also called the Dmax, because it is the maximum value for the dynamic range of a particular film emulsion.

Large increases in exposure beyond the shoulder of a film's HD curve results in *solarization* which is the reversal effect that results in a reduction of densities. Solarization was used extensively by the surrealist photographer Man Ray in the earliest part of the 20th century. **(Figure 5.4)** HD curves for different film emulsion types can be compared to demonstrate relative film speed. When two HD curves are compared on a graph, the film that requires the least exposure to reach the straight line section of the curve is said to have the higher film speed.

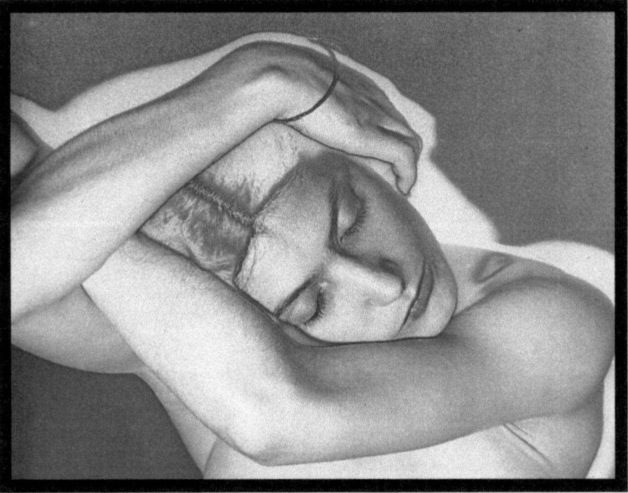

Figure 5.4
Solarization (Man Ray)

ASA/DIN/ISO

The sensitivity of a specific film emulsion to light is known as the film's speed. A given film's sensitivity to light or its film speed is expressed as an ASA (American Standards Association now ANSI) or DIN (Deutsches Institut für Normung or German Institute for Standardization) number. Low ASA or DIN numbers indicate that a given film emulsion has a slow film speed or low sensitivity to light. High ASA or DIN numbers indicate that a given film emulsion has a fast film speed or high sensitivity to light. As the ASA/ISO number doubles, the light sensitivity of the recording media doubles. For example, 100 ASA film is twice as sensitive to light as 50 ASA film and one-half as sensitive to light as 200 ASA film.

The American National Standards Institute (ANSI) was formed in 1918 as a consortium of five engineering societies whose charter was to coordinate the development of standards for products, processes, and services in the United States. An engineering committee within ANSI formed the American Standards Association in 1928. The American Standards Association is the United States contributor to the International Organization for Standardization (ISO) which was founded in 1947.

ISO currently supports the film speed standard known as ISO5800:1987. The 1987 standard defines the linear ASA film speed standard as well as the logarithmic DIN film speed standard. With the linear ASA scale, a doubling of the ASA number indicates that the film emulsion is twice as sensitive to light. For example, 400 ASA film has twice the light sensitivity as 200 ASA film and 200 ASA film has twice the light sensitivity of 100 ASA film which has twice the light sensitivity of 50 ASA film.

The logarithmic DIN scale increases three degrees for every doubling of ASA. For example, 100 ASA/DIN 21 degrees would be doubled to 200 ASA/DIN 24 degrees and doubled again to 400 ASA/ 27 degrees. The 1987 standard combined the ASA and DIN headings into one heading with the title ISO in order to accommodate digital photography. Most digital cameras have an ISO setting that is roughly equivalent to a film's ASA/DIN rating. ISO settings on digital cameras retain this light sensitivity relationship as it applies to CCD or CMOS light sensor arrays.

Film

Beginning in the 1890's and extending through most of the twentieth century, emulsion-coated cellulose or film dominated the world of photography. With the availability of high quality 35 mm format digital cameras in the 1990's, the sales of film have dropped precipitously. The trend for the future seems to be a continued decline in film sales and a narrowing of different available film choices provided by manufacturers; however, many professional photographers will continue to use film for a multitude of reasons. Like all of the other aspects of photography, the use of film is a personal choice that photographers make when they visualizes the end result that they are trying to achieve.

Calumet Photographic supply in Chicago lists three manufacturers of film – Fujifilm, Ilford, and Kodak. Many different sizes of film are available, but the primary film sizes are – 35 mm, medium format or 2¼, and large format sheet film (4 X 5 and 8 X 10). Thirty-five millimeter film is called 135, and it comes in cartridges containing twenty-four or thirty-six exposures. Thirty-five millimeter film can also be purchased in bulk rolls which can then be loaded to reusable film cartridges. Medium-format film is called 120 or 220. The 120 version of this film is composed of a film strip that is attached to a paper backing, and it allows for twelve exposures for each roll. The 220 version is a film strip that is twice as long as the 120 version, and it does not contain the paper backing; it allows for twenty-four exposures per roll. Film for large format 4 X 5 and 8 X 10 cameras is called sheet film. Sheet film needs to be loaded into a film carrier in total darkness, and each film carrier contains two exposures. Sheet film also comes in "ready load" format which requires a special attachment mechanism on the back of the large format camera. Ready load sleeves contain one exposure per sleeve.

The types of film for each of these three sizes can be divided into three basic categories – black and white negative film, color negative film, and color transparency or color reversal film. Black and white negative film was the first kind of roll film that became available in the 1890's, and is still widely used today. Because of the its black and white reversal structure, black and white transparency film is very interesting, but it is not widely used because only a few labs can process the exposed film. Color negative film is used to make color prints by using the RA-4 chemical print process. Color negative film is much less sensitive to contrast and exposure error problems that are inherent in color transparency film. Color transparency film is also called color reversal film or slide film. Color transparencies yield the highest quality color images because of the quality of the dyes contained in the emulsion layers of the film; however, color transparency film is very susceptible to exposure errors, color shifting, and contrast problems. Both color negative and color transparency films have Tungsten versions of the film, which is manufactured to compensate for the color temperature difference between artificial lighting at 3400 degrees Kelvin and natural day light at 5000 degrees Kelvin.

Black and white film is composed of light sensitive silver halide crystals that are bound together by gelatin, which is known as *emulsion.* **(Figure 5.5)** The emulsion is applied to a transparent cellulose material and anti-scratch layers are applied over the emulsion layer. When the

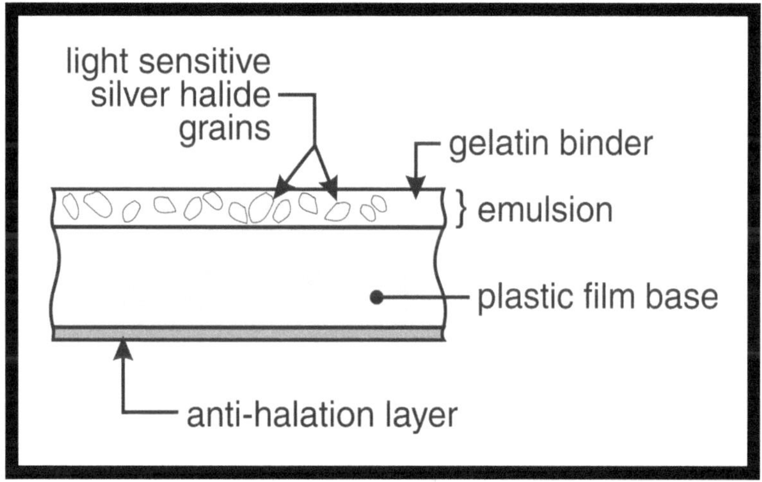

Figure 5.5
Emulsion

film is exposed to light the silver halide crystals respond to the light to form a latent image within the emulsion layer. The intensity of light that the silver halide crystals are exposed to determines the amount of black silver metallic particles that will remain in the emulsion layer when the film is chemically developed. The more light that strikes the crystals, the more silver will remain upon development. In lower light areas of the negative, very few black silver deposits will be formed during film development. The resulting negative contains black silver areas to represent the bright reflected light or high values of the subject, and sections with reduced silver deposits to represent the shadow or low values of the subject.

Color film contains at least three emulsion layers that are sensitive to red, green, and blue light. Each of the silver halide emulsion layers contain dye couplers which are capable of forming visible color dyes when the film is processed. In addition to the color- sensitive emulsion layers, color film often contains masking layers, which restrict the transmission of certain wavelengths of light to the lower color emulsion layers. Color transparency film goes through an additional process which reverses the color dyes in the emulsion layer to form the final real color transparency.

Film manufacturers make a distinction between consumer and professional quality film types. Consumer films have a wide exposure latitude and a long shelf life. The wide exposure latitude means that a good exposure can be obtained by an amateur photographer even with erroneous exposure settings. The long shelf life is necessary because consumer film may sit on a shelf for years before it is finally exposed. Professional quality film has a narrow exposure latitude and a short life span. Professional photographers usually have the equipment and knowledge necessary to obtain correct exposures. The narrow latitude and short shelf life of professional film yields a much higher quality end result at the expense of film durability.

Spectral Sensitivity

Another important characteristic of film is known as *spectral sensitivity.* Different film emulsions are sensitive to different portions of the light spectrum. Early black and white film was very sensitive to blue light which caused the sky in early landscape photographs to appear as white due to over-exposure. The German scientist Hermann Vogel solved the spectral sensitivity problem by adding different color dyes to early film emulsions leading the way to modern panchromatic films. Both modern black and white and color films retain color biases to certain sections of the light spectrum. The spectral sensitivity of modern films can be altered through the use of color filters, which will be discussed in Chapter 6.

Film Grain

The silver deposits on a film strip can be observed with a high powered magnifying glass. **(Figure 5.6)** The silver that remains after the film has been developed is referred to as the *film grain*. Film that is manufactured with a very fine film grain tends to be slower in film speed and higher in film contrast than film with a larger film grain. For example, 100 ASA film has a finer film grain than 400 ASA film. Fine-grain film reproduces a greater accuracy of detail for a given subject than large-grain film, but large-grain film has a higher film speed than fine-grain film. The granularity of film and the film speed should be taken into consideration when a film is chosen for a particular subject.

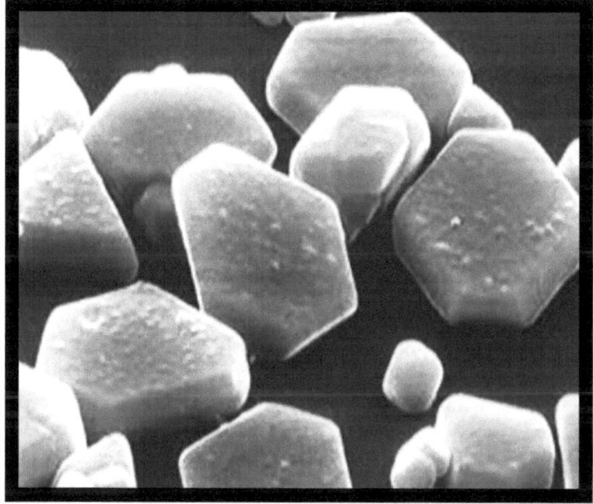

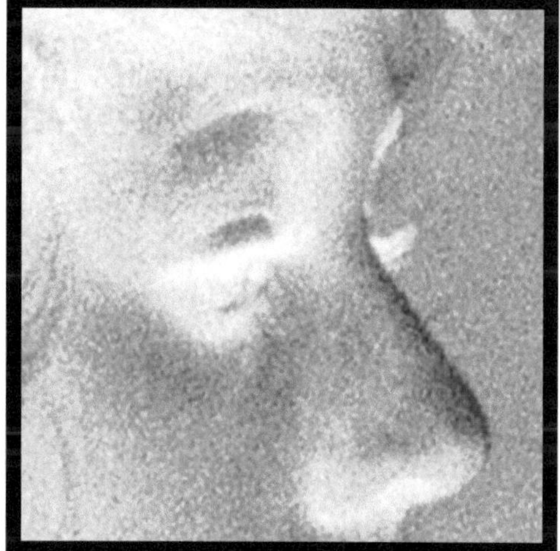

Figure 5.6
Film Grain

Film Storage

Professional quality film is not as durable as the consumer quality films that are available at your local drug store. Professional quality film is very sensitive to heat, and for that reason most retail film outlets store their professional film in refrigerated cases. Professional photographers also refrigerate their film, but they remove the film from the refrigerator at least an hour before use in order to avoid condensation on the film surface. Professional film should be processed as quickly as possible after exposure, but if the exposed film cannot be processed immediately, then it should be refrigerated. Refrigeration after exposure is more important than refrigeration prior to exposure.

Travel With Film

In today's high security environment, traveling with film has become a real challenge. The use of high powered X-Ray machines in airports have the potential to ruin a batch of once in a life time film images. Here are some rules to follow when traveling with film:

1. Never put your film in your checked luggage. The X-Ray machines that are used for checked luggage are so powerful that they will fog the film no matter what the ASA rating of the film may be.

2. Carry your film in lead lined bags in your carry-on luggage. Photographers used to be able to request that your film be manually inspected and not put through the X-Ray machine at the inspection station, but those days are over. In the heightened security world that exists today, all film must go through the X-Ray machine – so don't bother asking for a manual inspection. If the film is in lead lined bags in the carry-on luggage, then the inspectors will be forced to manually inspect the film. Always be prepared to always go through manual inspection and allow plenty of extra time to accommodate this inconvenience, it is part of being a professional photographer. Try to maintain a positive, friendly attitude no matter how frustrating the inspection experience may be. It does not pay to be confrontational with customs or security, and remember, some of the inspectors just want to admire your camera equipment!

Digital Light Sensors

Digital cameras use two types of light capture devices – Charge Couple Device (CCD) and CMOS (Complementary Metal Oxide Semiconductor). CCD devices contain an integrated circuit and an array of linked or coupled light sensitive capacitors. CMOS is composed of an integrated circuit that is driven by an array of lights sensors. CMOS sensors use less power and have a higher noise immunity than CCD instruments. Each of these devices contains an array of light sensitive *photosites* that create a voltage change in response to the amount of light that strikes the them. Each photosite in the array represents one pixel in the final image. The pixel arrays of the sensor are overlaid with a pattern of alternating red, green, and blue color filters that are known as the Bayer Filter.

The Bayer Filter is named after its inventor, Dr. Bryce E. Bayer of the Eastman Kodak corporation. Dr Bayer's pattern alternates red-green rows with green-blue rows to produce an array that is 25% red, 25% blue, and 50% green. The bias toward green is based upon human vision's bias toward green. **(Figure 5.7)** The sensors in the array record luminance values for each pixel and store the image as a grayscale file.

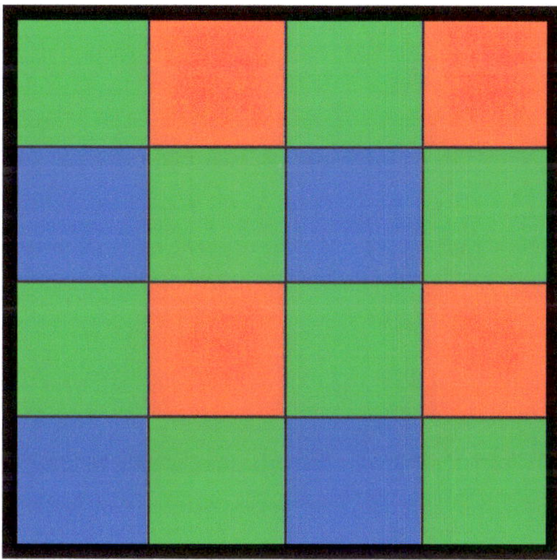

Figure 5.7
The Bayer Filter

A computer within the camera interprets the luminance values from the sensors to construct the final image in the correct digital file format. Each of the arrays has a specific height and width, and the area of the array is determined by multiplying the height of the array by the width of the array. For example, a light sensitive array that is 3264 pixels in width by 2448 in height forms a eight-megapixel array (3,264 X 2,448 = 7,990,272). The standard resolution of a high-quality print is 300 pixels per inch, so the 3,264 by 2448 pixel array would yield a 10.88 inch (3,264/300) by 8.16 inch (2448/300) print at 300 pixels per inch. Most digital camera sensor arrays are smaller than a standard 36 mm by 24 mm film frame, but many of the new digital cameras have a 36 mm by 24 mm "full frame" sensor array.

For the light capture that is involved in an exposure, digital light sensors behave differently than film. Digital light sensors and their associated integrated circuitry count the number of photons that strike the sensor, and a computer in the camera stores the sensor values as voltage levels in the image capture file. For the Camera Raw file format, the voltage level for each pixel is stored as a twelve or fourteen bit number depending on the camera manufacturer. For example, a twelve bit per pixel Camera Raw file could represent between zero and 4096 voltage levels for each pixel in the Raw file.

When the number of photons that strike the sensor is zero, then the pixel is said to be at its *noise floor.* When the number of photons that strike the sensor exceeds the voltage capacity of the sensor, then the pixel becomes burned out. Burned out pixels are expressed as pure white, and highly burned out pixels can have a burnout effect on adjacent sensors that is known as bloom.

There is a direct linear relationship between the number of photons that strike the sensor and the voltage level that is recorded within the Raw digital image file. Because of this linear relationship, the characteristic curve for digital media is a straight line unlike the S shaped characteristic curve for film. In addition to the image data, Raw files contain heading information and metadata. Like film negatives, Raw files cannot express the captured image directly. Like film development, it is the function of conversion software to convert the Raw file into an image file that can be displayed on a camera's LCD screen or a computer monitor. For the digital camera, the conversion computer and software is contained in the camera. In Adobe Photoshop, the Raw file conversion software is built into the Photoshop application. The process of converting the linear Raw data file into images that can be viewed by humans is a process that is known as Tone Mapping.

The Sensor's Light Sensitivity (ISO)

Most digital cameras have an ISO (International Organization for Standardization) setting which controls the light sensitivity of the camera's digital light sensors. The ISO setting on the digital camera is roughly equivalent to the ASA/DIN rating for film. Most manufacturers use the linear ASA numbers to determine the ISO setting. For example, an ISO 100 setting on a digital camera is roughly equivalent to a ASA 100 rating for film.

The relationships between ISO settings on a digital camera are equivalent to the relationships between ASA/DIN ratings for film. For example with a ISO 100 setting, the digital sensors are one-half as sensitive to light as when the ISO setting is at ISO 200, and the light sensors are twice as sensitive to light when the camera is set to ISO 400 as when the ISO setting is at ISO 200.

Most digital cameras use electronic amplification in order to increase the sensitivity of the light sensors as the ISO settings increase. As the ISO number increases, digital cameras have a tendency to pick up "noise". Noise is manifest as either brightness and/or color in the shadow areas of the captured image.

Images Expressed as Numbers

In the digital world images are expressed as numbers, so a short lesson in binary numbers will be helpful in understanding digital files. Most numeric expressions in the everyday world would use base-ten decimal numbers. The most common example of base ten numbers is our monetary system. Each position in the decimal system is a multiple of the number ten. For example,

Position	5	4	3	2	1
Base 10	10^4	10^3	10^2	10^1	10^0
Value	10,000	1,000	100	10	1

So the decimal number 10,459 could be expressed as:

$(10^4 \text{ X } 1) + (10^2 \text{ X } 4) + (10^1 \text{ X } 5) + (10^0 \text{ X } 9)$ in base 10.

The binary number system is a series of ones and zeroes where each position is expressed as a multiple of the number 2. For example,

Position	5	4	3	2	1
Base 2	2^4	2^3	2^2	2^1	2^0
Value	16	8	4	2	1

So the decimal number 27 could be expressed as:

$(2^4 \text{ X } 1) + (2^3 \text{ X } 1) + (2^1 \text{ X } 1) + (2^0 \text{ X } 1)$ in base 2.

The binary number system is the language that is used by digital technology, because computers and other digital equipment are based on millions of tiny transistors that can have a value of 1 or 0 (on or off). In the binary number system, each group of eight binary digits is referred to as a byte. So the binary number 11111111 is one byte and it has a value of 255 in decimal. The byte is the primary unit of storage for all digital equipment, and one byte can be used to express the decimal values from 0 to 255. The binary number 1111111111111111 has sixteen bits or two bytes and it has a value of 65,535. Two bytes can be used to express decimal values from 0 to 65,535.

Digital Files

Digital image files contain pixels that are represented as bytes. Digital files have no dimensions, but they do have a specific number of pixels in height and width. The image resolution of a digital file could be 1280 pixels by 960 pixels (1280 x 960 = 1.2 megapixels) or 4256 pixels by 2848 pixels (4256 x 2848 = 12.1 megapixels) or 6800 pixels by 6800 pixels (6800 x 6800 = 46.2 megapixels). The image resolution of a digital file is dependent on the sensors and software that are contained in the camera or scanner that created the file There are no dots in a digital file, so the only meaningful measurement for digital files is PPI or pixels per inch.

Each electronic capture device has a specific hardware resolution value that is expressed as pixels per inch. Simply stated, PPI is the number of pixels that an image file contains per inch. As the resolution increases, the quality of the image increases, so a 300 PPI image is of higher quality than a 50 PPI image. The 300 PPI image file has a higher resolution than the 50 PPI image. Be careful not to confuse Pixels Per Inch with Dots Per Inch (DPI), which refers to the number of dots that an ink jet printer can print.

Computer image files can contain either black and white or color images. The number of bits contained in each pixel in an computer image file is known as the file's *bit depth.* For each pixel that is created in a hardware dependent image file, the bit depth of each pixel can be eight, twelve, fourteen, or sixteen bits depending on the hardware device that created the file. Sixteen-bit pixels can express a much wider range of grayscale tones or color hues than eight-bit pixels. Pixels could theoretically have bit depths of 1, 2, 12, 14 or 16, but they are always stored and manipulated by a computer in increments of one or two bytes (eight or sixteen bits).

Black and white image files group the pixels in the image file into one channel known as the grayscale channel. Each pixel contained in an eight-bit black and white image file contains eight bits or one byte. All of the pixels in a black and white image file can be grouped together to form a grayscale channel. Each of the pixels in the grayscale channel can have a value from 0 (black) to 255 (white) with 254 shades of gray in between. The decimal value of 255 is expressed as 11111111 in binary.

Each pixel contained in a sixteen bit black and white image file contains two bytes (16 bits). This means that each pixel in the file is expressed as a sixteen bit binary number. Each of the pixels in this grayscale channel can have a value from 0 (black) to 65535 (white) with 65534 shades of gray in between. The decimal value of 65535 is expressed as the value 1111111111111111 in binary. As you can see sixteen-bit digital files contain much more detail than eight-bit files. The problem is that sixteen-bit files are twice as large as eight-bit files.

RGB color image files contain three channels – red, green, blue. Each channel is a representation of the complementary color pairs red/cyan, green/magenta, and blue/yellow. For a RGB color image file with a bit depth of eight, each pixel in the file is expressed by a twenty-four-bit binary number – eight bits for the red channel, eight bits for the green channel, and eight bits for the blue channel. For each pixel, the red channel can have a value from 0 to 255 with 0 representing cyan and 255 representing red. For each color pixel, the green channel can have a value from 0 to 255 with 0 representing magenta and 255 representing green. For each color pixel, the blue channel can have a value from 0 to 255 with 0 representing yellow and 255 representing blue.

The red, green, and blue channels for a given image can be viewed in the Channels Palette in Adobe Photoshop. Reviewing the individual red, green, and blue channels is a good way to analyze the strengths and weaknesses of certain aspects of an image. Each pixel in a RGB color image file with a bit depth of sixteen contains three sixteen-bit channels. For a sixteen bit RGB file, each of the channels for a pixel can have a value from 0 to 65535. The increased detail for sixteen-bit files doubles the total size of the image file.

Adobe Photoshop contains a handy file size calculator which is available by choosing:

FILE → NEW

however, it is useful to walk through the file size calculation manually in order to understand the process. Remember that digital files do not contain dimensions, they contain bytes which represent pixels. For this example, imagine an image file that has a bit depth of eight and is 4000 pixels wide by 3200 pixels tall. This file was created by scanning an image that was 10 inches by 8 inches at a resolution of 400 pixels per inch. The width of 4000 pixels is derived by multiplying the width of the source document (ten inches) times the resolution of 400 pixels per inch, and the height of 3200 pixels is derived by multiplying the height of the source document (8 inches) times the resolution of 400 pixels per inch.

The total pixels contained in the resulting file is 12,800,000 pixels (4000 pixels X 3200 pixels). The size of the file is determined by the number of channels contained in the file. Black and white files contain one channel or one byte per pixel, so the resulting file is 12.8 megabytes. Color files contain three channels or three bytes for each pixel, so the resulting file would be 38.4 megabytes. For image files with a bit depth of sixteen, the size of the resulting black and white image file would double to 25.6 megabytes, and the three channel color file would be 76.8 megabytes. The same numbers can be derived by entering the image dimensions and resolution into the Photoshop new file calculator.

Image File Formats

The basic unit of storage for all computer files is the byte which is made up of eight bits; however, beyond this basic unit of storage, image files come in a multitude of file formats. The RAW format alone represents more than one hundred manufacturer's proprietary file formats. Individual file formats can be identified by the three character extension following the period in the file name.

Image files are stored as either raster or vector file formats. Raster image files are the pixel-based image files that were discussed above. Because of the fixed nature of the raster file, the quality of the image decreases as the size of the output file increases. Vector-based image files contain mathematical formulas that are used to derive the image. The quality of vector-based files does not deteriorate as the size of the input file increases, because the mathematical formulas within the file are used to recalculate the file as the size increases. The file format that is used for the storage of digital images is very important, so a review some of the most common formats and their uses is warranted. Listed below are some of the common raster file formats:

- RAW
- JPEG
- TIFF
- GIF
- PNG
- BMP
- HDP
- XMP

RAW file formats are defined by each individual manufacturer, and they are based on the number of bits that can be recorded by each sensor within the manufacturer's camera. Adobe claims that CS3 has plug-in translators for more than one hundred-twenty manufacturer's RAW formats. Listed below are the file extensions for some of the major RAW formats:

- .RAF – Fuji
- .CRW and CR2 – Canon
- .KDC and .DCR – Kodak
- .MRW – Minolta
- .NEF – Nikon
- .ORF – Olympus
- .DNG – Adobe developed DNG in an attempt to standardize RAW formats.
- .PTX and .PEF – Pentax
- .ARW and .SRF – Sony
- .X3F – Sigma
- .ERF – Epson

The advantage of RAW files is that they usually contain more data per pixel than other file formats. Most RAW formats have 12 or 14 bits for each pixel plus and 1 or 2 pixels for brightness which can be translated into 8 or 16 bit depth pixels. The disadvantage of RAW formats lies in the file sizes as well as dependence upon the individual manufacturers for support. RAW files must be translated so that they can be used in Photoshop.

JPEG (Joint Photographic Experts Group) is a compressed file format that was approved by ISO in 1994. JPEG is a lossy compression algorithm which means that it takes advantage of limitations of the human eye to eliminate information that cannot be seen. JPEG uses eight bit per pixel bit depth and a quality gradation which shrinks the JPEG file size as the quality is reduced. The JPEG algorithm is used by Photoshop to create compressed PDF files. JPEG files suffer degradation when they are edited and saved.

TIFF (Tagged Image File Format) is a flexible image file format-that was developed in the 1980's in order to create an output standard for desktop scanners. TIFF supports both 8 and 16 bit per pixel bit depths for both color and black and white image formats. While TIFF is a widely used image format, the TIFF format is not supported by most Web browsers.

GIF (Graphic Interchange Format) is an eight bit per pixel image file format that was developed by Compuserv in 1987. Because of the eight bit per pixel format, GIF files are limited to 256 color variations. The GIF file format is widely used for the representation of simple color logos and symbols, and GIF formats lend themselves to portability and animation on the World Wide Web. GIF files can be compressed by using the LZW lossless file compression algorithm.

PNG (Portable Network Graphics) is an open source extension of the GIF file format that was developed in 1994 in response to a patent dispute involving the GIF format. The PNG file format supports a twenty-four bit per pixel RGB configuration which expands the color palette of GIF to more than 16 million colors.

BMP (Bit Mapped Format) is an image file format that was developed by Microsoft for the use with its graphics application within Windows. This simple and widely used format could encounter problems in non-Windows environments. BMP files can be created with 1,2,4,16, or 24 bits representing each pixel

HDP (High Definition Photo) is an image file format and lossless file compression algorithm that was developed by Microsoft. The Microsoft format was formerly known as WDP or WWP (Windows Media Photo) for the Microsoft Windows environment. The HDP file format is similar to the TIFF file format, but it can support bit depths of up to 32 bits per channel.

XPM (X PIXMAP) is the ASCII-based image format that was developed by French technicians Daniel Dardailler, Colas Nahaboo, and Armaud Le Hors in 1989. The XPM file format is based on the string manipulation capabilities of the C programming language. The XPM files can be created with any text editor, and the information is stored in human-readable text format. The disadvantage of XPM lies in the huge size of the image files – XPM files can be twice as large as the equivalent TIFF file.

PSD (Photoshop Document) is the Adobe file format that is used by Adobe Photoshop. PSD has the capability to store most of the imaging options available in Photoshop including layers, masks, ICC profiles, and many other features. Because of the popularity of Photoshop, the PSD format is widely used and supported throughout the software industry.

MRSID (Multiresolution Seamless Image Database) is a wavelet compression format that is primarily used by Geographic Information Systems to partition and display imagery in map software.

The Image Frame

The image frame that is used in the image capture process is defined by the image capture media. For film, the image frame can be 36 mm by 24 mm for 35 mm cameras, 55 mm by 55 mm for medium-format cameras, and 4 inches by 5 inches or 8 inches by 10 inches for large-format cameras. For digital cameras, the image frame is dependent upon the size of the light sensor array; the newest digital cameras have a 36 mm by 24 mm "full frame" light capture array. The image frame is a critical component in the standard exposure model because it defines the boundary and aspect ratio of the captured image. The image boundary defines a frame for the captured image, and the aspect ratio is the ratio of the width of the frame to the height of the frame. Aspect ratio is a critical component of both composition and the final products of the capture process – the print, or electronic image.

The Eye of the Photographer

The art of image capture is an exercise in learning to see. Photographers do see the world differently than other people, and the ability to see like a photographer can be learned. Because each individual is unique, each photographer's vision of the world is different. If five photographers were lined up at Glacier Point in Yosemite National

Park, the result would be five different images. The greatest photographs ever taken were composed approximately three to four inches from the front of the camera lens – in the photographer's eye.

Exposure

In the quest for the perfect negative or image file, the first step is to understand the criteria for a perfectly exposed image. The best case would be the creation of an image that would not need any corrections, either through manual or digital correction processes. A perfectly exposed image would contain the full range of tonal values that are expressed by the subject of the exposure. Since some subjects contain a tonal range that is outside the gamut of the film or light sensors, the capture of the full tonal range for a subject is not always possible.

In addition to the capture of a full tonal range, the perfect image should contain some detail in both the shadow areas for the subject as well as the highlight areas for the subject. An under-exposed image will have no detail in the low value areas of the image, and an over-exposed image will have no detail in the high value areas of the image. If detail is missing from either the high or low values, then nothing can be done to correct the image. Slight under or over exposures can be corrected through manual or automated procedures, but gross under- or over- exposure cannot be repaired.

The incident light emanates from either a natural or artificial light source, and it travels from the light source to the subject. The subject is the primary focus of the photographic composition. The incident light is reflected from the subject, and it moves along the exposure axis to the camera. While incident light has some influence in the creation of the reflected light, the incident light is not as important as the reflected light in the creation of the correct exposure. The determination of a good exposure is primarily concerned with the interpretation of the light reflected from the subject. The reflected light is the light that is reflected from the subject and travels between the subject and the camera.

Dynamic Range

The first step in the exposure process involves the determination of the correct exposure values for a given subject. Every photography subject has a range of values from the brightest aspects of the subject to the darkest aspects of the subject. The brightest areas of the subject are the areas that reflect the most incident light, and the darkest areas of the subject are the areas that reflect the least incident light. The difference between the brightest subject values and the darkest subject values is the subject's contrast or range of brightness. This range of brightness is also called the *dynamic range.*

According to Ansel Adams, a standard black and white photograph printed on glossy paper has a range of values that can be expressed as the ratio of 1:100. This means that the black areas of a print reflect 1/100th of the light in the light areas of the print. The problem lies in the fact that the range of brightness for a given subject on a bright sunny day could be as high as 1:10,000, and it is the job of the photographer to capture an image that can be translated into the photographer's output media of choice – print on paper, or display on a video screen. Remember that any photograph is an approximate representation of reality.

Exposure Value

The system of Exposure Values was developed in Germany in the 1950's in an attempt to simplify the understanding of the relationship between the light sensitivity of film and the correct exposure for a subject. Exposure Value is a number which represents a set of aperture and shutter speed settings that will yield a correct exposure for a specific ASA/DIN or ISO setting. Each of the EV numbers can be assigned to one of the zones in the Zone System; also, the dynamic range for a subject or a capture media can be expressed as a range of EV values. Each incremental EV value represents twice as much light as the next lower EV value. For example, the EV value of 14 represents twice the reflected light as the EV value of 13. Listed below are some light capture media with their dynamic range expressed as a ratio and a number of EV values.

Capture Media	Range of Brightness	Exposure Value Range
The Human Eye	1:1,000,000	19.9
Black and White Negative Film	1:16,000	14
Color Negative Film	1:1,000	10
Color Transparency Film	1:50	5.6
JPEG Image Data	1:400	8.6
Raw Image Data	1:4,000	12

Listed below are the dynamic range ratios and EV values for some output media:

Output Media	Range of Brightness	Exposure Value Range
Consumer Monitor	1:100	6.6
Professional Grade Monitor	1:1,000	10
Print Paper	1:250	8

The goal of the photographer is to:

- Capture as much of the subject's range of reflected light as possible
- Translate as much of the subject's range of reflected light to an output media

A successful photographer is the magician who transforms reflected light into a beautiful image.

Light Measurement

The three most important pieces of information for determining the correct exposure values for a given subject are the brightest subject value, the darkest subject value, and the middle gray subject value. The middle gray value is a point in the subject where there is 18% reflectance on the scale of black to white. The determination of the middle gray value is the object of the Zone System. So, how does the photographer go about measuring these values of the subject's reflected light?

The measurement of reflected light from a given subject can be achieved through the use of a light meter. There are three basic types of light meters – an incident light meter, an average light meter, and a spot meter.

The Incident Light Meter

The incident light meter uses a white diffuser bulb over the measurement sensor to measure the light that is falling on the subject. A measurement of incident light is interesting, but it does not tell the photographer much about the range of brightness values that are being reflected from the subject.

The Average Meter

The second kind of light meter is an average meter. Average meters are the kind of meters that are built into the view finders of both film and digital cameras. Hand-held average meters measure an area of approximately 30 degrees in width, and the meter averages the reflected light for the subject area. The problem with average meters is that they assume an average subject, and the meter is often fooled by problems like high-contrast back-lighting. Any time that the distribution of brightness, darkness, and middle values are not average, the average meter is prone to error.

The Spot Meter

The third type of meter used for measuring reflected light is the spot meter. Spot meters measure approximately 1 degree of the subject area, and they are by far the most useful tool for measuring the brightness range of a subject. Many spot meters output their measurements as Exposure Value numbers. The easiest way to measure the middle gray value of a subject is to use a gray card and a spot meter. Gray cards are manufactured so that their surface is be exactly equal to the 18% reflectance value of middle gray. One method for determining the correct exposure value for a subject involves the placement of a gray card in the subject scene and the measurement of the gray card surface with a spot meter to obtain the Exposure Value number.

Exposure Value

The understanding of Exposure Value is one of the keys to understanding photography. An understanding of Exposure Value lies in the fact that each combination of ASA/DIN rating or ISO setting and Exposure Value number yields a group of aperture and shutter speed settings that will give a correct exposure for a given subject. Tables A.1 through A.4 have been included in Appendix A in order to show the Exposure Value Tables for the ASA/ISO values of 50, 100, 200, and 400. The correct exposure for the subject can be determined with the following steps:

1. Determine the ASA/ISO value of your recording media. For film, this value is on the film box. For digital recording media, most digital cameras allow you to set the ISO value.

2. Place the gray card in the subject scene, and measure the reflected light from the gray card surface using your spot meter. This measurement will yield an Exposure Value number.

3. Determine the range of aperture and shutter speed settings that will give the correct exposure for the subject. Most spot meters provide a method for showing this range of values. For example, if you are using 100 ASA film, and your gray card shows an EV reading of 15, then the range of correct apertures and shutter speeds are from f/1 at 1/32,000 of a second to f/128 at ½ of a second. When using film, there are some variations on these values for long exposures that is discussed below.

4. Choose the correct aperture and shutter speed for your subject from the group of combinations represented by the Exposure Value. The aperture and shutter speed combination that you choose should be based on the desired depth of field for the subject and the motion of the subject. Depth of field is defined as the amount of the subject area that will be in focus for a given exposure. *Depth of field* is controlled by the aperture ring, with the depth of field increasing as the f-stop number increases. For example, an f-stop of f/22 yields a greater depth of field than f/5.6, which means that a larger portion of the subject area will be in focus at f/22 than at f/5.6. The second consideration in choosing the appropriate f-stop and shutter speed involves the motion of the subject. For events like sports photography or fast moving animals, fast shutter speeds are required in order to stop the motion of the subject, while for landscape photographs without any wind, a slow shutter speed would be appropriate. The general rule is that for a specific aperture as the shutter speed increases, the depth of field decreases which causes portions of the subject area to be out of focus.

The Exposure Value tables in Appendix A are also useful to demonstrate the doubling relationship for ASA/ISO values. For example, an f-stop of f/22 for EV 15 requires a shutter speed of 1/30 of a second for ASA 50, 1/60 of a second for ASA100, 1/125 of a second for ASA 200, and 1/250 of a second for ASA 400.

Variations in the aperture and shutter speed combinations for a given ASA or ISO and Exposure Value can be caused by the use of filters, extension tubes, bellows, and reciprocity failure. These variations are known as exposure factors. The exposure factors for filters are discussed in Chapter 6.

Extension tubes and bellows are used in macro photography to move a lens further away from the film or light sensor. By increasing the distance from the back of the lens to the capture media, the magnification power of the lens is increased. This increase in distance also increases the exposure due to the increased distance that the light must travel from the back of the lens to the capture media.

Reciprocity Failure

The final exposure factor is known as *reciprocity failure.* In photography, reciprocity refers to the linear relationship between apertures and shutter speeds for a given Exposure Value. For example, an EV of 12 for ASA 100 film yields a group of correct aperture/shutter speed combinations. On the Appendix A charts as you read from left to right, notice, that as the aperture decreases, the shutter speed doubles. Each incremental increase in f-stop causes one-half the amount of light to strike the capture media as the previous f-stop, and consequently requires a doubling of the amount of time that the shutter will remain open. For film, this reciprocity rule holds true until we get to a shutter speed of approximately one second.

For exposures of one second or longer, film responds to light much more slowly than usual due to the fact that film emulsions require a specific amount of light to activate the emulsion's light capture process. This variation in the aperture/shutter speed reciprocity relationship is known as *reciprocity failure.* Reciprocity failure results in the need for an additional increase in either the aperture size or length of time that the shutter remains open (a lowering of shutter speed). Some basic reciprocity failure values are as follows: a shutter speed of one second usually requires an increased aperture of one f-stop or an increase exposure time of two seconds. A shutter speed of ten seconds requires an increase in aperture of two f-stops or an increase exposure time of fifty seconds. A shutter speed of one-hundred seconds requires an increased aperture of three f-stops or an increase exposure time of 1200 seconds. Each film emulsion type has different reciprocity failure factors, so it is best to check the manufacturer's specifications for each film.

Image Proofing

Photographic media prior to the development of emulsion on glass plates and film required that the photographer process the media immediately. With the advent of emulsion on glass plates and film, the capture media required a secondary development process before the photographer could determine if the image process had been successful. This air of uncertainty motivated photographers in the middle of the twentieth century to develop procedures like the Zone System in order to bring some scientific certainty to the image capture process.

Instant Film

With the invention of instant film by Edwin Land in the late 1940s, film photographers had their first image proofing tool. Manufacturers quickly developed instant film magazines that could be attached to the back of medium and large format cameras. Instant film provided film photographers with the ability to proof the image before the final image was committed to film. Due to the popularity of digital technology, instant film became obsolete, and the Polaroid corporation discontinued the manufacture of instant film in 2008. As of this writing, Fujifilm remains the only manufacturer of instant film.

Liquid Crystal Display (LCD)

With the introduction of the Liquid Crystal Display screen in the mid 1990's, image proofing became extremely easy. So easy that many digital photographers spend more time staring at the LCD screen than they spend looking at and analyzing the subject. The LCD screen has become so popular that many of the small point-and-shoot cameras no longer have a view finder.

The LCD screen is a wonderful tool, but it does have some drawbacks. The LCD screen and its associated software tools are configured to display eight-bit compressed JPEG images; the JPEG conversion software is the default configuration for most digital cameras. Consequently, the image on the LCD screen is not an accurate rendering of the 12- or 14-bit Camera Raw image file. Also, the JPEG histogram software often indicates that the high values of the Camera Raw image are clipped, when in fact they are not really clipped. This false histogram reading is a direct result of the JPEG conversion software in the camera. LCD screens are excellent tools, but the photographer should be sure to take some time to analyze the subject.

Exposure Using Negative Film

After black and white or color negative film has been developed, the least amount of silver remains in the areas of the negative which represent the darkest shadow areas for the subject. If the shadow areas of the negative are under-exposed, then the shadow areas of the image will be pure black without any detail on the display monitor or in the resulting print.

For this reason, image capture using negative film is primarily concerned with the correct exposure for the shadow areas of the subject so that the least dense area of the negative will retain some detail. If there is no silver left in the least dense areas of the negative, then there is nothing that can be done to improve the negative.

Black and white negative film has a dynamic range of 14 Exposure Values. Traditionally, the rule for black and white film was to expose for the shadow areas of the subject and then use expansion and contracting techniques in development, as well as dodging and burning techniques while printing in order to accentuate the shadow and highlight areas of the print.

Color negative film has a dynamic range of 10 Exposure Values. Because of the layered nature of color negative film, the use of techniques such as expansion, contraction, dodging, and burning, is not possible. The application of these techniques to color negative film can cause color shifting because each of the emulsion layers respond differently to a specific technique.

Exposure Using Transparency Film

After transparency film has been developed, the least amount of silver remains in the areas of the film which represent the brightest areas for the subject. The remaining silver for negative film is exactly the opposite for transparency film; consequently, the exposure of transparency film is concerned with the highest values for the subject so that some detail can be retained for the brightest areas of the subject. Color transparency film is the most difficult of the film types to expose because it has a narrow dynamic range of only 6 Exposure Values.

Exposure Using Digital Media

Image exposure using digital media is a balancing act between the small amount of data that is captured for the shadow areas of the subject and the clipping of the highlight values that occurs with over-exposure.

The capture of light using CCD or CMOS sensors is a linear function that can be represented by a straight line, with the highest number of bits applied to the areas of the image that represent the brightest areas of the subject, and the lowest number of bits applied to the areas of the image file representing the darkest aspects of the subject. If the image is under-exposed in order to push data into the low values, then as the image data is spread in order to compensate for the under exposure. This stretching of the data can result in banding and posterization.

The highest-quality digital images have a continuous flow of captured values. When a range of values for an image is stretched, gaps occur where there is no data in the image file. These empty spaces or bands show up as white lines or bands in the image file's histogram. *Posterization* is similar to banding because it is an abrupt change in the image's tonality that is caused by the stretching of the image's range of values. The name posterization comes from the abrupt tonal changes that occur in posters. If an image is over exposed in order to move the shadow values to the right, then it is possible that the highlight values of the subject will be clipped and lost forever.

The solution to the digital image balancing act lies in the exposure procedure that is used for transparency film. For digital image capture, it is best to expose the image in the same way that color transparency film would be exposed – expose for the high values. So, how does the digital photographer accommodate the lack of data in the shadow areas of the image?

The Adobe Photoshop Camera Raw conversion software has some excellent features which can be used to recover lost highlights. So, the basic rule for digital images is to slightly over-expose the highlights and recover these high values with the Camera Raw conversion software. This approach is a compromise which addresses both highlight clipping and the small amount of data in the shadow areas. For digital images, expose for the highlights, and slightly over-expose them so that the shadow areas are recorded at a higher value. Also, remember that, as discussed above, the clipping warnings on the camera's LCD screen may be inaccurate.

The Zone System

In 1940, Ansel Adams and Robert Baker published their first version of the Zone System. The Zone System was developed in order to effectively map the range of reflected light coming from a subject onto the range of values from black to white that can be recorded on a capture media and ultimately printed on a piece of paper. In the case of Adams and Baker, the capture media that the Zone System represented was black and white film. In the modern world, the capture media could be black and white or color film and electronic light sensors. This section will discuss the representations of the values for the capture media or zones, and then it will discuss the process of mapping the reflected light values from the subject onto these zones in order to obtain a perfect exposure.

Baker and Adams divided the range of luminance values of the capture media into eleven zones which were numbered using zero and the Roman numerals I to X. This odd number of zones was established so that one of the zones (namely Zone V) could be placed in the middle of the range of zones; the numbering scheme is a bit contrived since traditional Roman numerals did not contain a zero. Each of the zones represents a tone of gray extending from pure black in Zone 0 to pure white in Zone X. Each of the zones represents one stop of incremental change in either aperture or shutter speed on a camera lens. For this reason, each zone corresponds to a doubling of exposure from the zone to its left. For example, Zone II represents twice the exposure value of Zone I and Zone VII represents twice the exposure value of Zone VI. It is also useful to think of each zone as representing an Exposure Value or a range of f-stops and shutter speeds. In the quest for the perfect exposure, the goal is to determine the Exposure Value for Zone V. Zone V represents middle gray or 18% reflectance in the range of tones from black to white.

For a given capture media, Zone 0 represents pure black, or 0% reflectance, with no detail in the low/shadow values of the capture media, and Zone X represents pure white, or 100% reflectance, with no detail in the high values of the capture media. Zones I and IX characterize the end points for the dynamic range for a given capture media. In Zone I the capture media begins to show some detail or texture for the low values, and in Zone IX the capture media begins to show some detail or texture in the high values. Zones II through VIII characterize the end points for the texture range of a given capture media. In Zone II, the capture media shows full detail for the low values, and in Zone VIII the capture media shows full detail for the high values. As we previously noted, Zone V represents middle gray of 18% reflectance.

Place and Fall

Place and fall refers to the process of mapping the brightness range for a subject onto the zones defined by a specific capture media. The final result of the place and fall process is a unique Exposure Value for Zone V which can be converted to specific set of aperture and shutter speed settings. Place and fall gets its name from the fact that the placement of a subject's brightness value into one of the eleven zones in the Zone System causes the other values to fall into the remaining ten zones. For example, our previous example yielded a gray card reading of EV 15 which was placed in Zone V. This zone placement results in the following values for the other zones:

Zones	0	I	II	III	IV	V	VI	VII	VIII	IX	X
EV	10	11	12	13	14	15	16	17	18	19	20

This range of values fall in the remaining ten zones. The place and fall values for a specific subject can be determined through the use of the following five different methods:

- Gray Card Measurement
- Key Stop Rule Application
- Shadow/Highlight Averaging

Gray Card Measurement

The gray card measurement technique has been discussed is previous sections. Gray card measurement involves the placement of a gray card in the scene under the same lighting conditions as the subject. The light reflected from the gray card is measured using a spot meter. The spot meter measurement yields an Exposure Value number which represents a group of aperture and shutter speed settings. The EV reading for the gray card is placed in Zone V and the EV conversion dial on the spot meter is used to choose the correct aperture and shutter speed settings based on depth of field and subject motion considerations. The disadvantage of a gray card approach to exposure lies in the fact that the highlight and shadow EV values for the subject are not taken into consideration which could cause either the highlight or shadow values for the subject to be over or under exposed.

The Key Stop Rule

The Key Stop Rule is a quick and easy method for determining the correct aperture and shutter speed setting for a particular subject. This method first determines the correct aperture setting by taking the square root of the ASA setting. For example, if you are using an ASA of 100 then your key stop would be f/10. The shutter speed for the subject is determined by estimating the reflected light from a subject in candle power per square foot. Ansel Adams gives the example of a subject in normal daylight where the Zone III reflected light is 30 candle power per square foot, which means that Zone IV has 60 c/ft2, and Zone V has 120 c/ft2. The Key Stop shutter speed is defined as the reciprocal of the Zone V candle power per square foot or 1/120th of a second at the aperture Key Stop of f/10. So, under normal daylight conditions an estimated aperture/shutter speed would be 1/125th of a second at f/10 (the square root of the ASA). The disadvantage of this approach is that we are not always dealing with normal daylight conditions, so the estimated shutter speed of 1/125th of a second has the potential for error. Also, this approach does not take into consideration the placement of highlight and shadow values in the correct zones.

Average Highlight and Shadow

The average highlight and shadow method of exposure requires the measurement of the brightest and darkest areas of the subject in order to obtain the middle or average value for Zone V. For example, if the darkest area of the subject yields and EV reading of 7 and the brightest area of the subject yields an EV reading of 17, then the middle or average value would be (17 + 7)/2 = 12, so 12 would be placed in Zone V, and the aperture and shutter speed would be chosen from the group of values associated with EV 12. The problem with the average method lies in the fact that some of the highlight and shadow detail values may fall outside of the textural range for the capture media. For example, if the photographer using negative film wanted to capture the detail for the shadow area represented by EV 7 in the example above, then this would be a problem, because the shadow area represented by EV 7 would fall in Zone 0 which will show up as pure black in the monitor or print output. Since there is no silver on the negative for Zone 0, there is no way to recover the detail from the shadow area of the subject.

Zone Calculation for Negative Film

For negative film, the darkest areas for a subject are represented by the portions of the film negative that contain the least amount of residual silver after film development. When working with negative film, the goal is to capture the correct amount of detail for the shadow areas or low values. Image capture is driven by the fact that the textural range for the zone system extends from Zone II to Zone VIII with slight detail manifest in Zones II and VIII, and full detail manifest from Zones III through Zone VII. For negative film, the darkest shadow areas of our subject are measured and then the Zone V value is calculated based on the fall for the other zones.

For example, if the shadow area of the subject is measured as reading EV 7 on the spot meter, then the Zone V value for our exposure will be 10. The EV reading of 7 is placed in Zone II to obtains slight texture and the resulting fall for the Zone V value would be EV 10. For a full texture rendering of the shadow area with the EV reading of 7, then the EV reading of 7 would be placed Zone III which would yield a Zone V reading of EV 9. The final exposure step involves the choice of aperture and shutter speed settings based on depth of field and subject motion considerations. This approach concurs with Ansel Adams' mantra for negative film, "expose for the shadows and develop for the high values." (Ansel Adams *The Negative* P. 74) For negative film, the bias should be toward slight over-exposure. Since the high values on the negative contain the most amount of residual silver, the high values can be enhanced through the use of development, printing, and digital manipulation techniques.

Zone Calculation for Transparency Film

For transparency film, the representation of highlight and shadow values from the subject are the reverse of highlight and shadow representation on negative film – the least amount of residual silver dye represents the brightest portions of the reflected light from the subject. For transparency film, the goal is to capture the correct amount of detail for the brightest areas of the subject. Another difference between negative film and transparency film lies in the shortened textural range for transparency film – the textural range extends from Zone III to Zone VII with slight detail manifest in Zones III through VII and full detail manifest in Zones IV through VI.

The goal is to measure the highlight areas of the subject, and then calculate the Zone V value based on the fall of the other values. For example, if the highlight area of the subject that needs to be captured has an Exposure Value reading of 16 from our spot meter, then the Zone V value for the exposure should be 14. The highlight EV reading of 16 is placed in Zone VII in order to obtain slight texture for the measured highlights and the fall for the resulting Zone V value is 14. In order to obtain full texture for the measured highlight area with the EV reading of 16, the measured EV value of 16 should be placed in Zone VI which would result in a Zone V reading of 15.

The final step would involve the choice of aperture and shutter speed settings based on depth of field and subject motion considerations. In the case of transparency film, the rule is capture the high values and enhance the low values using development, printing, digital manipulation techniques. The bias in the case of transparency film should be toward under-exposure.

Zone Calculation for Digital Exposures

The use of the Zone System for digital light sensors is a balancing act which results from the inherent characteristics of CCD and CMOS light sensors. This balancing act involves avoiding both the over-exposure of the highlights and the introduction of noise and posterization effects in the shadow areas of the image.

Digital light sensors record light based on the number of photons that strike the sensors. Since the least amount of reflected light is contained in the shadow areas of the subject, the least amount of digital data is captured for the shadow areas of the subject. The difference between negative, transparency, and digital sensor image capture lies in the fact that light capture for film is expressed as the S shaped HD curve, while light capture for sensors is expressed as a straight linear relationship. For light sensors, more photons means more recorded data and less photons means less recorded data. Consequently, the highlight areas of a digital image contain more detailed information than the shadow areas of the digital image. If a digital image is under-exposed, then banding and posterization will occur in the shadow areas of the image when the image data is spread out in order to compensate for the under exposure.

For the application of the Zone System using digital light sensors, the same approach should be used that was used for transparency film. First, use a spot meter to measure the highlight area of the subject, and place the exposure value from the spot meter reading in Zone VII. The Zone V value is calculated based on the fall of the other values. Finally, determine the aperture and shutter speed based on depth of field and subject motion considerations.

In addition, the nature of light sensors force us to keep in mind two important considerations:

1. For long exposures, light sensors have a tendency to create random signals. These random signals are known as noise, and this noise causes distortion of the shadow areas of the captured image. Shadow areas of digital files are also prone to posterization, which occurs when there is a sharp jump of tonal values in the shadow areas due to the small amount of available data.

2. For digital image capture, it is better to darken an over-exposed image file than to lighten an under-exposed image file. When an under-exposed digital image is lightened, the small amount of data is the shadow areas of the image is spread across several zones which introduces noise and distortion into the image.

For digital exposures, shooting for the high values with a bias toward slight over- exposure still applies; however, be sure to remain aware of the noise and distortion problems that can occur in shadow areas when long shutter speeds are used for digital exposures. Some of the highlight values for digital exposures can be recovered through the use of digital techniques in the Photoshop Camera Raw Function.

The key point to remember when you are trying to understand the application of the Zone System procedures is that detail cannot be created in the parts of the image where no detail has been captured. If the photographer has not captured at least slight detail or texture across all of the tonal values for the subject, then there is nothing that can be done later to recover the missing detail.

Each film type or film sensor has its own unique characteristics, so be sure to review the manufacturers characteristic curve and experiment with different exposure values in order to determine the behavior of each individual film type or digital sensor array.

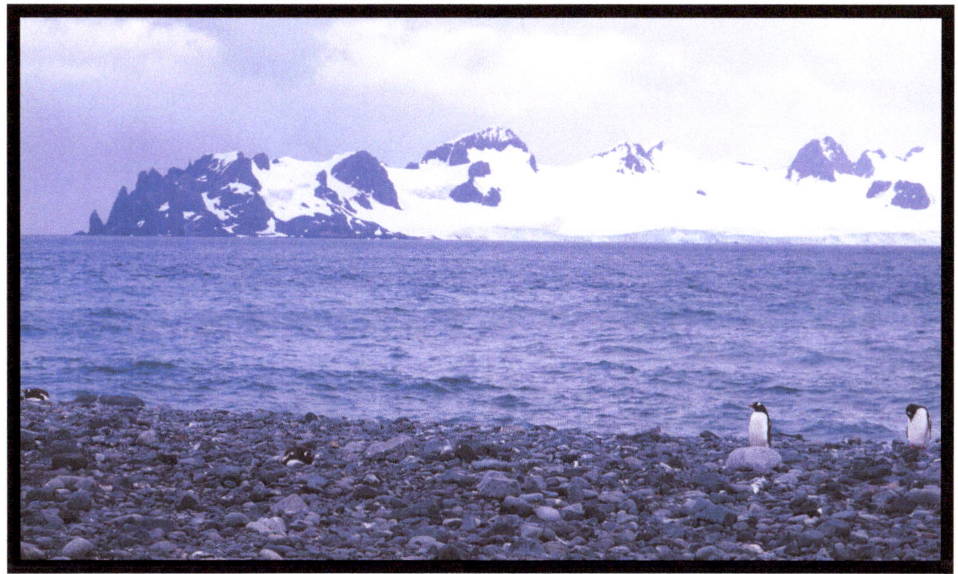

Figure 5.8
Yankee Harbour
Antarctica

It may be that you are not yourself luminous,
but that you are a conductor of light.
Some people without possessing genius
have a remarkable power of stimulating it.

-- Arthur Conan Doyle

Chapter Six

Filters and Pre-Exposure

Filters in Photography

The role of filters in photography is best understood when the filter is placed in the context of the Standard Exposure Model. The model has a light source which emanates incident light, a subject which reflects the incident light, and a camera which contains a capture media. Filters in photography can be used to either alter the incident light emanating from the light source or to alter the light reflected from the subject before it reaches the capture media.

Incident light is created by both natural and artificial light sources. The incident light emanating from a source has a specific color temperature. For artificial light sources, the light from the source can be modified with color filters that are placed in front of the source. For natural light photography, the primary light source is usually the sun. The color temperature of the sun's light can be altered by the earth's atmosphere as the angle of the sunlight changes due to the rotation of the earth. For example, sunlight in the morning and evening has a red cast because the sunlight is passing through the thickest portions of the earth's atmosphere due to the low angle of the sun at dawn and dusk. Sunlight at noon has a blue cast due to the thin atmosphere that the sunlight is passing through, combined with the blue tone of the sky caused by the sunlight reflected from the earth's oceans.

This chapter will explore the role of photographic filters as they alter the reflected light from the subject. Photo filters can provide three types of light alteration as it moves from the subject to the capture media – either film or electronic sensors. Filters can alter the wavelength of the reflected light, they can alter the amount of light that strikes the capture media, or they can alter the direction of the reflected light's oscillation.

Color filters that alter the wavelength of the inbound reflected light that strikes the capture media do so by absorbing some of the reflected light's wavelengths and transmitting the remaining wavelengths. For example, a green color filter transmits a high percentage of the green wavelengths of the color spectrum, and it absorbs all of the other wavelengths of color spectrum. The filters that limit the amount of light that strikes the capture media are known as neutral density filters, and the filters that alter the direction of the vibrating light are known as polarizing filters. There are also a large number of special effects filters, which will not be addressed here.

Because each of these filter types alter the reflected light from the subject, they also change the exposure value for the subject. This change in exposure value is known as the filter's *filter factor*. For example, a three stop neutral density filter requires a decrease in shutter speed or an increase in the aperture size by three stops.

Filters can be purchased with gelatin, glass, or plastic composition. Gelatin filters are fragile, and they are usually mounted in some sort of frame. Plastic filters are more durable than gelatin filters, but they are susceptible to scratches. Glass filters are both durable and somewhat scratch resistant, but glass filters are the most expensive of the three types. Filters can be screwed into the front of the lens or they can be mounted on a frame that sits either in front of or in back of the camera lens. The frame type of filter system eliminates the need for multiple sets of screw-mounted filters that would be required to accommodate the differences in lens diameters. A survey of retail photography outlets yielded the following list of filter manufacturers:

- Lee
- Cokin
- Tiffen
- Formatt
- Kodak
- Hasselblad
- Optiflex

Many of the photographic effects that were traditionally created through the use of filters are now created through photo editing software such as Adobe Photoshop.

Filters for Black and White Photography

Filters in black and white photography were used initially to compensate for the spectral sensitivity problems of film emulsions. Film emulsions in the late 19th century were primarily sensitive to blue light, which caused the sky portion of landscape photographs to appear white due to over-exposure. The German scientist Dr. Hermann Wilhelm Vogel introduced dyes into the film emulsions in order to make the emulsions sensitive to the portions of the spectrum that were not represented by the dye. Vogel's work led to the development of *orthochromatic* film emulsions which expanded film's light sensitivity into the green areas of the light spectrum. Today's black and white films are called *panchromatic* because they are sensitive to the full range of the visible lights spectrum.

Color filters can be used in black and white photography to alter the tonal representation of different colors reflected from the subject. The basic rule for filters is that the filter lightens its own color representations while darkening its complementary color representations. For example, a number twelve yellow filter lightens the yellow tones reflected from a subject while darkening the blue tonal values. This effect results from the fact that the yellow filter transmits most of the yellow reflected light from the subject and it absorbs the remaining colors reflected from the subject.

The filter's light transmission and absorption characteristics alter the amount of activated silver on the negative, which results in the darkening and lightening effects described above. The table below shows the number of stops in exposure compensation that are required for some of the most useful color filters.

Color	Filter Number	Daylight Exposure Increase	Tungsten Exposure Increase
Deep Red	29	+10	+5
Red	25	+4	+2.5
Light Red	23A	+3	+1.5
Orange	21	+2	+1
Deep Yellow	15	+1.25	+1
Yellow	8	+1	+.75
Light Yellow-Green	11	+2	+2
Yellow-Green	13	+2.5	+2
Green	58	+4	+4
Deep Green	61	+6	+6
Deep Bluish-Green	65	+8	+8
Cyan	44	+4	+4
Blue	47	+3	+6
Deep Blue	47B	+4	+8
Violet	34A	+4	+8
Magenta	33	+12	+6

The exposure increase translates to a reduction in EV of one unit. This EV reduction can be accomplished with decrease in shutter speed by one stop, or an increase in aperture size of one stop. The use of color filters in black and white photography provides an interesting method for controlling the subject's tonal values.

Filters for Color Exposures

Incident light has a property that is known as temperature which is either expressed in degrees Kelvin or as a number known as the mired number. The mired number is derived from the following equation.

$$M = 1000000/K$$

where K is the color temperature in degrees Kevin and M is the mired number. For color exposures, color negative and transparency films are manufactured to capture images in daylight (color temperature of 5500 degrees Kelvin or mired number 181.8) or under artificial light (color temperature of 3200 degrees Kelvin or mired number 312.). The film that is used for artificial light is known as tungsten film. The color temperature of the incident light can be measured with a light temperature meter like the Gossen ColorPro 3F.

Each of the filters used in color photography have an identification number, a filter factor, and a mired shift value. The filter factor identifies the required change in exposure value for the filter, and the mired shift value represents the number of degrees Kelvin that the filter will shift the color temperature. The mired shift index is expressed by the equation:

$$MSI = 1000(1000/T2 - 1000/T1)$$

where T1 is the current color temperature, and T2 is the desired color temperature. For example, if daylight film was being used under artificial lighting conditions, then a filter with a mired index of -131 would need to be used:

$$-131 = 1000(1000/5500 - 1000/3200)$$

The filter with the appropriate mired index is the 80A filter. If tungsten film were being used in daylight conditions, then a filter with a mired index of 131 would be required:

$$131 = 1000(1000/3200 - 1000/5500)$$

The filter with a mired index of 131 is the 85B filter.

Photographic filters that are used to alter color temperature can be divided into the following three categories:

- Color Conversion Filters
- Light Balancing Filters
- Color Correcting Filters

Color conversion filters are used when a significant change in color temperature is required. Listed below are filters with their identification number, filter factor, temperature shift, and mired shift index number:

Color Conversion Filters			
Filter ID	**Filter Factor (Increase Number of Stops)**	**Color Temperature Shift (Degrees Kelvin)**	**Mired Shift Index Number**
80A	2	2300	-131
80B	1 2/3	2100	-112
80C	1	1700	-81
80D	1/3	1100	-56
85C	1/3	-1700	81
85	2/3	-2100	112
85N3	1 2/3	-2100	112
85N6	2 2/3	-2100	112
85N9	3 2/3	-2100	112
85B	3-Feb	-2300	131

Light balancing filters are used when small increments of temperature shift are required. Listed below are the light balancing filters with their identification, filter factor, temperature shift, and mired index number:

Light Balancing Filters			
Filter ID	**Filter Factor (Increase Number of Stops)**	**Color Temperature Shift (Degrees Kelvin)**	**Mired Shift Index Number**
82C + 82C	1 1/3	710	-89
82C + 82B	1 1/3	630	-77
82C + 82A	1	550	-65
82C + 82	1	480	-55
82C	2/3	400	-45
82B	2/3	300	-32
82A	1/3	200	-21
82	1/3	100	-10
81	1/3	-100	9
81A	2/3	-200	18
81B	1 2/3	-300	27
81C	2 2/3	-400	35
81D	3 2/3	-500	42
81EF	2/3	-650	52

Color correcting filters are used to control specific primary colors (red, green, or blue) or complementary colors (cyan, magenta, or yellow). Color correcting filters are identified by a standard label CCnnX where nn is the absorption percentage, and X is the first letter of the filter's color. These filters transmit their own color while they absorb their complementary color. For example, the CC25Y (yellow with 25 % absorption) would transmit yellow wavelengths while absorbing 25 % of the blue wavelengths. Listed below are the color correction filters for the six primary and complementary colors with their filter factors:

Color Correcting Filters			
Color/ Filter ID	**Filter Factor (Increase Number of Stops)**	**Color/ Filter ID**	**Filter Factor (Increase Number of Stops)**
RED		CYAN	
CC025R	---	CC025C	---
CC05R	1/3	CC05C	1/3
CC10R	1/3	CC10C	1/3
CC20R	1/3	CC20C	1/3
CC30R	2/3	CC30C	2/3
CC40R	2/3	CC40C	2/3
CC50R	1	CC50C	1
GREEN		MAGENTA	
CC025G	---	CC025M	---
CC05G	1/3	CC05M	1/3
CC10G	1/3	CC10M	1/3
CC20G	1/3	CC20M	1/3
CC30G	2/3	CC30M	2/3
CC40G	2/3	CC40M	2/3
CC50G	1	CC50M	2/3
BLUE		YELLOW	
CC025B	---	CC025Y	---
CC05B	1/3	CC05Y	---
CC10B	1/3	CC10Y	1/3
CC20B	2/3	CC20Y	1/3
CC30B	2/3	CC30Y	1/3
CC40B	1	CC40Y	1/3
CC50B	1	CC50Y	2/3

Filters for B & W and Color Photography

Finally, there is a group of filters that can be used for both black and white and color film as well as digital capture media. These filters include UV/Skylight filters, neutral density filters, graduated filters, and polarizing filters. The ***Skylight*** (1A) and ***Ultra-Violet*** absorbing (2A, 2B) filters are used to remove haze from landscape compositions without modifying the remaining portions of the image. The Skylight filter is useful for the removal of the bluish cast contained in open shade caused by both blue and extreme violet wavelengths. UV filters are effective at the removal of visible radiation that exists below 400 nanometers. Neither of these filter types have an exposure factor, because they do not alter the exposure values for the image.

Neutral density filters are natural gray filters that are used to reduce the amount of light that strikes the capture media across the entire spectrum. Neutral density filters do not alter the image in any way, but they do alter the exposure value for the subject. For example, if the subject is a waterfall on a bright sunny day **(Figure 6.1)**, then the fast shutter speed that would be required for the correct exposure would make the waterfall appear to be frozen. A three-stop neutral density filter would reduce the shutter speed by three stops, which would give the waterfall a pleasing ribbon appearance.

Neutral density filters are rated in density units which define the filter's opacity. For example, a ND of .3 results in a one stop exposure reduction, a ND of .6 results in a two stop exposure reduction, and a ND of .9 results in a three stop exposure reduction. Neutral density filters can be combined, and when they are combined the filter reduction factors are simply added together.

A close cousin to the neutral density filter is the group of filters known as ***graduated filters***. For example, a graduated gray filter is a neutral density filter where the gray density is gradually reduced from the bottom of the filter to the top of the filter where the gray effect virtually disappears. The graduated gray filter results in more light striking the capture media at the bottom of the image, and less light striking the capture media at the top of the image. Graduated gray filters can be

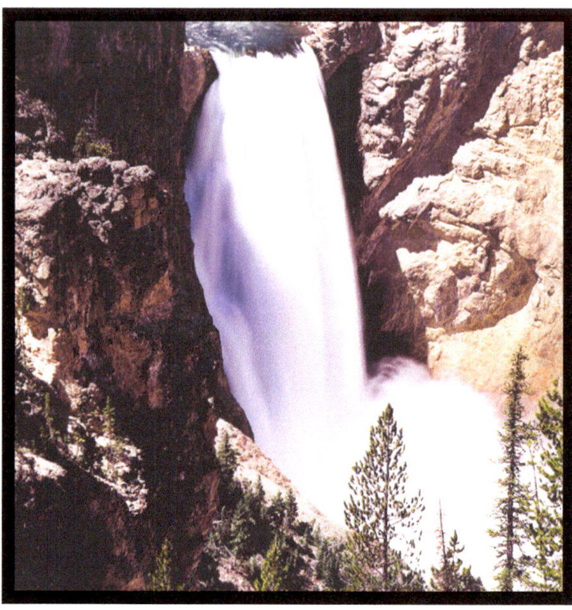

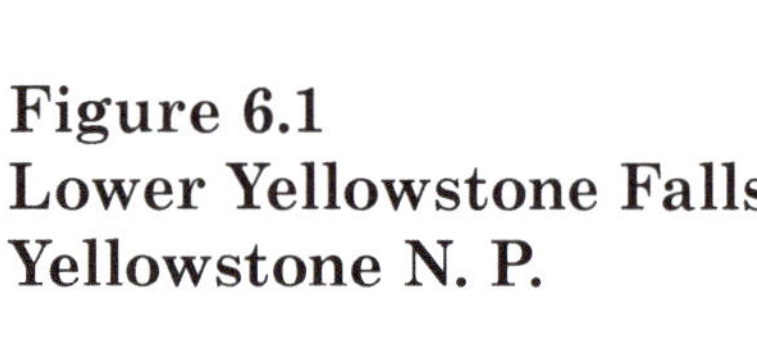
Figure 6.1
Lower Yellowstone Falls
Yellowstone N. P.

very useful for darkening the sky in landscape compositions. Graduated filters also come in a multitude of colors which can change the color tone of the subject as well as altering the exposure values for the image.

Polarization filters are used to increase contrast for the image and remove reflection from the composition. Light waves vibrate in all directions as they travel along the exposure axis from the subject to the camera. **(Figure 6.2)** Polarizing filters can be used to alter the direction of these light vibrations. Polarizing filters are made up of two pieces of glass which when rotated can channel the vibrating light waves into one plane. The limitation of polarizing filters lies in the fact that they are only effective when the light source is at a ninety degree angle from the exposure axis between the subject and the camera.

A polarizing filter is ineffective when the light source is behind the subject or behind the camera. As the angle of the light source increases to ninety degrees from the subject/camera path, then the polarization effect increases for the image. The polarization effect of the filter is realized by rotating one of the glass elements until the desired effect is achieved.

The increase in contrast is useful for darkening the sky in landscape photographs. The removal of reflection can be useful in reducing glare from high reflectance objects, also the removal of reflection will increase color saturation in flowers and other aspects of landscape photography. The standard filter factor for a polarizing filter results in a 1.5 stop in exposure value reduction.

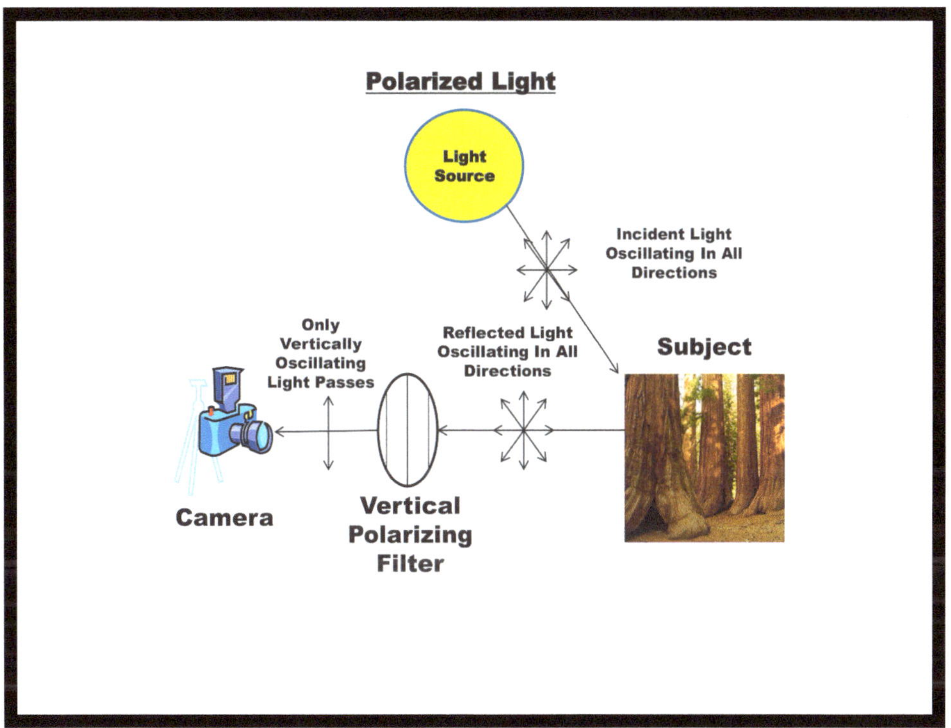

Figure 6.2
Polarized Light Filters

Filters in Digital Photography

All of the filters described above can be used effectively with digital camera technology, but like all things digital there are other electronic temperature controls. Most quality digital cameras have electronic white point and color temperature controls that can be used to alter the color temperature of the incident light.

White point is the digital setting control which causes a white surface (0 % reflectance) to appear white under daylight lighting conditions (a color temperature of 5500 degrees Kelvin). Most high quality-digital cameras allow the photographer to record and store a number of white point settings. Consequently, the digital camera could store one white point setting for daylight settings and a different white point setting for artificial light conditions. In addition, most good digital cameras have a color temperature control that can be used to control the temperature of the incident light. For example, the color temperature could be set to 5500 degrees Kelvin for normal daylight conditions and it could be set to 3200 degrees Kelvin for artificial light conditions.

The white point and color temperature settings on digital cameras control the color temperature of the captured light in much the same way that color filters adjust the temperature of the incident light. The advantage of the digital white point and temperature settings lie in the fact that they can be easily changed and stored for later use.

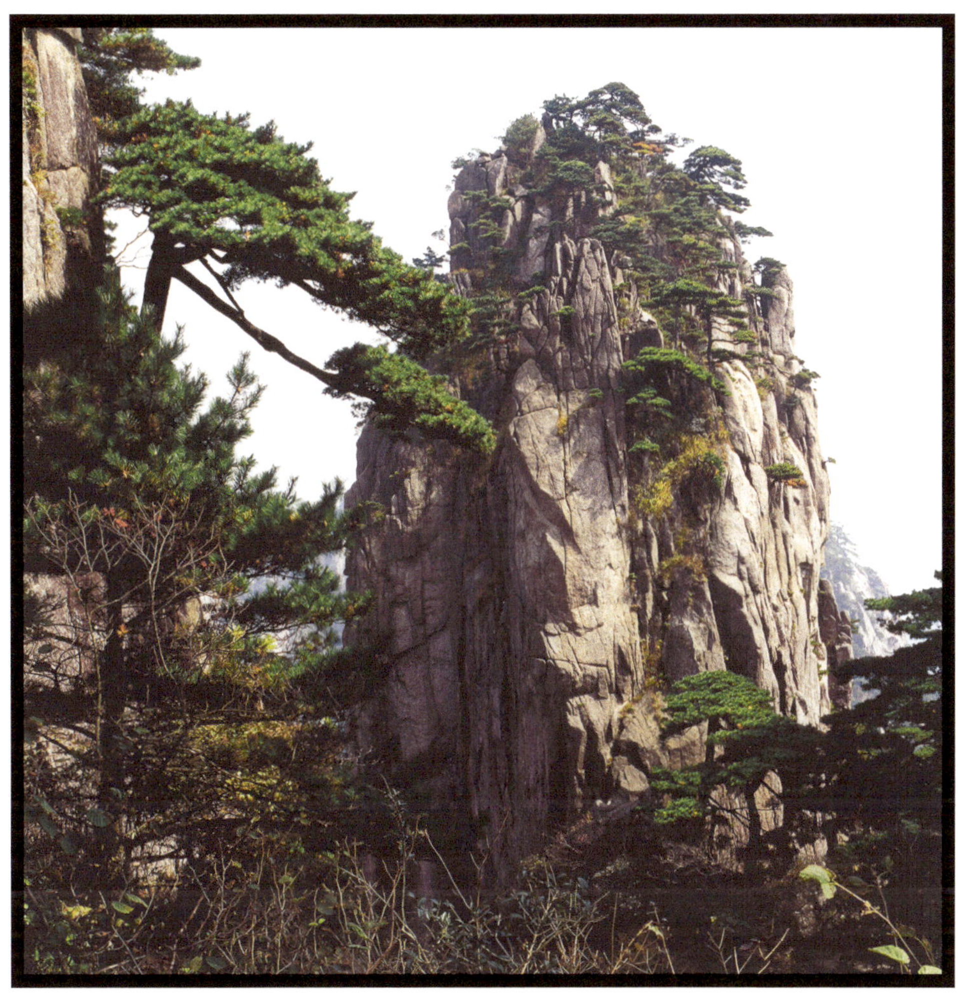

Figure 6.3
Yellow Mountain W. H. S.
Anhui, China

There is a pleasure in the pathless woods
There is a rapture on the lonely shore
There is society, where none intrudes,
By the deep sea, and music in its roar;
I love not man the less, but Nature more

-- George Gordon Byron

Chapter Seven

Natural Light Photography

Natural light photography is similar to surfing. Young surfers realize early on that it is futile to try to dominate the awesome force of the ocean. They come to understand that the only way to succeed at the art of surfing is to learn to take what the forces of nature gives them and then apply their knowledge and physical prowess to become part of the flow of nature. The surfing community has adopted the Taoist yin/yang symbol as an expression of the need to become integrated with the flow of nature. The writings of the Taoist masters Lao Tzu and Chang Tzu stress that inevitable change comes about through the dialectic interactions of the dynamic forces in nature, and that the best approach to the human encounters with nature involves the integration of the human forces with the dynamic interplay of nature's forces. This Taoist mindset is also very useful in the quest for high quality natural light photographs.

The review of natural light photography in this chapter will continue to use the Standard Exposure Model as the framework for the analysis. This chapter's organization is based on the following components of the model:

- The Light Source (Incident Light)
- The Subject/Reflected Light
- The Exposure Axis
- The Camera

Light Sources/Incident Light

Listed below are some of the available natural light sources:

1. **Sunlight** – Sunlight or daylight is available from sunrise to sunset. The nature of sunlight changes as the angle of the sun changes during the day.

2. **Moonlight** – Moonlight is available during both day and night time. Moonlight during night time hours usually requires long exposures; however, a full moon is a very bright subject. The moon during day-light hours makes for an interesting addition to landscape photographs. **(Figure 7.1)** A polarizing filter is useful for darkening the sky and increasing the contrast between the moon and the surrounding sky.

3. **Starlight** – Stars and planets are only available as a photographic subjects during night time hours. Stars and planets can be photographed at night using either fixed or rotating platforms. If a fixed platform is used to photograph celestial objects, then the objects will appear to be streaks or trails of light in the resulting image. The objects' light trails are caused by the rapid rotation of the earth. The objects can also be photographed as fixed points of light if the camera is mounted on a device with a tracking motor like a telescope **(Figure 7.2)**. The telescope tracking motor compensates for the rotation of the earth.

4. **Firelight** – Firelight is a very interesting natural light source. Firelight has a distinctive red cast, and fires contain rapid motion due to the movement of the flames.

5. **Lava** – Brightly colored lava is a very interesting light source, especially at night. The capture of lava images often includes the movement of the subject at very high speeds.

6. **Lightning** – Lightning is also a light source, but due to the random nature of lightning strikes, the capture of lighting can be difficult. The capture of lightning as a subject is most dramatic at night. The easiest approach to photographing lightning at night involves pointing the camera in the direction of anticipated lighting flashes, and locking the shutter open using the bulb setting on the lens. After the lightning flashes, the lens should be closed immediately.

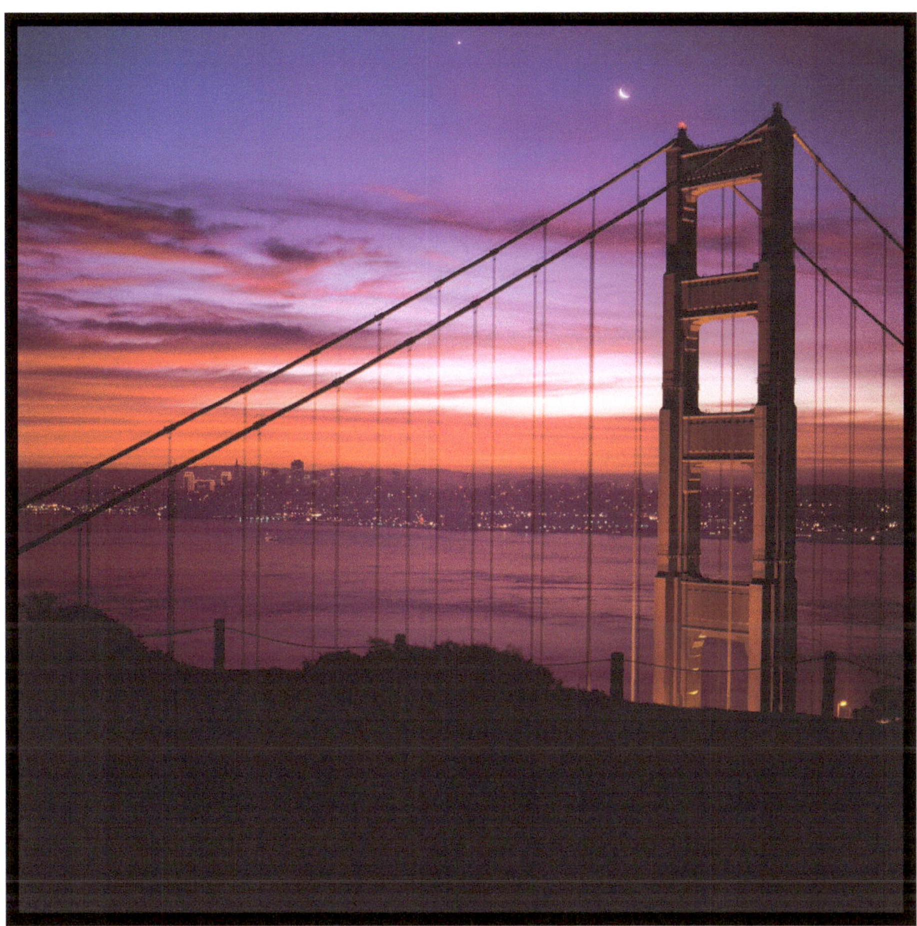

Figure 7.1
Venus and the Waning Moon

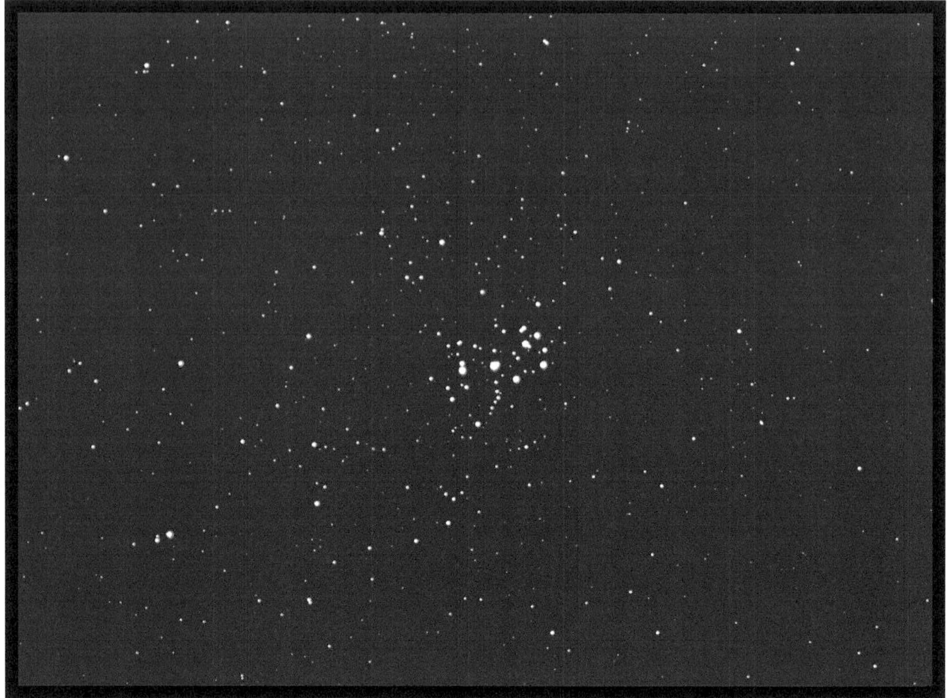

Figure 7.2
Pleiades Star Cluster

Diffuse Light

Diffuse light refers to the scattering of sunlight that occurs with either intermittent cloud cover or solid overcast. Clouds passing between the sun and the intended subject can cause rapid and significant changes in the luminescence values for the subject. When fast moving clouds are involved, it is best to take several meter readings prior to exposure.

When fog or solid overcast dominate the scene, the nature of the subject's highlight and shadow values change completely. Under solid overcast lighting conditions, the range of luminescence values becomes much shorter compared to bright sunlight. In addition, shadows under overcast conditions become broad and dispersed as opposed to the small and acute shadow areas that occur during bright sunlight conditions.

For diffuse light conditions, it is important to remember Ansel Adams' warning regarding the artificial expansion of the luminescence range through over exposure: "Do not strive to achieve "Luminosity" by contrast alone." (Ansel Adams, The Negative, P. 136) Care should be taken to retain the subtle low value areas of the subject through proper zone placement – especially when reciprocity failure is involved.

Atmosphere

Industrial haze, air pollution, and smoke in the atmosphere can greatly reduce the contrast and range of luminescence for a subject. For example, the Grand Canyon in Arizona is surrounded by coal-fired power plants that significantly impact the air quality and visibility within the national park **(Figure 7.3)**. Skylight (1A), UV absorbing (2A,2B), and polarizing filters can be used to cut through some of the haze, but their effect is limited. The best approach when working in hazy and smoky conditions involves limiting the vistas for the subject. If the camera's attention is focused on subjects closer to the camera, then the camera will be viewing the subject through much less haze and smoke.

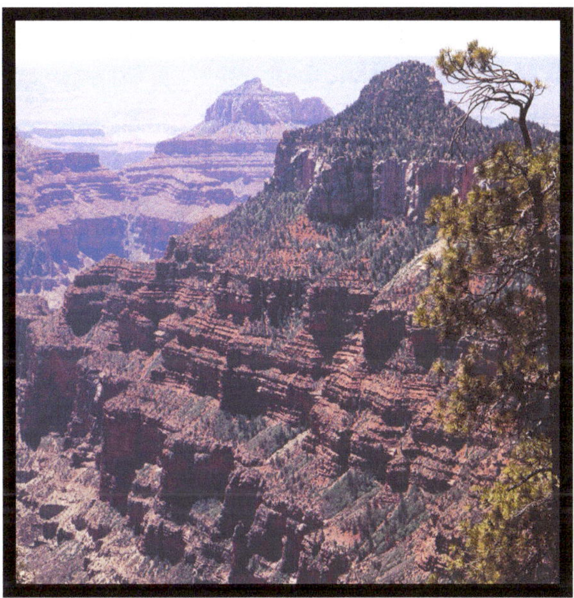

Figure 7.3
Grand Canyon N. P.

The Subject/Reflected Light

The key to working with the subject in the standard exposure model lies in the understanding of the range of luminescence for the light reflected from the subject. After the range of luminescence for the subject has been measured with a spot meter, then the correct aperture and shutter speed settings can be determined for the exposure. Listed below are the luminescence characteristics for some common subjects in natural light photography.

Foliage

The human eye is acutely sensitive to the yellow and green segments of the visible light spectrum. For this reason, green foliage appears to be brighter than it will be recorded by the capture media. Also, some green leaves have a very reflective surface which causes specular reflection from the leaves. Scenes containing a large amount of foliage can also contain some very dark shadow areas. Because of the dark shadow areas, the bias in photographing foliage should be toward a slight increase in exposure. This means that the exposure values should be shifted one or even two zones higher than usual. The exposure increase will preserve the dark shadow areas while increasing the luminescence of the green foliage. The correct exposure can be accomplished by measuring the shadow areas of the scene with a spot meter and placing the shadow readings in Zone III or even Zone IV depending on the range of luminescence for the subject. One exception to this zone shifting for foliage occurs with autumn foliage which can be very bright and colorful.

For photographing highly reflective sunlit foliage, the use of a polarizing filter can be quite useful in removing some of the reflection emanating from the subject. The understanding of the master photographer Edward Weston's notion of color as form can be very difficult; however, when the array of green tones that are contained in a foliage subject are considered **(Figure 7.4),** then a hint at Weston's conceptual meaning might be revealed:

"You find a few subjects that can be expressed in either color or black and white. But you find more that can be said only through one of them. Many I photographed would be meaningless in black-and-white; the separation of forms is possible only because of the juxtaposition of colors." (Edward Weston, Color Photography, Back Cover)

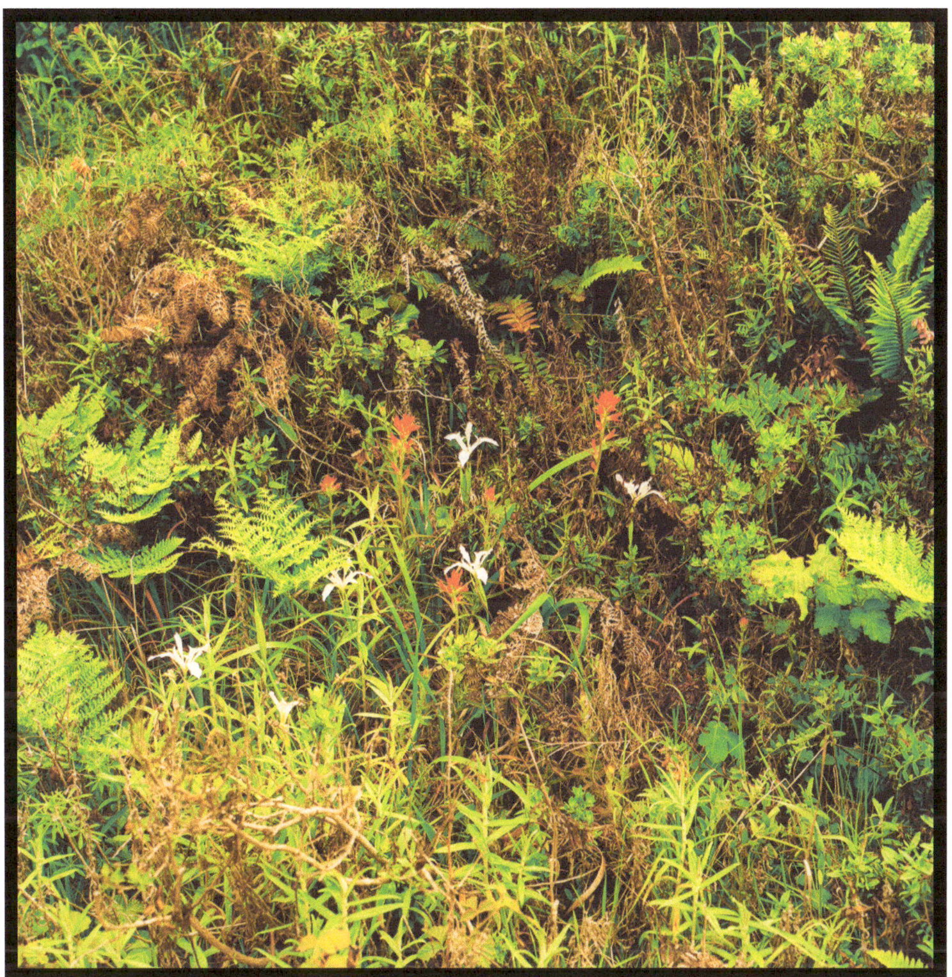

Figure 7.4
Phillip Burton W. A.
Marin County, California

Clouds

The capture of clouds in natural light photography involves a balancing act between the almost pure white areas of the clouds and the remainder of the subject area. **(Figure 7.5)** The bias when photographing a scene containing bright sunlit clouds should be toward a slight decrease in the exposure in order to retain some detail for the bright white areas of the clouds. If the white areas of the clouds are over-exposed, then these aspects of the clouds will become blocked and without texture. If the bright white areas of the clouds are under-exposed, then they will take on the gray look of concrete. When photographing a scene with bright sunlit clouds, the lightest areas of the clouds should be measured with a spot meter, and they should be placed one or even two zones lower than normal. The low values for the subject should be measured so that the remainder of the scene does not become too dark. Polarizing filters can be useful with scenes that contain clouds, because a polarizing filter darkens the sky and increases the contrast between the sky and the clouds.

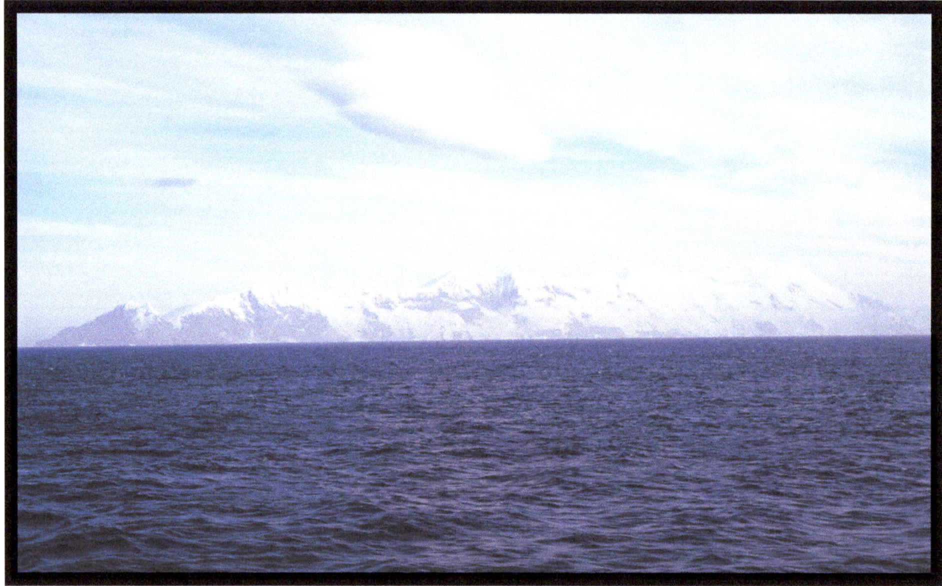

Figure 7.5
Lenticular Clouds
King George Island, Antartica

The Moon

The inclusion of the moon in a daylight landscape photograph adds an interesting detail to the uninteresting monotone blue sky. **(Figure 7.6)** Like bright clouds, the moon in a bright sunlit sky can be difficult to capture. The inclusion of the moon follows the same procedures and biases that were described above for clouds. A polarizing filter can be especially useful to accentuate the contrast between the sky and the moon.

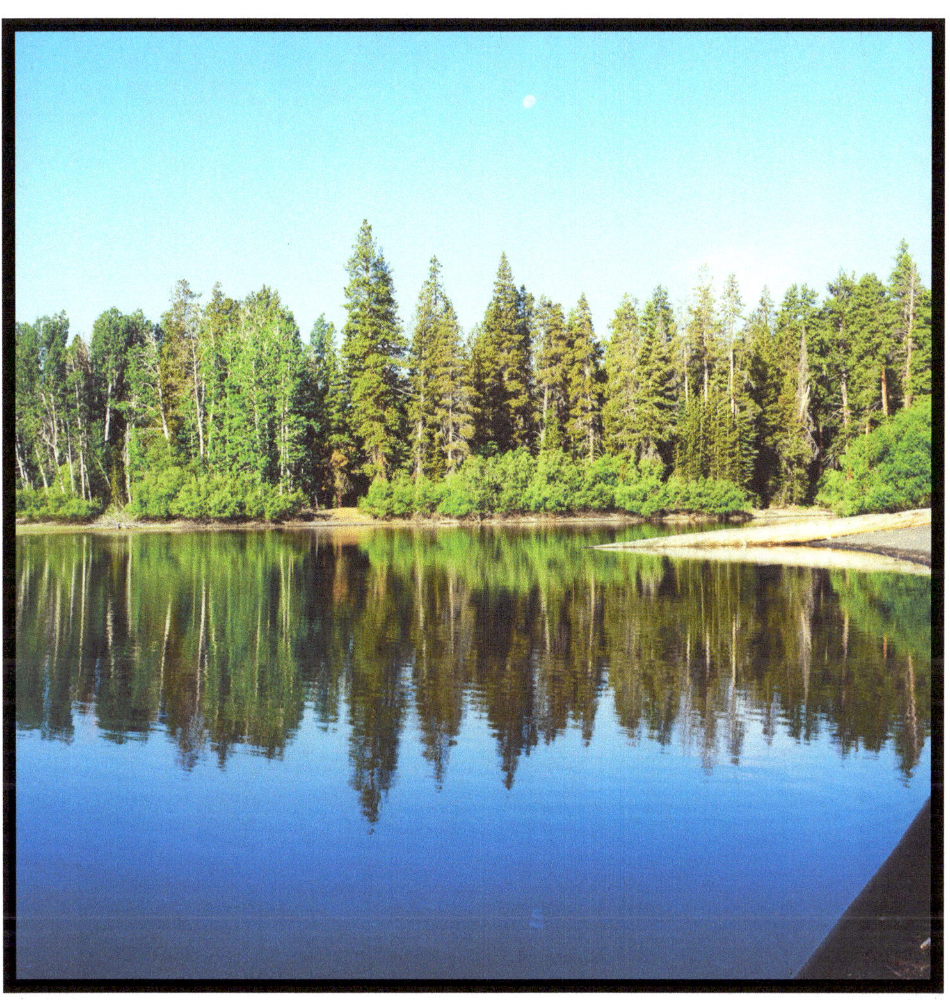

Figure 7.6
Moon and Reflection
Lassen N. P., California

Snow

Photographing snow on a sunny day involves the same pitfalls that are encountered with bright clouds. Over-exposed snow leads to burned out high values without texture, while under-exposed snow takes on a gray concrete-like cast. Snow in bright sunlight should be placed in Zone VIII or even Zone VII, while snow in shadows should be placed in Zone VI or even Zone V. **(Figure 7.7)**

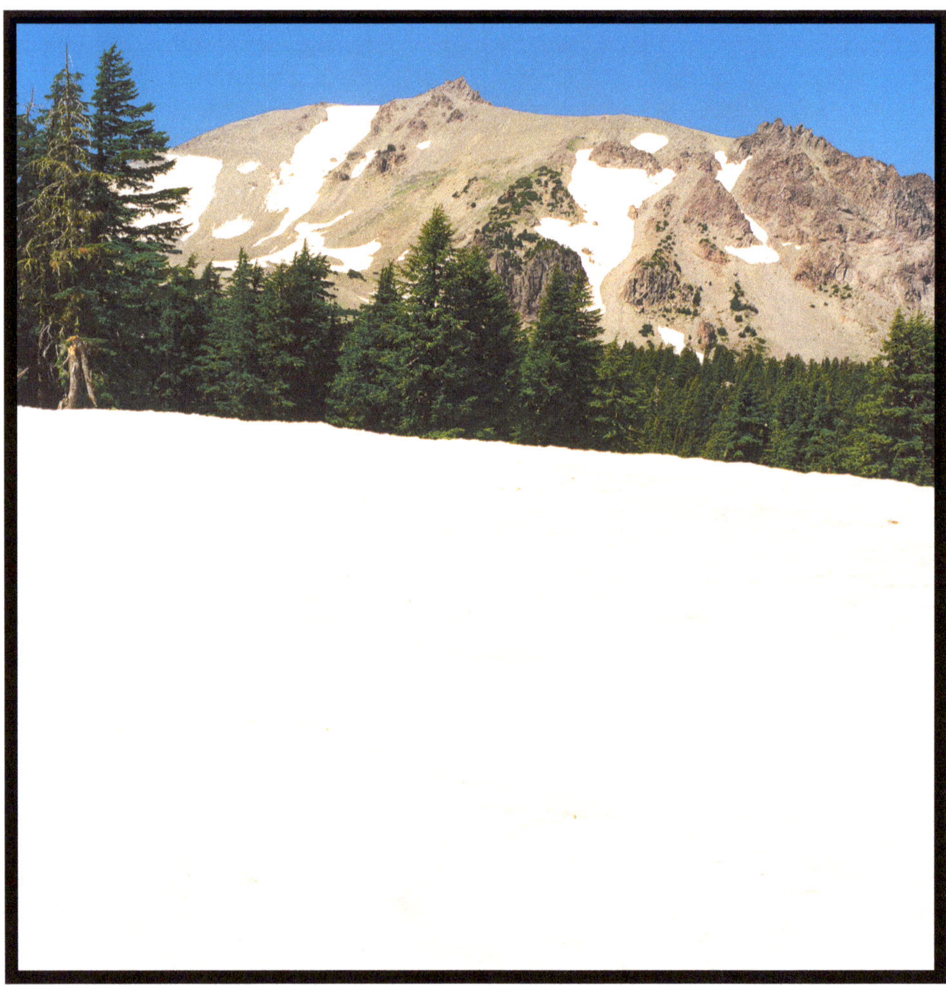

Figure 7.7
Snow
Lassen N. P., California

Fog

Accurately measuring the range of luminescence for a scene that includes fog is an essential step toward capturing a high-quality image. The diffuse light emanating from fog is brighter than it may seem; so, underestimating the brightness of the fog causes a tendency to under-expose a foggy scene. Fog itself has very little texture, so the secret to capturing an image that includes fog involves the accurate measurement of the low values for the subject. Also, measure the values for the foggy areas of the subject, but do not place the low values below Zone III, so that the detail in the shadow areas will be retained. **(Figure 7.8)**

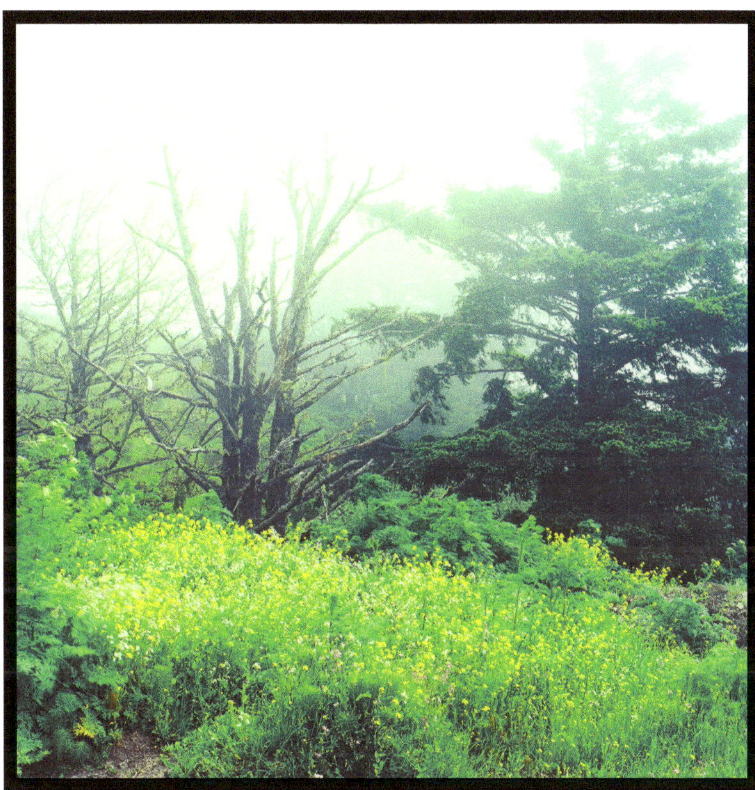

Figure 7.8
Fog
Cape Mendocino, California

The Ocean

The first thing to understand about photographing the ocean or any large body of water is that the body of water takes on the color of the sky. On a bright sunny day, the ocean appears to be blue, while on a gray over-cast day, the ocean appears to be gray. The second thing to realize about photographing the ocean is that it is in motion, and high shutter speeds cause the waves to appear frozen **(Figure 7.9)**. Neutral density filters are useful for making the wave action of the ocean appear to flow.

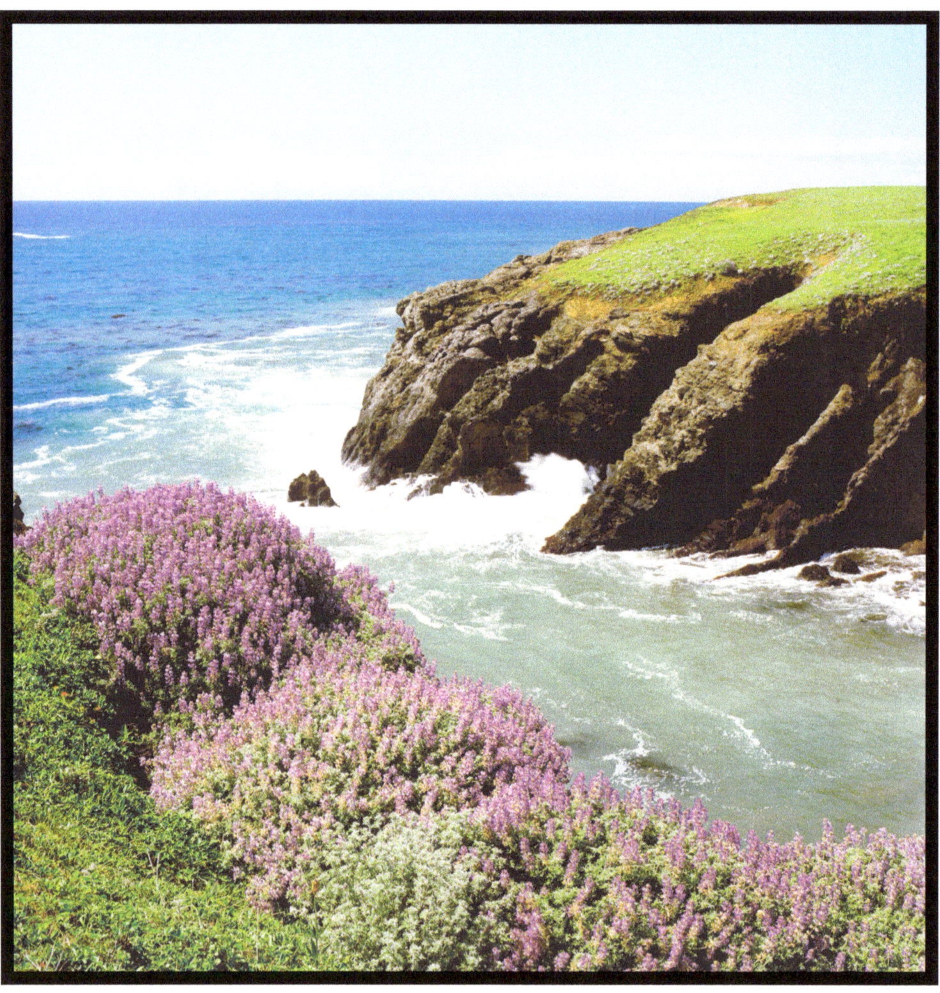

Figure 7.9
Mendocino Coast
California

The ocean also presents two additional challenges involving the range of luminescence. The first problem involves the high values representing the white wave foam, and the second problem involves the bright specular highlights that are reflected from the crests of the waves. The white foam should be handled in the same manner as white clouds and snow. The white values of the foam should be measured with a spot meter, and a bias toward the reduction in exposure should be considered. Be sure to take into consideration the low luminescence values when you are placing the values for the foam. Sometimes the slight reduction in exposure solves both the placement problems for the foam and the flow problems of the waves at the same time.

On bright sunlit days the uneven surface of the ocean has a tendency to emit bright specular highlights. A polarizing filter can be used to reduce some of this reflection; however, the complete removal of these highlight would make an ocean scene seem very unnatural. Also, remember that the polarizing filter only works when the sun is at a ninety degree angle to the exposure axis for the scene.

Mountains

The problem with photographing mountain landscapes is that your eye/brain seems to think that the mountain is much larger than it appears to the camera lens. Mountain landscape photographs are more interesting when the subject fills the frame. Filling the frame can be accomplished by using a larger fixed focal length lens or by increasing the zoom of a zoom lens **(Figure 7.10)**. For mountain scenes where snow is involved, be sure to follow the rules for snow that were that were previously discussed.

Flowing Water (Rivers, Streams, and Waterfalls)

The primary issue that is encountered when photographing flowing water involves the motion of the water. The high shutter speeds that are required to photograph rivers, streams, and waterfalls on a bright sunny day cause the flowing water to appear frozen. The use of a neutral density filter(s) will rectify the frozen effect of the flowing water to yield a pleasing ribbon effect in the image **(Figure 7.11)**.

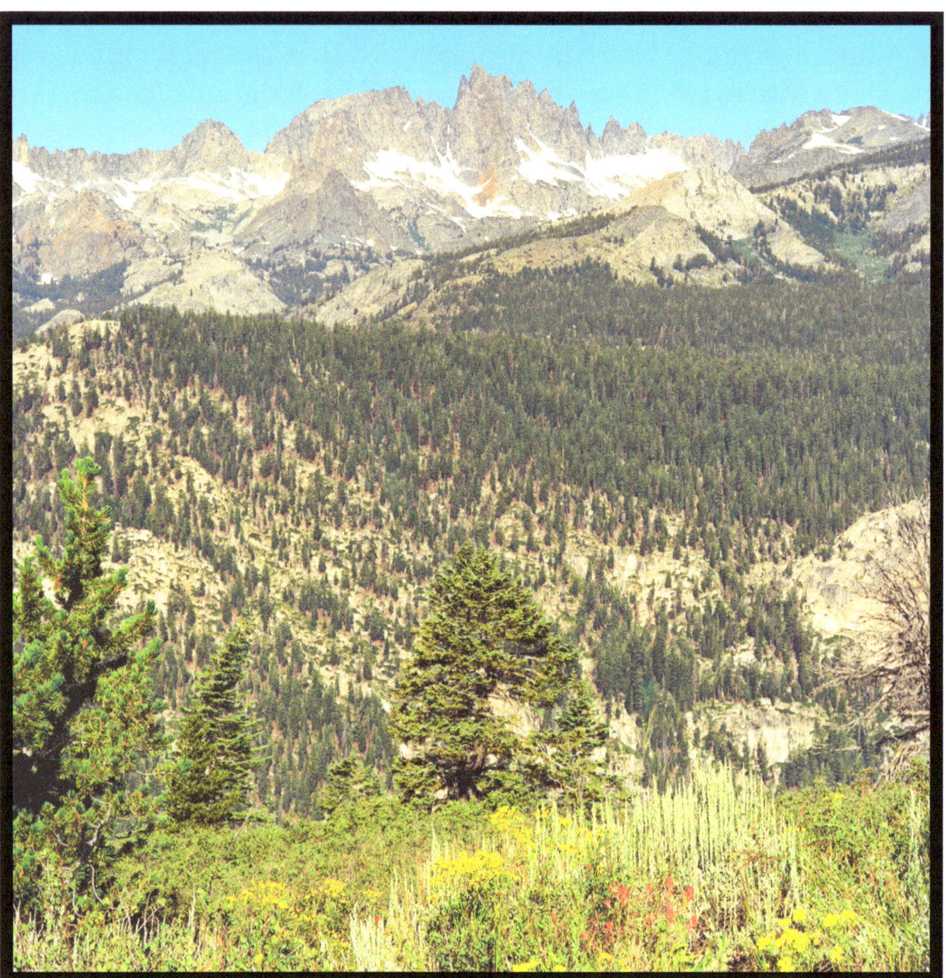

Figure 7.10
Ansel Adams W. A.
California

Neutral density filters require a reduction in exposure in order to obtain the correct exposure for the flowing water. It is the long shutter speeds that are required by the neutral density filter that cause the flowing water to appear like a continuous flow.

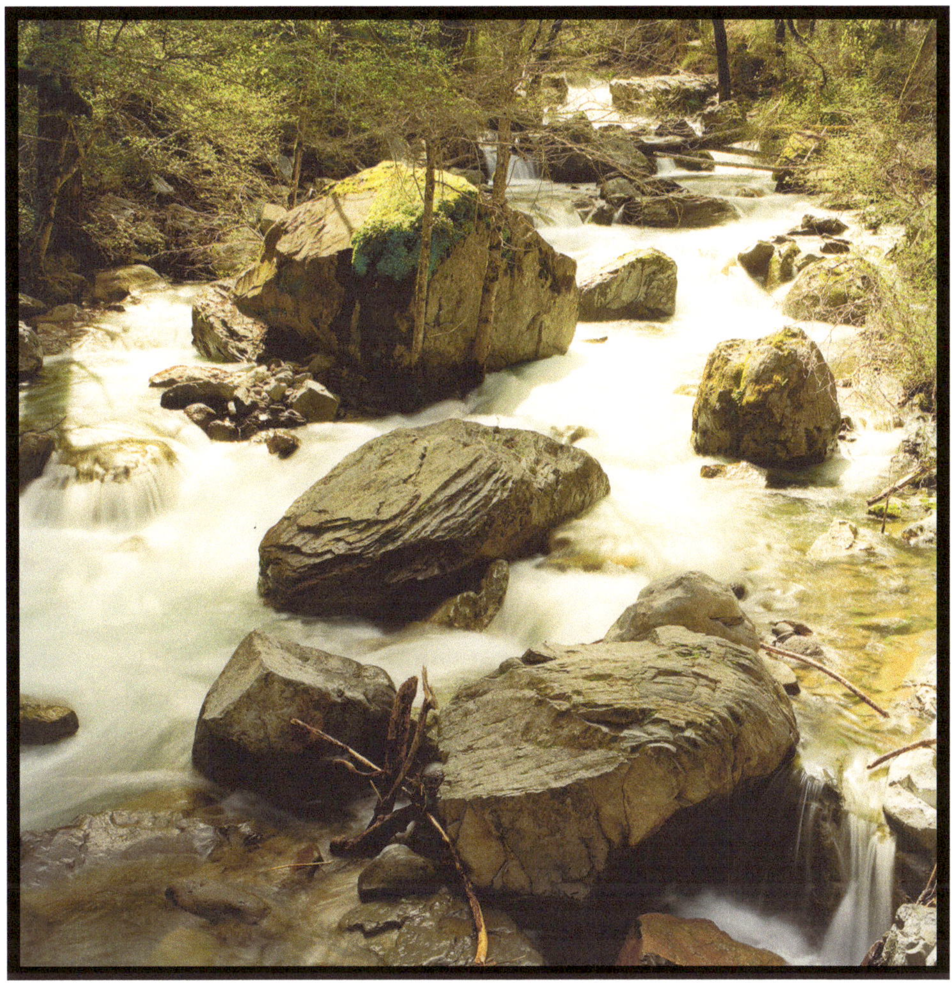

Figure 7.11
Ishi W. A.
California

Animals

The problem with the capture of animals in wildlife photograph involves the problem of subject motion. When a wild animal is encountered while hiking, the animal is often gone by the time the equipment set up in order to capture the image. The problem of capturing wildlife can be greatly improved by setting up a blind in the area where the animals are expected to appear. Wildlife photography takes research, stamina, and patience. Research is involved with the determination of the best locations for the setup of an animal blind. Stamina involves the porting of the blind and camera equipment to the chosen location, and patience involves keeping a watchful eye while waiting for the animals to appear. Once the animals do appear, the photographer's adrenaline levels will spike as they scramble to capture the fleeting image. This phenomenon is often referred to as buck fever by experienced hunters. The frenzy of buck fever can be avoided if the meter readings are taken and the aperture/shutter speed settings are made prior to the arrival of the animals. Animals in motion require a high shutter speed at the sacrifice of depth of field. Even the slight turn of an animal's head can cause blurring in the final image.

Flowers

The main problems in photographing flowers involve the small size of the subject and wind which causes the subject to move. There are many excellent macro lenses on the market that are specifically designed to photograph small objects at close range. Due to the focal length of macro lenses, close up photography requires long exposures which can limit the depth of field for a subject. The trick to photographing flowers involves obtaining the correct focus for the middle of the subject, and maximizing the depth of field by using the smallest aperture available. **(Figure 7.12)** This approach results in long exposures that are susceptible to the blowing wind blurring the image. Waiting for the wind to stop can be very frustrating, but this exercise will teach one of life's most important lessons – patience. If all else fails a plea to Vayu – the Hindu god of the wind – might be appropriate.

Macro photography often involves a bellows or extensions tubes which effectively increases the focal length for the lens that is being used. Also, polarizing filters can be useful for photographing flowers. Polarizing filters remove reflection from the subject, and they increase the color saturation within the image.

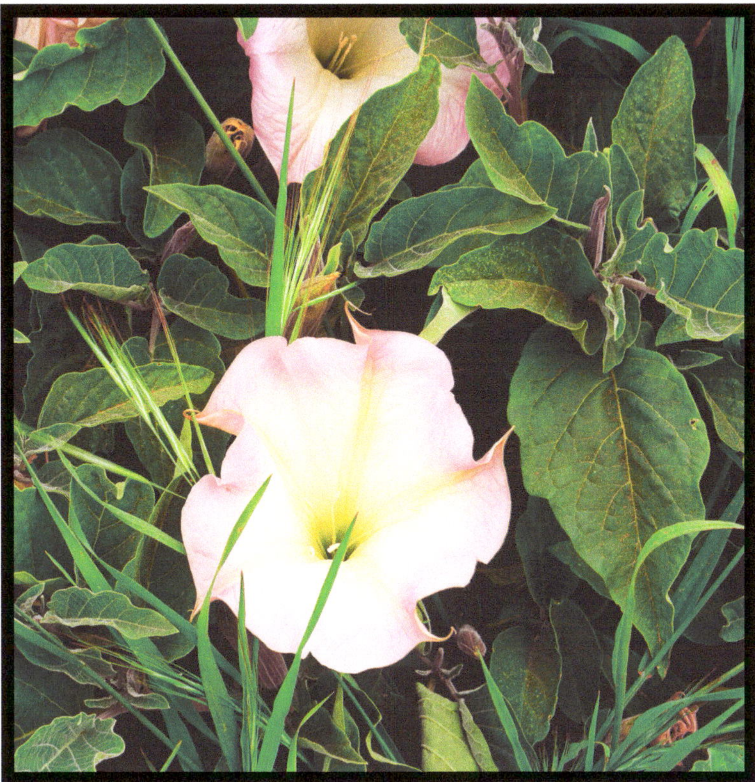

Figure 7.12
Flowers
Channel Islands N. P., California

Reflections

Some of the most striking and enigmatic natural light photographs involve the reflection of an object on a still body of water. It is when the waters in the image are at rest that the true nature of the reflections can be seen, similar to the knowledge that is attained when the activities of mind are at rest in the Hindu discipline of Yoga.

With the symmetric reflected images **(Figure 7.13)**, it is often difficult to determine which part of the photograph is the real subject and which part of the image is the reflection. This confusion can capture the viewer's attention much like the momentary confusion caused by Zen koan statements. In these types of reflected images, the reflected image is often darker than the original image. A graduated neutral density filter can be used to solve this problem.

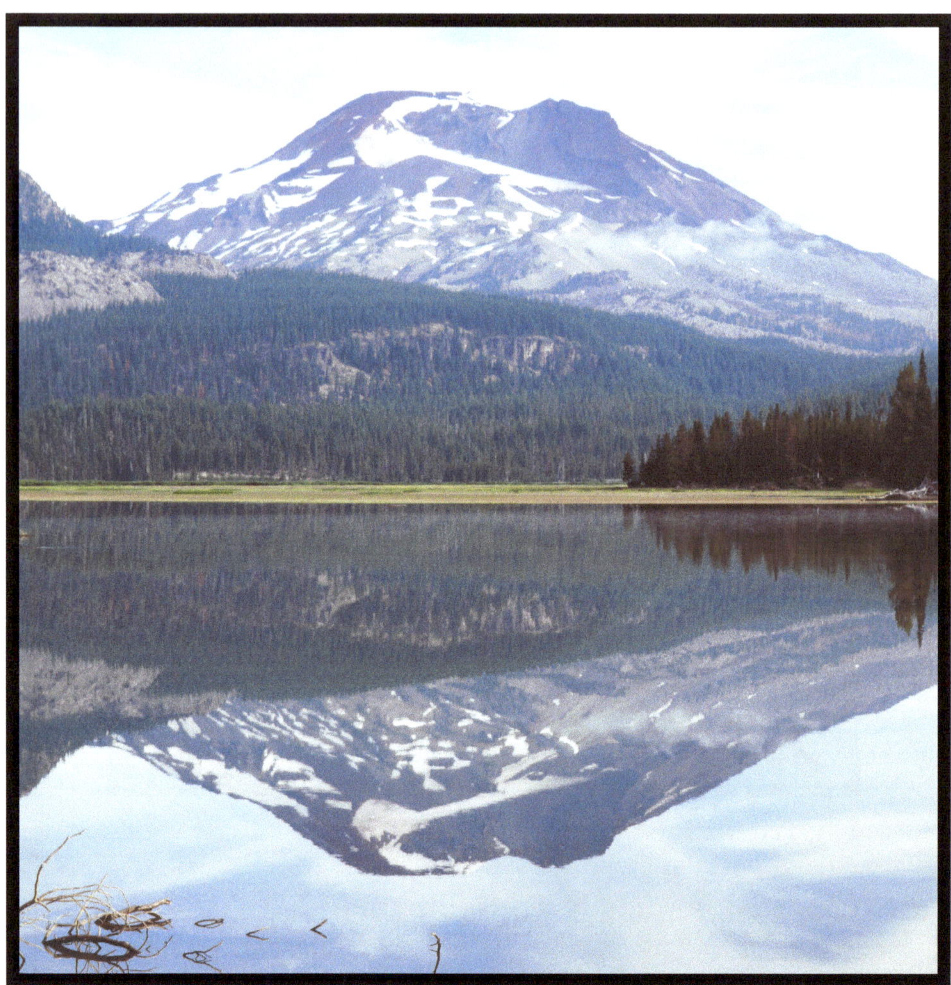

Figure 7.13
South Sister
Three Sisters W. A., Oregon

Exposure Axis\Angle of Illumination

For natural light photography, the most important light source is the sun. Using the sun as a primary light source requires an understanding of two important concepts – the exposure axis and the angle of illumination. The exposure axis is the straight line that is drawn from the subject to the front of the camera lens. The exposure axis is perpendicular to the capture media, and it is the path along which the reflected light from the subject moves toward the camera lens.

The second important concept in the review of natural light photography is the notion of the angle of illumination. The angle of illumination refers to the angle of the light source (the sun) in relation to the exposure axis. When the sun is directly in line with the exposure axis and behind the camera, the subject is fully illuminated and the shadow areas of the subject seem to disappear. Under these lighting conditions, the photographer has maximum control over the range of luminescence and the contrast values for the subject. The two problems that can occur at this angle of illumination are the limb effect and camera shadow problems. The limb effect occurs when is sun is in line with the exposure axis, and the lines of the subject curve away from the camera. Under these circumstances the curved areas of the subject take on a dark appearance especially when the subject has a light background. **(Figure 7.14)** The second problem encountered at this angle of illumination involves the shadow of the camera and tripod being cast on the subject being photographed. This is a particularly difficult problem when the sun is low on the horizon.

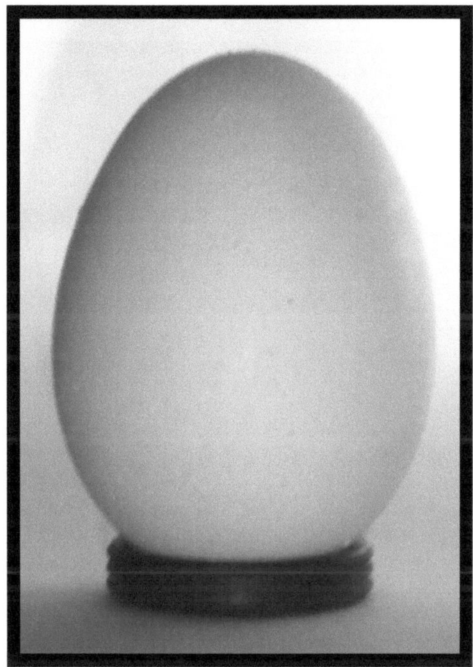

Figure 7.14
The Limb Effect

When the sun is at a right angle to the exposure axis, then the subject's shadows become more pronounced and the control of the range of luminescence and contrast values become more pronounced. During sunrise and sunset, sunlight at a ninety degree angle to the exposure axis casts a long shadow which magnifies the texture and depth of the subject. Sunlight at sunrise and sunset has a distinctive red cast which is due to the light passing through a large amount of the earth's atmosphere as the light travels from the sun to the subject.

As the sun appears to move overhead at noon, the long shadows for the subject become shorter and more acute as the subject takes on a harsh, flat appearance. The sunlight during the middle of the day is at its brightest, which accentuates the wide differences between the sunlight and shadow values for the subject. This large difference between the highlight and shadow values define the luminescence range or contrast for the subject. The range of contrast will increase as the sun appears to move directly over-head, and the subject will take on a harsh appearance.

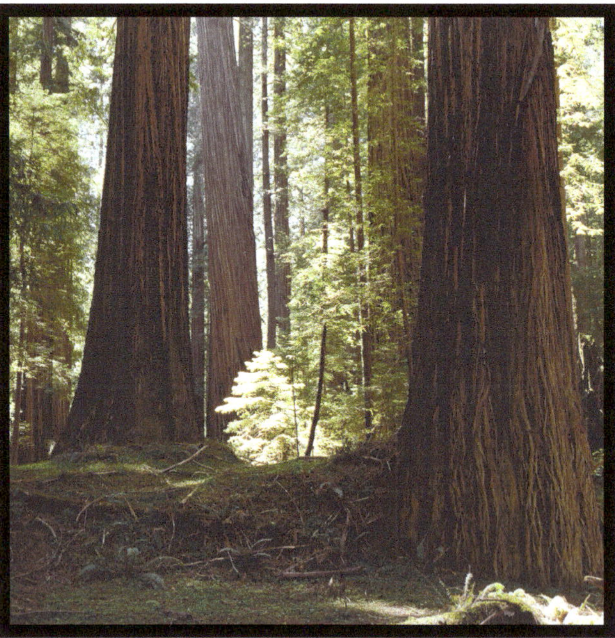

Figure 7.15
Rockefeller Grove, California

The best example of this harsh contrast problem is the redwood forest at noon on a bright summer day. The normal ratio of sunlight to shade for a subject is approximately one to eight, while the ratio of brightness in the redwood photograph **(Figure 7.15)** can be as high as 1 to 800. The capture of detail in a 1:800 range is virtually impossible. The sunlight striking the small redwood tree from the sun directly overhead causes the high values to be blocked or burned out. As the angle of the light source increases past ninety degrees in relation to the exposure axis, the use of a lens shade becomes more important.

When the sun is directly in line with the exposure axis and behind the subject, the subject is said to be back-lit. Under these lighting conditions, the front portion of the subject appears in shadow and the subject appears to be surrounded by a halo of light. The best approach to dealing with difficult back-lighting conditions is to place the darker values for the subject as high as Zones V or VI. Another approach involves the use of a reflector to bounce the light from the source onto the shadow areas of the subject. In either case, the use of a lens shade for back-lit subjects can be very important.

The Camera

Natural light photography often requires long exposures, and with long exposures, the stability of the camera is a critical concern. For natural light landscape photography the smallest aperture opening is often used in order to maximize the depth of field for the image. Also, long exposures are used to give flowing water a pleasing ribbon-like appearance. For long exposures, a tripod and cable release are essential tools. Ansel Adams stated that the main difference between amateur and professional photographers was that professional photographers always used a tripod.

The need for a tripod and cable release is especially true when telephoto lenses are used in natural light photography. It is virtually impossible for the human hand to hold a camera with a telephoto lens steady no matter what shutter speed is used. The use of a tripod and cable release greatly improves the quality of all natural light images.

I always prefer to work in the studio.
It isolates people from their environment.
They become in a sense... symbolic of themselves.

-- Richard Avedon

Chapter Eight

Artificial Light Photography

For artificial light photography, the photographer has complete control of all aspects of the image capture process. Unlike natural light photography where the artist is subject to the whims of nature, the studio photographer has the ability to manipulate all of the components of the Standard Exposure Model. For studio photography, the artist's role is similar to the role of a stage manager who has control of all of the details for the set.

Artificial Light

When artificial light is used in the studio environment, three main sources of light can be used:

- Key Lighting
- Fill Lighting
- Effects Lighting

Key Lighting

For studio photography, the *key light* is the light that creates the shadows and principal highlights for a composition. Shadows are a very important part of artificially lit images, and the creation of shadows have three basic rules:

1. For each composition, there should be only one set of shadows, and all of the shadows should be pointing in the same direction. Multiple shadows pointing in multiple directions can be very confusing for the viewer of the composition.

2. The subject should be far enough away from the background so that unwanted shadows from the subject can be eliminated with fill lighting.

3. Any shadows that are included in the image should be considered part of the composition. Shadows can be a very effective tool in artificial light photography, but they should be carefully planned as part of the composition.

Fill Lighting

Fill lighting includes secondary light(s) or reflective surfaces that are used to eliminate or fill the shadow areas of a composition. Fill lighting does not necessarily have to be a light. Mirrors or reflective "bounce" tools can be used for the function of fill lighting.

Effects Lighting

Effects lighting refers to small directional light(s) or reflective surfaces that are used to create specialized lighting within a composition. Effects lighting is used to light separate aspects of the composition. Effects lighting includes background lighting and the creation of individual highlights through the use of side lighting. Like fill lighting, effects lighting does not necessarily have to be a light. Effects lighting can be achieved through the use of mirrors or reflective surfaces.

Light Sources

For photography, there are three primary light source categories:

- Natural Light
- Electronic Light
- Static Light

Natural Light Sources

Natural light that is emanating from a window or door can be used as an effective source for light in studio photography. The problem with using natural light in a studio environment involves the balance of natural light temperature at 5500 degrees Kelvin with the temperature of artificial lights at 3200 degrees Kelvin. If the only light source being used is natural light, then daylight film can be used. If artificial light is used in conjunction with natural light, then tungsten film should be used, as tungsten film causes natural light to have a bluish cast. The balancing of natural and artificial light sources can be accomplished with the use of color conversion and color compensating filters **(Chapter 6)**.

Electronic Flash

Electronic flash is a pulse of light that is used to illuminate the subject at the time of exposure. Flash lighting has a tendency to create a harsh high contrast appearance for the subject. The iconic photographer Diane Arbus used a flash attached to her Rolleiflex camera in order to obtain a harsh high contrast appearance for some of her subjects. **(Figure 8.1)**

Most modern point-and-shoot 35 mm format cameras come equipped with a built-in flash that is triggered with the exposure button. The problem with a built-in flash is that the light intensity of the flash is very weak. In order for the built-in flash to be effective, the subject has to be within fifteen feet of the camera lens.

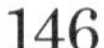

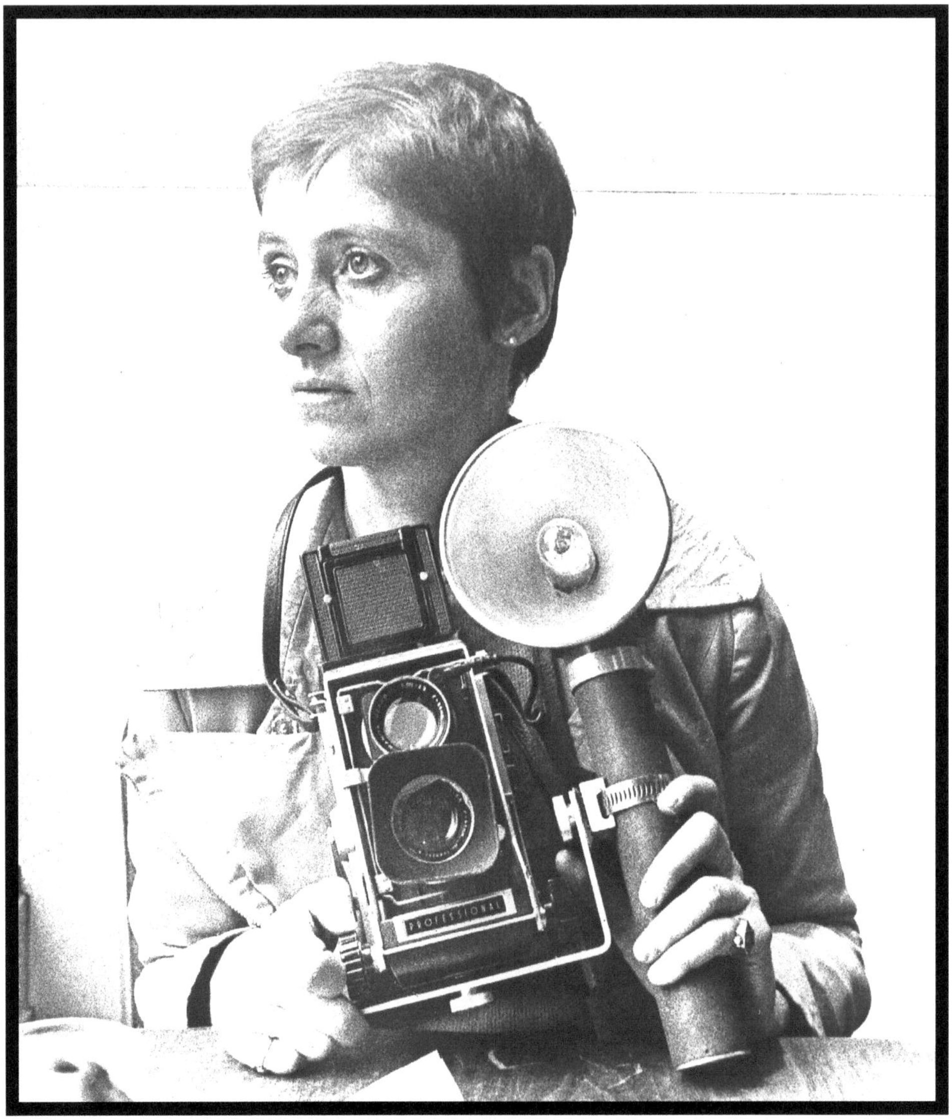

Figure 8.1
Diane Arbus

Studio flash units are high-intensity light sources that can be either masters or slaves. The master units can be triggered by the exposure button either through a cable from the camera or by a radio signal generated from an electronic device. The slave units are triggered by the light emanating from the master unit. The intensity of the flash can be varied by controls on the flash unit, and many professional flash units are powered by high voltage power packs.

Static Lighting

The primary distinction between flash units and static lighting lies in the fact that static lighting is always on. Static lighting is identified by the watt consumption of the light source, and static lights have a tendency to be very hot. Extreme caution should be exercised when using static lights, because the power consumption and heat generated from this type of lighting can cause fires.

Static lights can have a power consumption that ranges from one hundred watts to thousands of watts. A standard twenty amp electrical circuit can only support a maximum load of nine hundred watts. Consequently, the use of several high wattage lights on one twenty amp circuit can cause an electrical fire. A professional electrician should be consulted before any high voltage lights are used on any electrical circuit. Also, due to the high temperatures of static light sources, care should be taken to avoid skin burns caused by contact with the light sources.

Static light sources can use either incandescent or tungsten light bulbs. Incandescent light bulbs can be used with reflectors to generate high intensity light. Tungsten lamps are often used with Fresnel lenses to create a concentrated, high-intensity light beam.

Modifying the Light Source

Within the controlled studio environment, there are a wide range of tools that can be used to alter the intensity, direction, and temperature of light from both flash and static light sources. Listed below are some of the principal light source control mechanisms:

Barn Doors

Barn doors are adjustable matte black flaps that can be mounted on the front portion of the light source. Barn doors are used to eliminate light from certain areas of the composition.

Black Card

A black card is a black surface area that is used to prevent light from striking or being reflected to certain areas of the composition.

Bounces

Bounces are reflective surfaces that are used to direct light into select areas of the composition. Bounces are normally used to direct light to key shadow areas of the composition. Bounces can be purchased in different colors such as white, gold, and silver.

Diffusers

Diffusers are made from translucent material that is used to scatter and soften light as it travels from the source to the subject. In order to be effective, diffuser material needs to scatter at least 50% of the light source.

Flags

A flag is a piece of black material that is used to block source light from certain areas of the composition.

Gelatin Filters

Gelatin filters are transparent color gelatin material that is mounted in front of the light source in order to change the color of the incident light. Color filters transmit their own color, and they absorb all the other colors of the spectrum. **(*See* Chapter 6)**

Gobos

A gobo is a flag with irregular holes in the surface. The irregular holes create a dappled lighting effect on the subject.

Honeycombs

A honeycomb is a grid pattern of hexagonal cells that is placed in front of the light source. The honeycomb pattern increases the directionality of the light emanating from the light source.

Reflectors

Reflectors are highly polished and shaped surfaces that surround the light source. Reflectors are used to concentrate and direct the light emanating from the light source.

Scrims

A scrim can be a thin translucent material that is placed between the source light and the subject in order to reduce the intensity of the source light; they can also be a white cloth that is placed over a light source in order to soften the incident light.

Snoots

A snoot is a metallic device that is placed in front of the light source in order to control the direction of the light emanating from the source.

Softboxes

A softbox is a lighting device that is placed over the light source. Softboxes diffuse and soften the light emanating from the light source.

Umbrellas

Umbrellas are reflective lighting devices that are placed in front of the light source. Umbrellas can be used to control the direction of the incident light. Umbrellas can also be used to soften and diffuse (scatter) the incident light.

The Subject

Artificial lighting is used in commercial photography to capture three basic types of subject:

- Portraits
- Still Lifes
- Interiors

Portraits

Portrait photography is usually used to record specific human events such as births, and rites of passage like graduations, weddings, and family gatherings. It is photography's ability to stop time that makes it such an integral component of these life events.

Portraits are also used for individual and corporate promotion and advertising. **(Figure 8.2)** The social networking fad has fostered an explosion of individual portraits(*selfies*) that can be used on the internet. Corporate portraits are used for both yearly corporate statements and advertising. Whole volumes are available which address the lighting of portrait photography for both commercial and personal use.

Still Life

Artificial lighting is used extensively for both artistic and commercial product still life photography. **(Figure 8.3)** Artistic still life images have a long and varied history in the visual arts. The portrayal of everyday objects using paint or mosaics have been recorded by visual artists for thousands of years. Contemporary master photographers such as Irving Penn and Robert Maplethorpe have dedicated whole books to their still life images. Artificial lighting also plays a critical role in the lighting of products for commercial advertising.

Interiors

Artificial lighting is used extensively by architects and interior designers in the capture of interior scenes. The capture of indoor events like weddings would be impossible without the use of artificial lights.

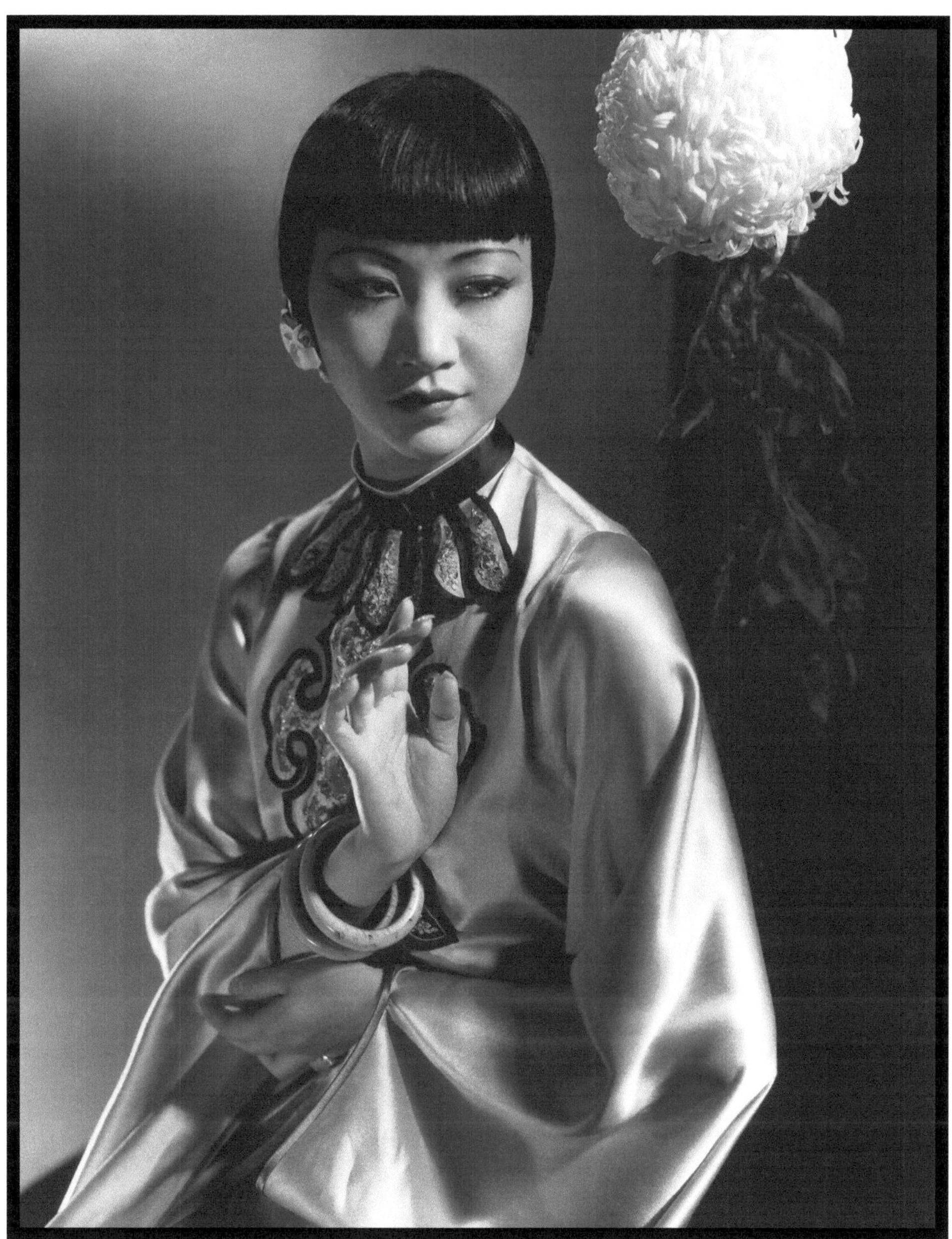

Figure 8.2
Anna May Wong (1930)
By Edward Steichen

Excellent examples of interior lighting and photography are available in the publications *Architectural Digest* and *Interiors.*

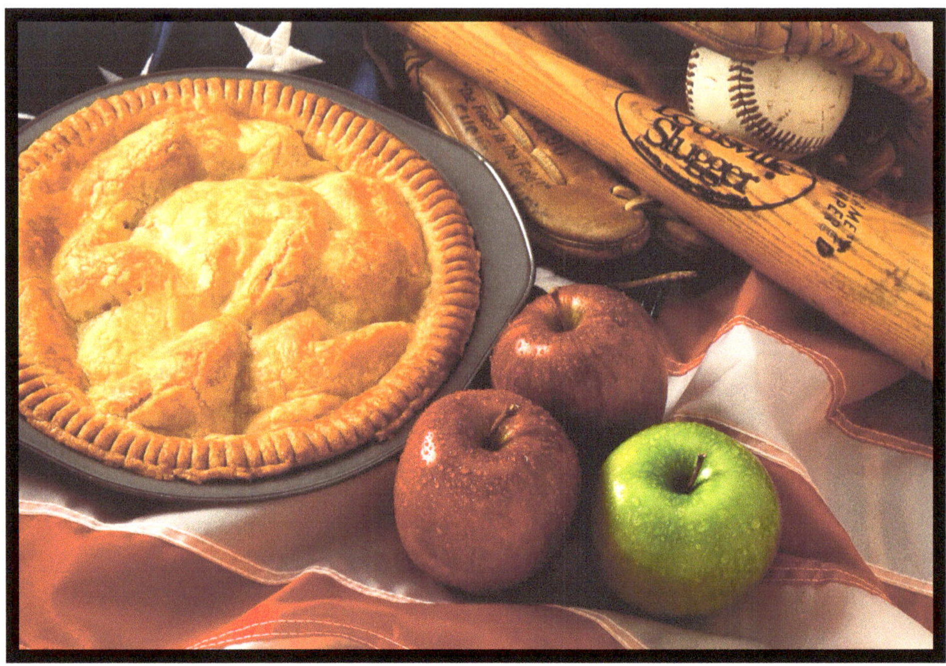

Figure 8.3
Still Life

Set Design/Lighting Diagrams

Studio photography using artificial lighting is very similar to the set design techniques that are used for theatres and movies. Like dramatic set design, the equipment used for studio photography includes tables, backgrounds, rear projection devices, booms and weights. For still life photography tables and props are an essential ingredient. Background materials and background projection devices such as slide projectors and fill lights are key components for all studio photography. Booms and weights are used to hold background material, cameras, and lighting. Booms and counter weighting material are used extensively for the configuration of the studio photography set.

Finally, lighting diagrams are an extremely helpful tool for the design of the studio photography set **(Figure 8.4)**. Most lighting diagrams are an overhead drawing of all of the components that make up a particular studio composition. By designing the studio set with the use of a lighting diagram, the photographer is forced to visualize object, light, and camera placement before the composition of the photograph begins.

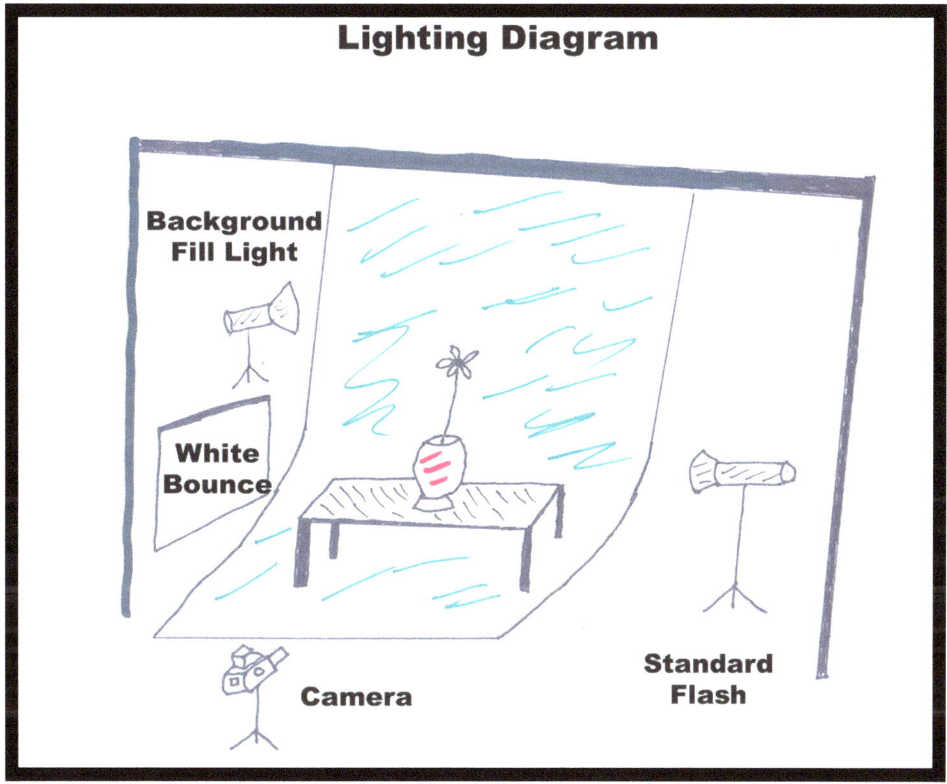

Figure 8.4
Lighting Diagram

Measuring the Light

Measuring the incident and reflected light for an artificially lit studio scene is very similar to the measurement of natural light. The key components of light measurement involve the intensity and temperature for both the incident light and the reflected light from the subject. Incident light meters can be used to measure the intensity of the incident light. A color temperature meter is needed to measure the temperature of both the incident and reflected light, and a spot meter should be used to measure the highlight, shadow, and gray card values for the subject. Once the light intensity and temperature for a scene is understood, the light modification devices outlined above can be used to balance the light.

The measurement of light values for the scene is fairly simple when static lighting equipment is being used. A problem arises when measuring light from flash equipment, because the lighting values will be different for the scene when the flash occurs. The flash measuring problem can be solved through the use of a flash triggering interface from the meter to the flash. Some light meters have an interface which allows the flash to be triggered from either a cable or a radio signal module that is attached to the meter. When the meter reading button on the meter is pressed, the flash is triggered and the meter can record the light level reading for the studio scene. The Sekonic L-558r light meter is an example of a light meter which contains the required flash activation interface.

The Camera

The use of the Standard Exposure Model's camera component under artificial light is very similar to camera use under natural light. For long shutter speed exposures, the use of a tripod to steady the camera is very important. If film is being used, the rules for reciprocity failure apply when the exposure is one second or more. Polarizing, color compensating, and conversion filters can be used to balance and alter the incident and reflected light.

The only difference for the camera component under artificial light involves the need to trigger flash equipment with the shutter mechanism on the camera. Most camera shutters have a flash interface which allows for the synchronization of the flash with the camera shutter. Flash synchronization is accomplished with the attachment of a cable or radio frequency module from the flash to the camera. With flash synchronization, the flash is triggered when the exposure button on the camera is pressed. Finally, when there is a doubt about an exposure value, instant film or LCD screen proofing tools should be used.

Creativity takes courage.

-- Henri Matisse

Chapter Nine

Image Capture

"I would like to repeat here that *the making of photographs is the prime function of photographer.* Once the craft is under intuitive control, the creative objective is more positive and assured. Proficiency of craft should by no means be considered the goal in itself. The emphasis today on technique, equipment, and materials can be overpowering" (Ansel Adams, *The Negative*, P. 125)

The Visual Language

The Ansel Adams quote above seems intuitively obvious, but there is a tendency among photographers to become preoccupied with the technical details of data capture. The point has been reached in the exploration of the tools and concepts involved in data capture that it is time to create some photographs.

The viewer of a painting or photograph usually scans the image starting in the upper left corner of the image frame and they continue the scanning process until the eye reaches the bottom of the frame. The goal of the visual artist is to contain and ultimately to stop the viewer's attention within the image frame. This visual arrest has the potential to trigger a enlightened moment in the viewer – the epiphany moment as described by James Joyce, quoted in **Chapter 2.**

Over the centuries, visual artists have developed a visual language that is used to control the viewer's process of scanning an image. Like auditory languages, the expression of the language differs from culture to culture, but the elements and principles of the visual language are the same for all cultures. The elements of the visual language are similar to words in the auditory language, while the visual principles are similar to the rules of grammar used in an auditory language. Human beings are inundated by this visual language on a daily basis through painting, drawing, television, movies, and advertising. The examination of the elements and principles that make up a visual language is not limited to photography. The father of modern photography, Paul Strand **(Figure 9.1)** was once confronted by one of his photography students who asked why Strand was making the students study the work of the painter Goya. Strand replied that there were lessons to be learned throughout all of the visual arts.

The design of any visual image can be decomposed into the elements and principles of its visual language.

Visual Language Elements

The elements of the visual language are as follows:

- Point
- Line
- Shape
- Form
- Texture
- Pattern
- Color

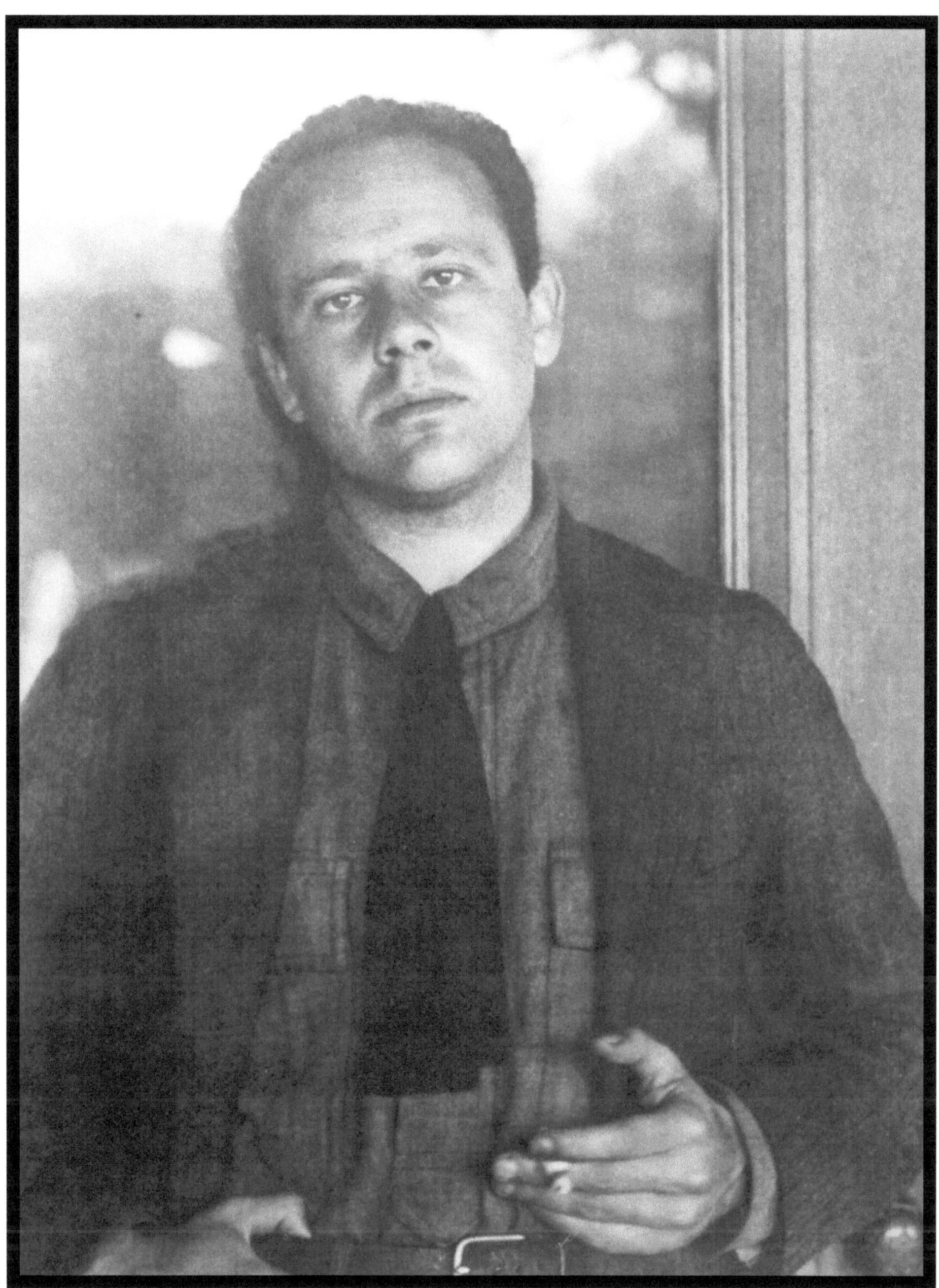

Figure 9.1
Paul Strand

Point

A point is that which has not part. – Euclid

A location in two or three dimensional space. – Webster

Line

A line is a breadth-less length.

The extremities of a line are points

A straight line is a line which lies evenly with the points on itself. – Euclid

A locus of points; a continuous mark that is made by a pen or pencil applied to a surface; a set of points – Webster

A line is a mark made by a moving point and having psychological impact according to its direction, weight, and variation in its direction and weight.

"The line is the strongest and most basic component of the visual language" – *Visual Design*

Attributes of a Line:

Straight Line – the shortest distance between two points

Horizontal Line – the sideways articulation of a line. Suggests a feeling of rest or repose

Vertical Line – the up/down articulation of a line. Communicates a feeling of loftiness and spirituality

Diagonal Line – the angular articulation of a line. Diagonal lines suggest dynamic motion or direction

Curved Line – curved lines are dominant in nature. Acutely curved lines suggest confusion and turbulence while shallow curved lines suggest a feeling comfort, safety, and relaxation.

Weight – Lines can be thick or thin

Shape

A shape is the use of line to define a mass in two dimensional space. Because a shape has only two dimensions it has no depth. In photography shapes occur when they are either front or back lit. This type of lighting causes the form and texture of the shape to disappear while increasing the contrast between the object and its surroundings. The silhouette is a classic example of a shape.

Form

A form is the use of line(s) to define a three dimensional mass in either a two- or three-dimensional space. The primary difference between shape and form lies in the fact that shape is two-dimensional, while form has depth and is three-dimensional. In photography forms are characterized by side lighting. It is the contrast between the light and shadow areas of a side-lit form that gives the form depth.

Texture

Texture is an attribute of a surface that can be discerned through the human sense of touch. When texture is described, words like rough, smooth, wet, dry, sharp, dull, sticky, or bristly are used. Texture is important in visual images because all surfaces have texture, and texture can contribute a strong emotional impact to a visual composition. In photography, side lighting can be used as one method to expose the texture of a surface. Also, the illusion of texture can also be introduced to an image through the manipulation of color gradation and contrast.

Pattern

A pattern is a recognizable motif within a surface or structure that repeats itself in a consistent and regular manner. Patterns can exist in both nature and man-made objects. Due to their relative nature, patterns evoke the emotional feelings of safety, consistency, and predictability. In photography, one of the most widely used methods for causing visual arrest is the disruption of a pattern within an image.

Color

Listed below are some of the psychological implications of the spectral colors:

Red – The positive aspects of red are passion, high energy, and the eroticism. The negative aspects are aggression, anger, and violence.

Orange – The positive aspects of orange are warmth, approachability, and informality. The negative aspects are lack of discrimination or quality.

Yellow – The positive aspects of yellow are the color or sunshine and an upbeat modern attitude. The negative aspects are blinding overwhelming brightness.

Green – The positive aspects of green are naturalness, life, and stability. The negative aspects of green are decay, mold, toxicity, and artificiality.

Blue – The positive aspects of blue are coolness, distance, spirituality, and elegance. The negative aspects of blue are sadness, alienation, and depression.

Violet – The positive aspects of violet are fantasy, dream state, and playfulness. The negative aspects of violet imply nightmares and madness.

Visual Language Principles

The principles of a visual language and visual design include the following concepts:

- Balance
- Proportion
- Ryythm
- Emphasis
- Unity

Balance

Balance is an attempt to render a visual composition with a sense of equilibrium. Equilibrium in a visual composition can be achieved by a reconciliation of opposing forces. Balance in a visual image is achieved through the use of symmetrical or asymmetrical visual techniques. Formal balance refers to the repetition of image components on both sides of the vertical or horizontal lines or equally around a central point in the image. For example, a mountain scene reflected in a perfectly still lake is an example of the use of horizontal symmetry to achieve formal balance in the visual image. Approximate symmetry is the use of similar objects that are placed to achieve balance in an image. The second visual balancing technique is referred to as asymmetrical or informal balance. Asymmetrical balance involves the use of objects of unequal weight that are placed within the image to bring a sense of balance to the image. For example, a large shape close to the center of an image can be balanced by a small object close to the edge of the image, or a large light-colored object can be balanced by a small dark-colored object. Dark objects in a visual composition appear to have more weight than light-colored objects.

Proportion

Proportion refers to the size and scale of various elements within a visual image. The relationship between the size and scale of the elements within an image can be used to express normal or abnormal manifestations of the total image. Normally proportion is a tool that is used by visual artists to represent depth. Depth can be expressed through the representation of large objects in the foreground of a scene and smaller objects in the middle and far ground of a scene. Abnormal proportions can be used to shock and arrest the attention of the viewer. For example, a ten-foot fly swatter next to a normal sized human can elicit a range of human emotions such as humor, fear, and shock.

Rhythm

Rhythm in the visual arts refers to the repetition, alternation, or gradation of motifs in order to direct the viewers eye through a visual space. Visual rhythm can be achieved through the effective use of any of the visual elements. Repetition refers to the use of patterns to achieve visual movement in a visual space. Alternation is the use of repetition in the visual space to represent alternating representations of visual elements. The alternation of dark/light, round/square, or thick/thin visual elements can prove to be more interesting than the straight forward repetition of the same visual elements. Gradation in a visual image refers to the use of patterned visual elements in a regular progression of steps. Gradation of size and scale within an image is used to portray perspective. The gradation of color and tone can be used in a visual image to represent aerial perspective. Aerial perspective refers to the fact that the contrast of an object decreases as the distance of the object from the viewer increases. Leonardo da Vinci used color and tone very effectively to represent aerial perspective in landscape paintings. Gradation of tones from dark to light within an image can be used to direct the viewer's eye in one direction within a visual image.

Emphasis

Emphasis within a visual image refers to the primary and secondary points of focus within the visual space The points of emphasis are the locations within the image that draw the viewer's attention. As the viewer's eye scans an image, it is stopped or arrested at the primary and secondary points of emphasis. Points of emphasis interrupt the normal pattern, movements, or rhythm within the image; they cause the eye to stop and be drawn to certain key points in the visual image. Emphasis within the image can be achieved through the use of repetition, contrast, or dominance. The repetition of a visual element is an obvious technique for emphasizing a particular motif within the image. The use of visual contrast is another technique that is used for emphasizing certain aspects of the image. The placement of color texture, shape, size, or scale within the image can be used to contrast the strongest point of emphasis with the other elements of the composition. Dominance of a particular visual element within an image is the final technique which can be used in a composition to express emphasis. The dominance of a color, shape, or line within a composition is an effective tool for eliminating confusion or monotony within the composition.

Unity

Unity involves the coordination of all of the visual elements within a composition in support of the ideas being expressed. All of the visual elements in a composition should work together to create a coherent whole. When all of the visual elements are unified, then they are said to be working in harmony. The use of a consistent pattern within a visual image is an excellent example of harmonious unity. Unity and harmony together can also be achieved through the consistent application of form and color, while unity alone can also be achieved through the use of a variety of visual elements such as round or sharp angled shapes.

Visual Style

The expression of a visual style comes from the artist's imagination, sense of adventure, flexibility of mind, and a confidence in the artist's sense of judgment. Creative artists use their imagination to visualize connections and relationships that others do not see. A creative artist is not afraid to try new approaches to solving a problem, and the creative artist has a flexibility that allows them to adjust to different problem situations as they arise. Visual style is the result of choices that the artist makes when they combine the components of the visual language to arrive at the final composition of the image. Making choices regarding how to combine the visual elements and principles for a specific subject is a very personal process, unique for each individual artist. For example, if ten photographers were placed in Times Square New York, and they were asked to compose a photograph, the result would be ten different photographs. The visual components that are used in capturing a photograph are similar to the words, phrases, and intonation choices that are used in human speech.

After years of verbal practice, the verbal choices that are made when speaking become almost an unconscious decision. Similarly, the visual choices that are made while capturing photographic images arise from experience and intuition. The execution of the image capture choices require both reflection and concentration. The development of a unique photographic style combines the photographer's unique interpretation of the subject matter with their openness to the voice of intuition.

The magic of photography lies in the medium's mysterious ability to stop time. The popularity of photography among hobbyists lies in the photographic medium's ability to record events that can cause the viewer to remember the slice of time that the snap shot represents. Taking snap-shots is fun; taking professional quality images is hard work that comes from the heart of the artist.

Learning to Play the Blues

The last two practices involved in the development of a photographic style are *scrutiny* and *imitation*. The best way to understand the processes of scrutiny and imitation is to apply these practices to another art form; for example, learning to play the blues.

Twelve-bar blues is a simple, elementary music form that is the basis for a large body of contemporary popular music. Twelve-bar blues is an auditory language that uses three basic music chords that are repeated in a specific pattern over twelve bars of music. The first step in learning the blues involves listening.

Anyone who wants to learn the blues will find themselves listening to as many of the blues masters as possible. As the listener absorbs the work of various blues masters, they will scrutinize the music to pick out the styles that they like and dislike. This lesson in style development also applies to photography. Good photographers spend a great deal of time reviewing the work of both past and current masters of the visual arts. As the work is scrutinized, good photographers try to identify the aspects of the work that like and dislike.

The final step in learning to play the blues involves the controversial notion of imitation. Pablo Picasso's comments on imitation are very insightful:

> "Copiers don't bother me provided they copy frankly and not for too long a time: if they have any temperament, it'll appear eventually to disclose the personality of an artist. The best means is to make him draw a perfect circle. He won't succeed, but this failed circle will reveal his temperament. Or ask him to copy a painting. His copy will not be exactly like the model, but something that belongs to him will appear." (Pablo Picasso **(Figure 9.2)**, PICASSO ON ART – A Selection of Views, P. 51)

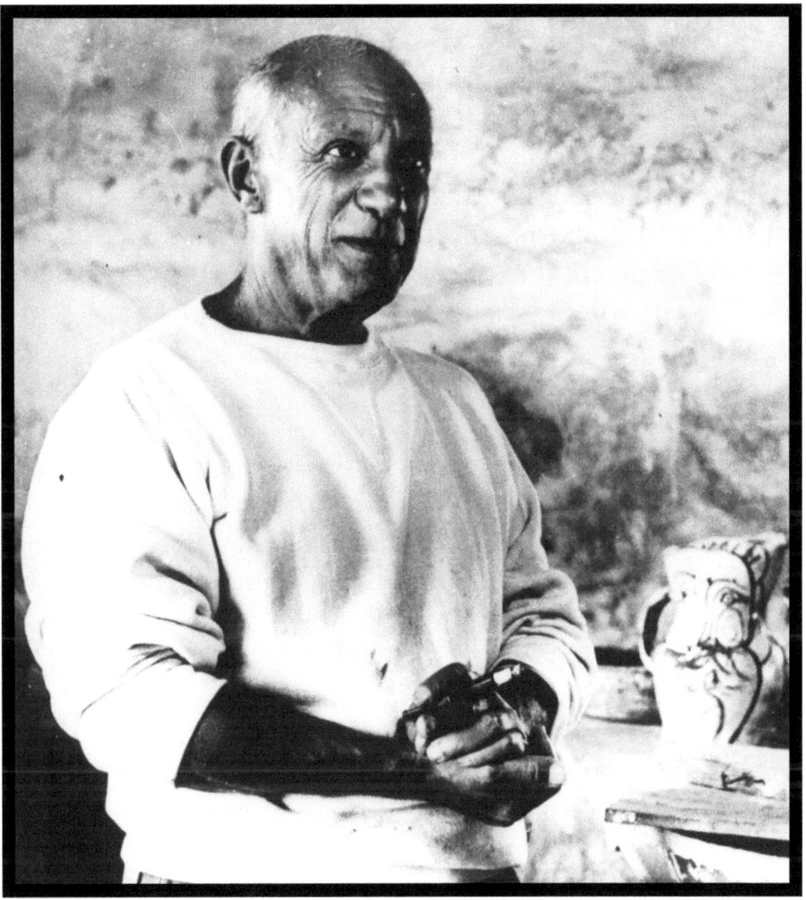

Figure 9.2
Pablo Picasso

The process of emulating the style and technique of the master blues artists will surely help in the development of the aspirant's own musical style. As stated above by Picasso, it is impossible for the artist to exactly replicate the work of a master, and the process of emulation will help to reveal the beginnings of the artist's personal style. Many artists are threatened by imitation, but they do not realize that imitation is the highest form of flattery.

Imitation also puts the artist into a mode of action. An artist cannot develop their own style unless they begin to practice the art. As the artist progresses, they should always take the time to scrutinize their own work in the same way that they analyzed the work of the masters. This self-correction analysis loop will inevitably lead to the emergence of a unique photographic style.

As the photographer's own distinctive style emerges, they should always be open to experimentation with different combinations of the visual elements and principles. Very often, the mistakes that are made, and the questions that are asked during experimentation, become more important than the original experiment. Also, experimentation puts the photographer into the field of action where then are sure to learn new techniques.

The Composition Process

Image composition is one of the most difficult tasks in the visual arts; however, the composition process can be aided by following a pre-defined set of steps or procedures. Some ideas for a composition routine are outlined below.

Avoiding "Buck Fever"

As mentioned above, buck fever is a phenomena that occurs with hunters when they finally encounter their prey. When the prey is encountered, the hunter's adrenaline levels spike and his heart begins to race. Buck fever causes a veil of confusion to descend over the rational mind of the hunter. When buck fever takes over, the hunter's concentration is broken and very often the hunter makes mistakes which result in the prey escaping without a shot being fired.

Photographers experience something similar to buck fever when they encounter an exciting photo opportunity. Ansel Adams' comments on this phenomena are very enlightening:

> "Consideration of design – in the photographic sense – is of extreme importance in visualization of the image. Great enthusiasm for the subject sometimes veils a clear conception of the image of it! An exciting subject may exist in an environment of field and sky, but in the print this "space" may appear as dull, neutral areas of distressingly low interest. Space in nature is one thing, space confined and restricted by picture edges is quite another thing." (Ansel Adams, *The Negative,* P. 129)

Outlined below are some suggested steps that can be incorporated into the photographer's standard image capture routine. The purpose of this routine is to help the photographer avoid the lapses in concentration and subsequent mistakes that can occur when buck fever takes over. The steps outlined below may seen to be highly detailed and time consuming, but eventually these image capture procedures will become second nature for the photographer; they will provide the framework for an image capture ritual that will go a long way to the limiting of mistakes.

Find the Spot

The first decision to be made when composing a photograph involves the location of the tripod. The position of the camera in relation to the subject is one of the most important aspects of the composition process. The subject is always viewed from the eye level of the photographer, so time should be taken to consider different heights for the composition. The composition may be better at a camera angle that is higher or lower than the eye level of the photographer.

Once the camera has been positioned at the appropriate spot, it should be leveled. Most professional cameras have a bubble level which allows the photographer to level both the horizontal and vertical axis of the camera. Small cameras that do not have leveling devices can be leveled with a small plastic string level that can be purchased at the hardware store.

After the camera has been set up, the photographer should take some time to look at the subject and let the image become crystallized in the mind's eye of the photographer. The visualization of the subject image is a key component of the composition process.

Human beings have eyes that are used to view reality, but it is the human brain that interprets reality. The main function of the brain is to order the chaos that is received through the senses. The ordering and filtering of sensory input is a human survival mechanism that has developed through millions of years of evolution. The mental interpretation of the subject image involves some basic precepts:

- The human brain has a tendency to lower the overall contrast of a scene.

- The human brain has a tendency to average the tonal range of the subject toward middle gray.

- Important objects in a scene may seem larger to the human eye than they will appear in the eye of the camera. Mountain ranges and beautiful flowers may seem larger than the camera lens will interpret them because the brain zeroes in on the most striking aspects of the subject. Some professional photographers recommend that after the initial composition is complete, the photographer should take two steps toward the subject.

The final step in the setup process involves an awareness of the subject's light sources. Each scene has one or more light sources. The photographer should take the time to become conscious of the direction of the light source(s). The lighting of the subject with either bright direct light or scattered diffuse light from an overcast sky as well as the subject's lighting from the front, back, or sides present the photographer with different sets of problems that need to be solved. Bright direct sunlight introduces contrast problems that are expressed in the wide range of luminescence values. Front and back lighting of the subject present unique metering problems while side lighting presents the opportunity to use polarizing filters. (see the exposure section of **Chapter 5**)

Frame the Subject

As the photographer begins the composition process, s/he should be sure to keep in mind the notions of visual arrest, visual containment, and natural framing. *Visual arrest* refers to the points in the composition where the viewer's eye is forced to stop; for example, lines which break the frame of the composition contribute to both visual arrest and the containment of the viewer's eye within the image frame **(Figure 9.3)**. The key visual stopping points within the composition are essential to the retention of the viewer's attention. *Visual containment* refers to the process of keeping the viewer's attention contained within the frame of the composition; for example, the horizon or vanishing point for a scene provide natural exit points for the viewer's eye. Finally, the photographer should always be conscious of objects within the scene that have the potential to create a natural frame for the subject **(Figure 9.4)**; for example, vertical trees can be used to vertically frame other aspects of the scene.

These visual considerations culminate in the photographer's choice of the lens focal length that is appropriate for the subject. The lens' focal length could be macro, wide angle, or telephoto. Traditional photography stressed the use of primary focal length lenses over the use of zoom lenses. Primary lenses have a fixed focal length while zoom lenses have a variable focal length. In order to accomplish the variation in focal length, traditional zoom lenses required a large number of glass elements. This large number of glass elements in the older zoom lenses degraded the quality of the image; therefore, professional photographers preferred primary lenses. With the dawn of the visual age, the bias toward primary lenses is no longer justified. Camera manufacturers have invested heavily in optical research which has significantly improved the quality of modern zoom lenses. The choice of a lens focal length should always be driven by the mandate to ***Fill The Frame***!!!

A successful photographic image is an illusion. The illusion is rooted in the photographer's application of visual techniques that make images represented on two dimensional media like a piece of paper or a

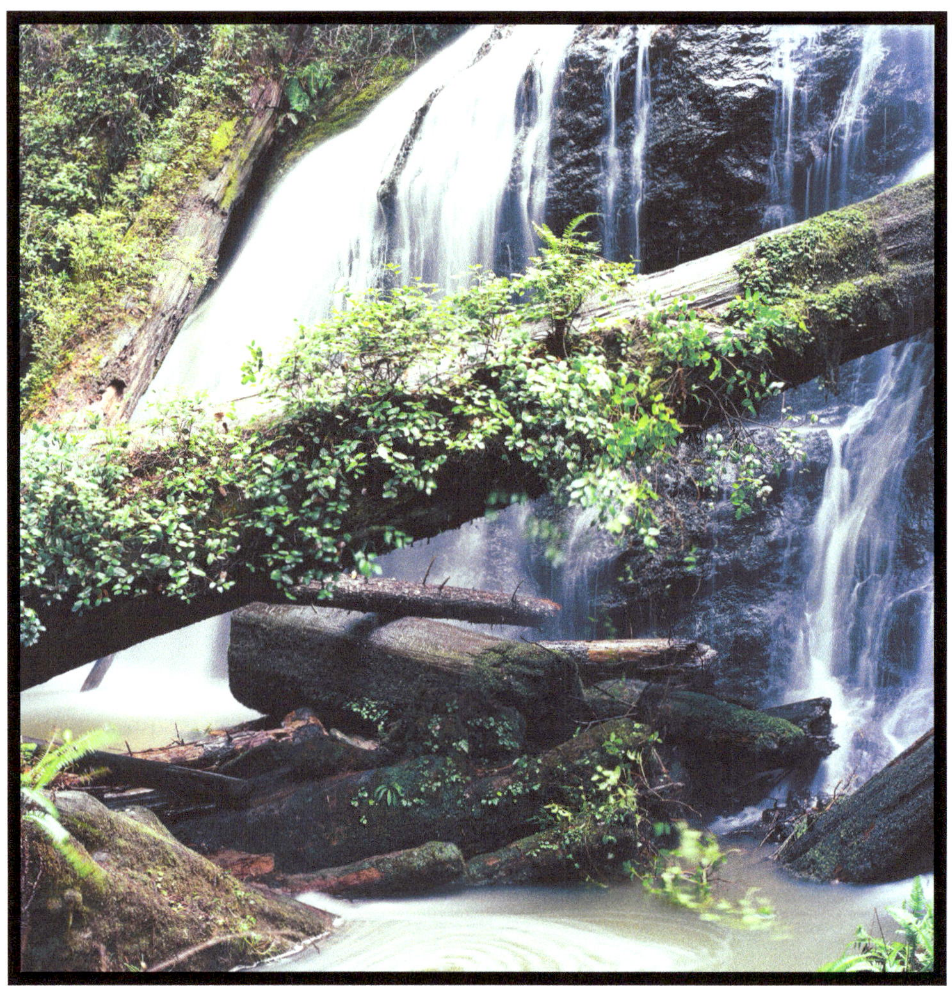

Figure 9.3
Russian Gulch State Park
Mendocino County
California

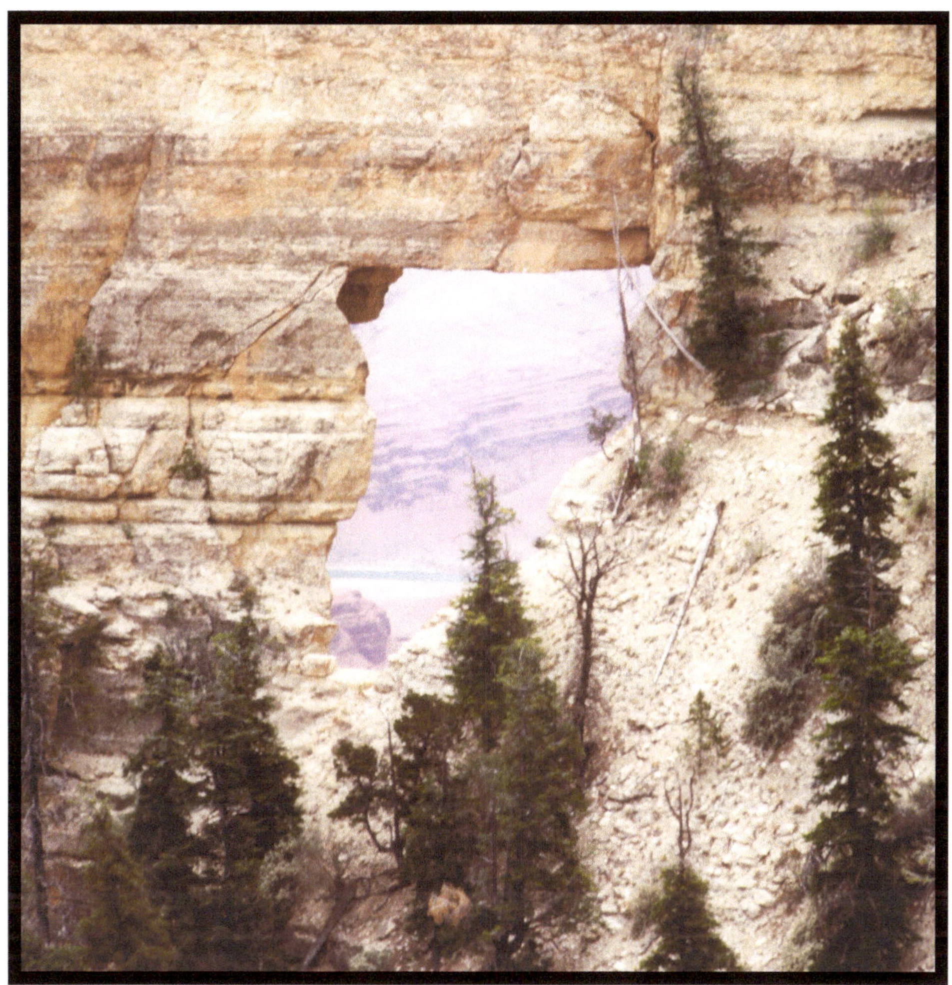

Figure 9.4
Grand Canyon N. P.
Arizona

display screen appear to be three dimensional. These visual techniques include "The Rule of Thirds" and three different types of visual perspective.

The Rule of Thirds is defined as the division of the scene as viewed in the viewfinder or LCD screen into three distinct horizontal and vertical segments **(Figure 9.5)**. The horizontal segments are referred to as the foreground, middle ground, and far ground. For example, objects placed in the foreground of the frame contribute to a feeling of depth for the composition. The three vertical segments are referred to as the left third, the middle third, and the right third. The photographer should pay special attention to the lines in the scene as they flow from one segment of the composition to other segments in the composition.

During the European Renaissance, the rule of thirds was a tool used by artists to correctly replicate the depth proportions of a scene onto the painter's canvas. The painter would view the scene through a frame which used strings to divide the interior of the frame into equally divided horizontal and vertical segments. When the painter reproduced the proportions of the scene that were contained within each segment of the frame, the resulting painting reproduced the illusion of depth that was observed through the frame. Many camera manufacturers offer viewfinder glass with an etched grid that provides the same aid to composition as the renaissance frame.

The points where the top and bottom horizontal middle ground lines intersect the vertical third lines are called power points within the *Rule of Thirds* **(figure 9.5)**. These four power points are important to the composition because the placement of important aspects of the scene at the slightly off center positions creates tension and energy within the composition. Objects placed at the power points with the composition give the image an interesting perspective.

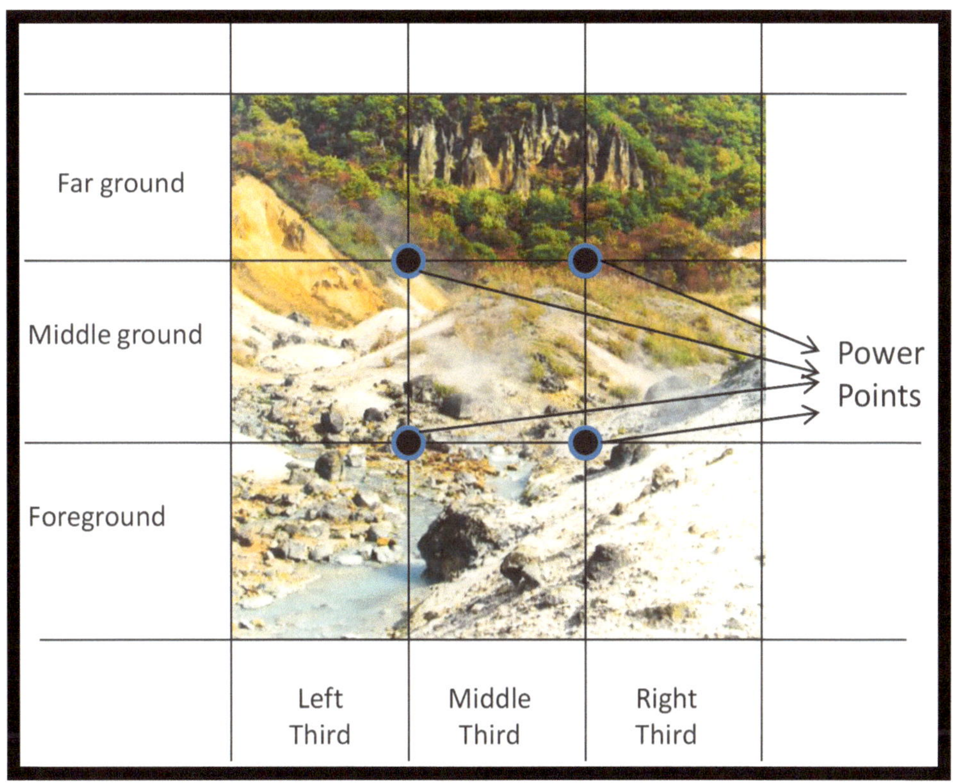

Figure 9.5
Rule of Thirds

The other techniques that can be used to create the illusion of depth come under the title of visual perspective. The five types of visual perspective that contribute to depth perception are:

- Overlapping
- Size Relationships
- Linear Perspective
- Foreshortening
- Aerial Perspective

Overlapping is an effective perspective tool which adds depth to a composition. When one object within a composition overlaps another object, then it seems obvious to the viewer of the image that the overlapped object is behind the foreground object.

Size Relationsips create an illusion of depth because the size of an object appears to become smaller as the distance from the viewer increases. The size of objects in relation to each other objects within a visual image can create the illusion of depth. For example, a large human form in a composition will appear to be closer to the viewer than a smaller human form in the same composition.

Linear Perspective refers to the fact that lines within a visual image can be made to converge at a point on the horizon of the image known as the vanishing point. The vanishing point within the image creates the illusion of depth within the image. For example, parallel railroad tracks appear to converge at a vanishing point on the horizon. The illusion of convergence for the railroad tracks gives depth to the image. A vanishing point is dependent upon the presence of a horizon within the visual image. Images without a horizon have a tendency to appear flat. The horizon always rises to the eye level of the viewer, and the horizon is also a natural exit point from the image frame.

Foreshortening refers to the property of perspective that distorts the geometry of objects based on the angle from which the viewer observes the object. For example, a coffee cup when viewed from the top obviously forms a circle, but when the cup is viewed from the side, the top of the cup appears to be an ellipse. Likewise, the lines of a cube change from a square to an irregular rectangle when the cube is rotated in reference to the viewer. The tools of foreshortening can be used to give the illusion of depth to a visual image.

Aerial Perspective refers to the distortion of an image caused when light is scattered due to atmospheric conditions. The farther an object is from the viewer, the more atmosphere the reflected light must pass through which causes the distortion of the reflected light. As the distance from the subject increases, the contrast and saturation values for the subject decrease. Also, as the distance from the subject increases, the reflected light from the subject shifts toward the blue range of the visual spectrum.

Measure the Light

The next step in the composition process includes the measurement of the range of luminosity for the reflected light from the subject. The measurement of the subject's reflected light can be accomplished with an average meter, a spot meter, or matrix metering. Average meters can be either hand held or imbedded in a viewfinder, and they are the kind of light meters that were traditionally use in film based single lens reflex cameras. Average meters take in the lighting values for large portions of a scene, and they provide an averaged value reading. Average meters are easily fooled by non-average high contrast scenes. Some of the problems with average meters can be avoided by taking several readings.

The most useful tool for measuring the reflected light from a subject is the spot meter. Spot meters measure exposure values for a one degree segment of the subject. The photographer should take as many spot meter readings as are necessary to obtain an accurate range of luminosity for the subject.

Matrix metering is a descendent of a technology known as AMP (automatic multi-pattern metering) which has been available since 1984. Matrix metering is a hybrid of the average and spot metering approaches. For matrix metering, the camera takes several readings at multiple points in the scene, and the camera's computer interprets the multiple readings in order to provide one Zone V exposure value. Matrix metering can be a very powerful tool when it is used with the digital camera's histogram display software.

Even though it takes a little extra time, the spot meter remains the most accurate tool for measuring the three most important luminescence values for the subject:

- The brightest value
- The darkest value
- The middle gray Zone V value

The brightest and darkest luminescence values and the middle zone five value are used to define the correct exposure value for the subject. If the subject does not contain a middle gray value, then a spot meter reading of a gray card should be used to determine the Zone V exposure value. The brightest, darkest, and middle spot meter values should then be mapped onto an eleven square zone chart. As part of his book *The Negative* Ansel Adams included an exposure log which contains a useful zone chart. In the book, Adams gave the reader permission to replicate the log, and this very useful document has been included in Appendix B of this volume.

In the processing of mapping the place and fall of the spot meter readings, close attentions should be paid to Zones II, VIII, and V. For negative film, the photographer needs to pay close attention to the placement of the low values for the darkest aspects of the scene. For transparency film and digital capture media, special attention should be paid to the placement of the high values, or the brightest aspects of the scene.

Once the initial Zone V exposure value has been determined, consideration needs to be given to the exposure value adjustments that are required for any filters that will be used. For example, if a #8 yellow filter will be used for an exposure, then a Zone V exposure value of 13 would need to be adjusted to 12. This is because the #8 yellow filter has a daylight filter factor of 2x or a doubling of exposure. A decrease of exposure by 1 stop effectively doubles the exposure. If the filter being used was a #21 orange filter then the Zone V exposure value would be decreased by 2 to 11 because the filter factor for this filter is 4X.

Finally, the aperture and shutter speed settings need to be derived from the adjusted Zone V exposure value. Each exposure value number represents a range of aperture and shutter speed settings that will yield a correct exposure for the ASA/ISO value being used. For example, the exposure chart in Appendix A demonstrates that for an ASA/ISO setting of 100 with a Zone V exposure value of 13, the aperture/shutter speed settings range from f/1 @ 1/8000 sec. to f/128 @ 2 sec.

The choice of the aperture and shutter speed setting that will be used is determined by the desired depth of field for the scene and the motion of the subject within the composition. Depth of field, as previously stated, refers to the portion of the scene that appears to be in focus. The aperture size determines the depth of field for the scene. For a given exposure value as the aperture size decreases, the depth of field increases and the shutter speed increases. As the aperture size increases for the EV range, the depth of field decreases and the shutter speed increases. If the goal of the photographer is to stop the motion of the subject, then a faster shutter speed is required.

Each of the aperture and shutter speed settings within an EV range has minimum and maximum depth of field values. This refers to the minimum and maximum distance from the camera that will retain sharp focus. Many traditional cameras have a depth of field range index printed on the barrel of the lens. For maximum depth of field, the lens should be set to its hyper-focal distance. The hyper-focal distance for the lens is set by aligning the infinity setting on the focus ring to the correct aperture setting on the lens' depth of field index **(Figure 9.6)**.

If film is being used and the shutter speed is one second or longer, then a final adjustment will need to be made to compensate for reciprocity failure. The exposure section of **Chapter 5** should be consulted for the discussion of reciprocity failure.

If there is any uncertainty about the chosen aperture and shutter speed settings, then it is wise to take a test exposure. Traditionally instant film was used for test exposures, but in the digital age LCD displays with histogram software provide excellent tools for image proofing.

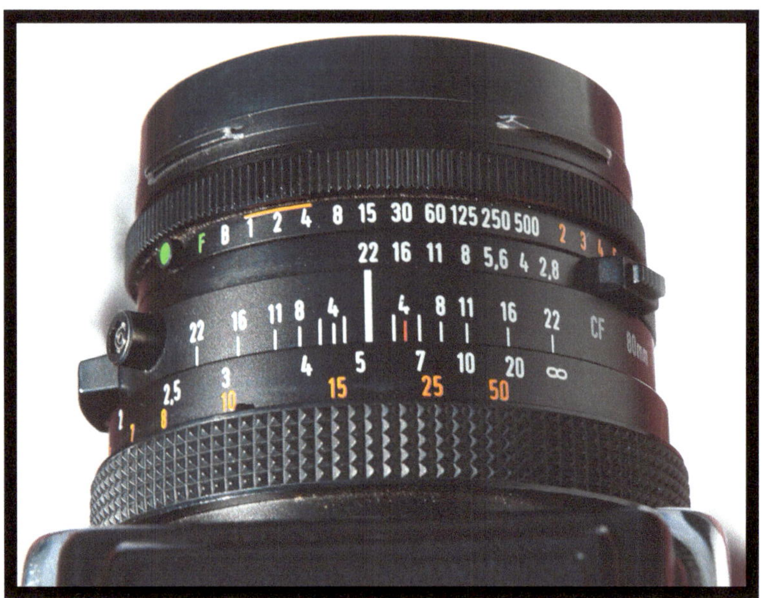

Figure 9.6
Hyper-Focal Distance

The safest approach to actually capturing the scene always includes the capture of multiple images. The practice of capturing multiple images is known as bracketing. Bracketing involves the variation of either the aperture or shutter speed in increments of 1/3, ½, or 1 full stop above and below the Zone V aperture and shutter speed settings. In most cases, this alteration is to the shutter speed setting so that the depth of field controlled by the aperture is not changed. For example, an exposure of f/22 @ ¼ sec., could be bracketed at f/22 @ ½ sec and f/22 @ 1/8 sec. This bracketing approach will result in three different exposures at three different shutter speeds. Many of the new digital cameras provide an automatic bracketing feature. Bracketing increases the probability that a correct exposure will be captured, and it also provides the safety of multiple image capture. In addition, new Photoshop software allows the photographer to combine multiple images in order to compensate for the exposure inadequacies of each individual image. Bracketing is an excellent technique for creating the input to the multiple image combination process.

Panoramas

The use of extreme wide-angle lenses to capture panoramic landscapes has some pit falls. Wide-angle lenses can cause image distortion especially when the image plane of the camera is tilted either up or down. When the image plane is tilted up, the vertical lines in the image tend to converge toward the center of the image. When the image plane of the camera is tilted down, then the vertical lines in the image tend to diverge toward the edge of the frame. One approach to limit the image distortion in wide-angle compositions involves the use of multiple images to represent a panorama, a technique that has been used for years by the likes of Timothy O'Sullivan. Modern panoramic tools provided by Adobe Photoshop and Panotools make the construction of multiple panoramic images much easier than in the past.

The first step in taking multiple panoramic images involves knowing the angle of view for the lens that is being used. Each lens has a specific angle of view that is specified by the manufacturer. Many tripods contain panoramic heads that have degree indices as part of the tripod head. The degree index combined with the angle of view for the lens helps to make a decision on how many images will be needed for the panorama.

The gridded view finder is also helpful in keeping each segment of the panorama correctly aligned. As the view is moved from one segment of the panorama to the next, an effort should be made to keep the specific lines of the grid aligned with the lines from the previous image. The camera should be kept level by using a bubble level, and a small portion of the edge of each image should be overlapped with the adjoining image. Also, the photographer should be conscious of the fact that the exposure may change as the camera pans from one segment to the next. The spot meter is very useful for determining the change in exposure from one segment to the next. Multiple image panoramas are a great way to capture majestic landscapes without the image distortion that you encounter with wide angle lenses.

Document the Work

The last and probably most important step in the composition process involves the documentation of the work. It is true that modern digital cameras provide a wealth of data about the photographs, but this metadata (data about data) is only useful if a computer is used to view the image and data.

Appendix B contains a data sheet that was developed by Ansel Adams to record all of the critical information regarding the images that are captured. Adams' data sheet includes places for recording the date, film type, lens, filter, and aperture/shutter speed information for each frame. This record of image data will provide critical information when the images are sorted and organized. Nothing is more frustrating than trying to sort through a mountain of images several weeks after they were captured without an exposure record and notes for guidance. The image record and any additional notes associated with the image record are indispensable learning tools and organizational aids that can be used when sorting through your finished images.

Time should be taken to record as much of the image data as possible. Notes regarding range of luminescence, test exposure values, direction of the light source, and other impressions of the scene can provide powerful feed back when the final result is analyzed.

Break the Rules – Your Choices

The world is filled with millions of camera owners who believe that they are experts in the art of photography. There are many photographers, both amateur and professional, who will not hesitate to instruct you in the right and wrong ways to capture images. Keep an open mind and listen to others' ideas, but remember that the final choices are yours. Visualize and compose your images the way you want to see them. Remember that the final image should speak to you – or why else would you waste your time capturing the image? The final image may not speak to some of the viewers, but that's OK – the final image should reflect your view of the world.

Once you have established a composition routine that works for you, then you should try to experiment with variations in the routine that will improve the end result. Be brave, and always remember that how you arrive at the final product that you have visualized is your own personal choice. Techniques that work for others may not work for you, but in the end be sure to be true to your own vision.

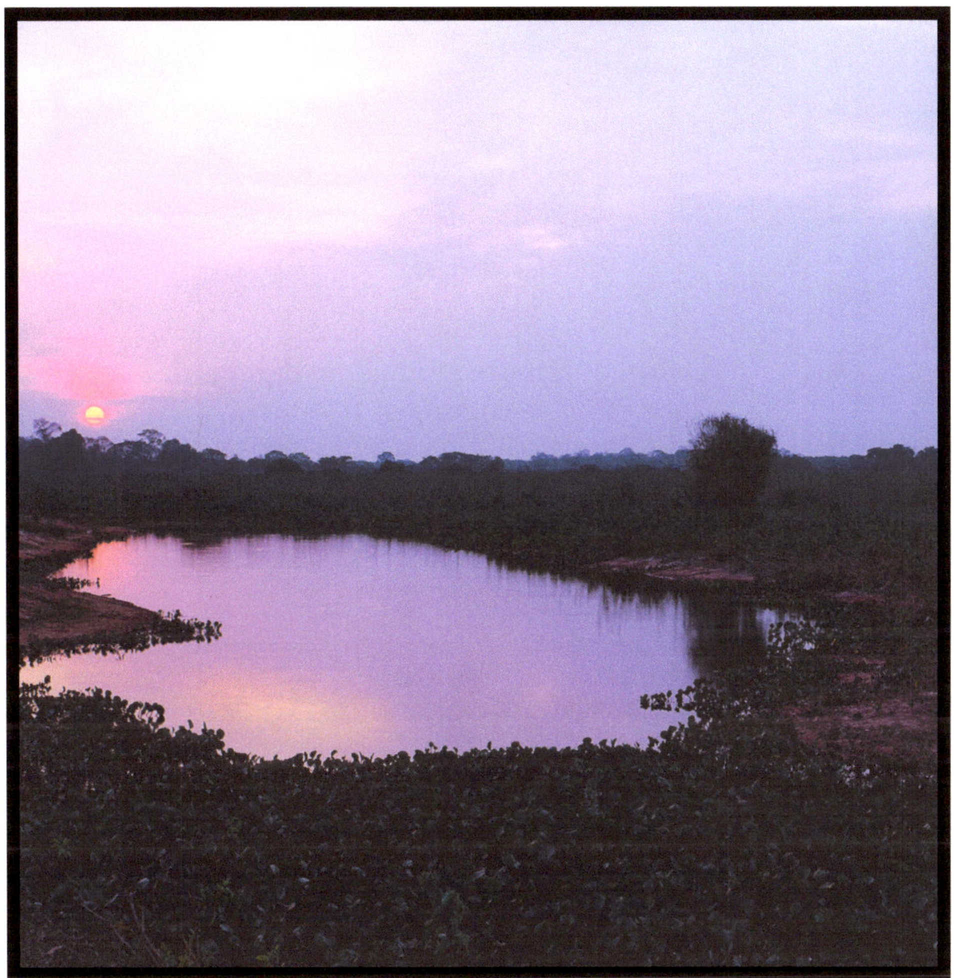

Figure 9.7
Sunset
Pantanal N. P.
Brazil

The owl of Minerva bigins its flight
only with the coming of the dusk

-- Georg Wilhelm Fredrich Hegel

Appendix A - Exposure Value (EV)

Figure A.1

	ISO 50														
EV/Aperture	**1**	**1.4**	**2**	**2.8**	**4**	**5.6**	**8**	**11**	**16**	**22**	**32**	**45**	**64**	**90**	**128**
1	1	2	4	8	16	32	64	132	264	528	1056	1112	2224	4448	8896
2	1/2	1	2	4	8	16	32	64	132	264	528	1056	1112	2224	4448
3	1/4	1/2	1	2	4	8	16	32	64	132	264	528	1056	1112	2224
4	1/8	1/4	1/2	1	2	4	8	16	32	64	132	264	528	1056	1112
5	1/15	1/8	1/4	1/2	1	2	4	8	16	32	64	132	264	528	1056
6	1/30	1/15	1/8	1/4	1/2	1	2	4	8	16	32	64	132	264	528
7	1/60	1/30	1/15	1/8	1/4	1/2	1	2	4	8	16	32	64	132	264
8	1/125	1/60	1/30	1/15	1/8	1/4	1/2	1	2	4	8	16	32	64	132
9	1/250	1/125	1/60	1/30	1/15	1/8	1/4	1/2	1	2	4	8	16	32	64
10	1/500	1/250	1/125	1/60	1/30	1/15	1/8	1/4	1/2	1	2	4	8	16	32
11	1/1000	1/500	1/250	1/125	1/60	1/30	1/15	1/8	1/4	1/2	1	2	4	8	16
12	1/2000	1/1000	1/500	1/250	1/125	1/60	1/30	1/15	1/8	1/4	1/2	1	2	4	8
13	1/4000	1/2000	1/1000	1/500	1/250	1/125	1/60	1/30	1/15	1/8	1/4	1/2	1	2	4
14	1/8000	1/4000	1/2000	1/1000	1/500	1/250	1/125	1/60	1/30	1/15	1/8	1/4	1/2	1	2
15	1/16000	1/8000	1/4000	1/2000	1/1000	1/500	1/250	1/125	1/60	1/30	1/15	1/8	1/4	1/2	1
16	1/32000	1/16000	1/8000	1/4000	1/2000	1/1000	1/500	1/250	1/125	1/60	1/30	1/15	1/8	1/4	1/2
17	1/64000	1/32000	1/16000	1/8000	1/4000	1/2000	1/1000	1/500	1/250	1/125	1/60	1/30	1/15	1/8	1/4
18	1/128000	1/64000	1/32000	1/16000	1/8000	1/4000	1/2000	1/1000	1/500	1/250	1/125	1/60	1/30	1/15	1/8
19	1/256000	1/128000	1/64000	1/32000	1/16000	1/8000	1/4000	1/2000	1/1000	1/500	1/250	1/125	1/60	1/30	1/15
20	1/512000	1/256000	1/128000	1/64000	1/32000	1/16000	1/8000	1/4000	1/2000	1/1000	1/500	1/250	1/125	1/60	1/30

Figure A.2

	ISO 100														
EV/Aperture	1	1.4	2	2.8	4	5.6	8	11	16	22	32	45	64	90	128
1	1/2	1	2	4	8	16	32	64	132	264	528	1056	1112	2224	4448
2	1/4	1/2	1	2	4	8	16	32	64	132	264	528	1056	1112	2224
3	1/8	1/4	1/2	1	2	4	8	16	32	64	132	264	528	1056	1112
4	1/15	1/8	1/4	1/2	1	2	4	8	16	32	64	132	264	528	1056
5	1/30	1/15	1/8	1/4	1/2	1	2	4	8	16	32	64	132	264	528
6	1/60	1/30	1/15	1/8	1/4	1/2	1	2	4	8	16	32	64	132	264
7	1/125	1/60	1/30	1/15	1/8	1/4	1/2	1	2	4	8	16	32	64	132
8	1/250	1/125	1/60	1/30	1/15	1/8	1/4	1/2	1	2	4	8	16	32	64
9	1/500	1/250	1/125	1/60	1/30	1/15	1/8	1/4	1/2	1	2	4	8	16	32
10	1/1000	1/500	1/250	1/125	1/60	1/30	1/15	1/8	1/4	1/2	1	2	4	8	16
11	1/2000	1/1000	1/500	1/250	1/125	1/60	1/30	1/15	1/8	1/4	1/2	1	2	4	8
12	1/4000	1/2000	1/1000	1/500	1/250	1/125	1/60	1/30	1/15	1/8	1/4	1/2	1	2	4
13	1/8000	1/4000	1/2000	1/1000	1/500	1/250	1/125	1/60	1/30	1/15	1/8	1/4	1/2	1	2
14	1/16000	1/8000	1/4000	1/2000	1/1000	1/500	1/250	1/125	1/60	1/30	1/15	1/8	1/4	1/2	1
15	1/32000	1/16000	1/8000	1/4000	1/2000	1/1000	1/500	1/250	1/125	1/60	1/30	1/15	1/8	1/4	1/2
16	1/64000	1/32000	1/16000	1/8000	1/4000	1/2000	1/1000	1/500	1/250	1/125	1/60	1/30	1/15	1/8	1/4
17	1/128000	1/64000	1/32000	1/16000	1/8000	1/4000	1/2000	1/1000	1/500	1/250	1/125	1/60	1/30	1/15	1/8
18	1/256000	1/128000	1/64000	1/32000	1/16000	1/8000	1/4000	1/2000	1/1000	1/500	1/250	1/125	1/60	1/30	1/15
19	1/512000	1/256000	1/128000	1/64000	1/32000	1/16000	1/8000	1/4000	1/2000	1/1000	1/500	1/250	1/125	1/60	1/30
20	1/1024000	1/512000	1/256000	1/128000	1/64000	1/32000	1/16000	1/8000	1/4000	1/2000	1/1000	1/500	1/250	1/125	1/60

Figure A.3

	ISO 200														
EV/Aperture	**1**	**1.4**	**2**	**2.8**	**4**	**5.6**	**8**	**11**	**16**	**22**	**32**	**45**	**64**	**90**	**128**
1	1/4	1/2	1	2	4	8	16	32	64	132	264	528	1056	1112	2224
2	1/8	1/4	1/2	1	2	4	8	16	32	64	132	264	528	1056	1112
3	1/15	1/8	1/4	1/2	1	2	4	8	16	32	64	132	264	528	1056
4	1/30	1/15	1/8	1/4	1/2	1	2	4	8	16	32	64	132	264	528
5	1/60	1/30	1/15	1/8	1/4	1/2	1	2	4	8	16	32	64	132	264
6	1/125	1/60	1/30	1/15	1/8	1/4	1/2	1	2	4	8	16	32	64	132
7	1/250	1/125	1/60	1/30	1/15	1/8	1/4	1/2	1	2	4	8	16	32	64
8	1/500	1/250	1/125	1/60	1/30	1/15	1/8	1/4	1/2	1	2	4	8	16	32
9	1/1000	1/500	1/250	1/125	1/60	1/30	1/15	1/8	1/4	1/2	1	2	4	8	16
10	1/2000	1/1000	1/500	1/250	1/125	1/60	1/30	1/15	1/8	1/4	1/2	1	2	4	8
11	1/4000	1/2000	1/1000	1/500	1/250	1/125	1/60	1/30	1/15	1/8	1/4	1/2	1	2	4
12	1/8000	1/4000	1/2000	1/1000	1/500	1/250	1/125	1/60	1/30	1/15	1/8	1/4	1/2	1	2
13	1/16000	1/8000	1/4000	1/2000	1/1000	1/500	1/250	1/125	1/60	1/30	1/15	1/8	1/4	1/2	1
14	1/32000	1/16000	1/8000	1/4000	1/2000	1/1000	1/500	1/250	1/125	1/60	1/30	1/15	1/8	1/4	1/2
15	1/64000	1/32000	1/16000	1/8000	1/4000	1/2000	1/1000	1/500	1/250	1/125	1/60	1/30	1/15	1/8	1/4
16	1/128000	1/64000	1/32000	1/16000	1/8000	1/4000	1/2000	1/1000	1/500	1/250	1/125	1/60	1/30	1/15	1/8
17	1/256000	1/128000	1/64000	1/32000	1/16000	1/8000	1/4000	1/2000	1/1000	1/500	1/250	1/125	1/60	1/30	1/15
18	1/512000	1/256000	1/128000	1/64000	1/32000	1/16000	1/8000	1/4000	1/2000	1/1000	1/500	1/250	1/125	1/60	1/30
19	1/1024000	1/512000	1/256000	1/128000	1/64000	1/32000	1/16000	1/8000	1/4000	1/2000	1/1000	1/500	1/250	1/125	1/60
20	1/2048000	1/1024000	1/512000	1/256000	1/128000	1/64000	1/32000	1/16000	1/8000	1/4000	1/2000	1/1000	1/500	1/250	1/125

Figure A.4

EV/ Aperture	ISO 400														
	1	**1.4**	**2**	**2.8**	**4**	**5.6**	**8**	**11**	**16**	**22**	**32**	**45**	**64**	**90**	**128**
1	1/8	1/4	1/2	1	2	4	8	16	32	64	132	264	528	1056	1112
2	1/15	1/8	1/4	1/2	1	2	4	8	16	32	64	132	264	528	1056
3	1/30	1/15	1/8	1/4	1/2	1	2	4	8	16	32	64	132	264	528
4	1/60	1/30	1/15	1/8	1/4	1/2	1	2	4	8	16	32	64	132	264
5	1/125	1/60	1/30	1/15	1/8	1/4	1/2	1	2	4	8	16	32	64	132
6	1/250	1/125	1/60	1/30	1/15	1/8	1/4	1/2	1	2	4	8	16	32	64
7	1/500	1/250	1/125	1/60	1/30	1/15	1/8	1/4	1/2	1	2	4	8	16	32
8	1/1000	1/500	1/250	1/125	1/60	1/30	1/15	1/8	1/4	1/2	1	2	4	8	16
9	1/2000	1/1000	1/500	1/250	1/125	1/60	1/30	1/15	1/8	1/4	1/2	1	2	4	8
10	1/4000	1/2000	1/1000	1/500	1/250	1/125	1/60	1/30	1/15	1/8	1/4	1/2	1	2	4
11	1/8000	1/4000	1/2000	1/1000	1/500	1/250	1/125	1/60	1/30	1/15	1/8	1/4	1/2	1	2
12	1/16000	1/8000	1/4000	1/2000	1/1000	1/500	1/250	1/125	1/60	1/30	1/15	1/8	1/4	1/2	1
13	1/32000	1/16000	1/8000	1/4000	1/2000	1/1000	1/500	1/250	1/125	1/60	1/30	1/15	1/8	1/4	½
14	1/64000	1/32000	1/16000	1/8000	1/4000	1/2000	1/1000	1/500	1/250	1/125	1/60	1/30	1/15	1/8	¼
15	1/128000	1/64000	1/32000	1/16000	1/8000	1/4000	1/2000	1/1000	1/500	1/250	1/125	1/60	1/30	1/15	1/8
16	1/256000	1/128000	1/64000	1/32000	1/16000	1/8000	1/4000	1/2000	1/1000	1/500	1/250	1/125	1/60	1/30	1/15
17	1/512000	1/256000	1/128000	1/64000	1/32000	1/16000	1/8000	1/4000	1/2000	1/1000	1/500	1/250	1/125	1/60	1/30
18	1/1024000	1/512000	1/256000	1/128000	1/64000	1/32000	1/16000	1/8000	1/4000	1/2000	1/1000	1/500	1/250	1/125	1/60
19	1/2048000	1/1024000	1/512000	1/256000	1/128000	1/64000	1/32000	1/16000	1/8000	1/4000	1/2000	1/1000	1/500	1/250	1/125
20	1/4096000	1/2048000	1/1024000	1/512000	1/256000	1/128000	1/64000	1/32000	1/16000	1/8000	1/4000	1/2000	1/1000	1/500	1/250

Appendix B - Data Sheet

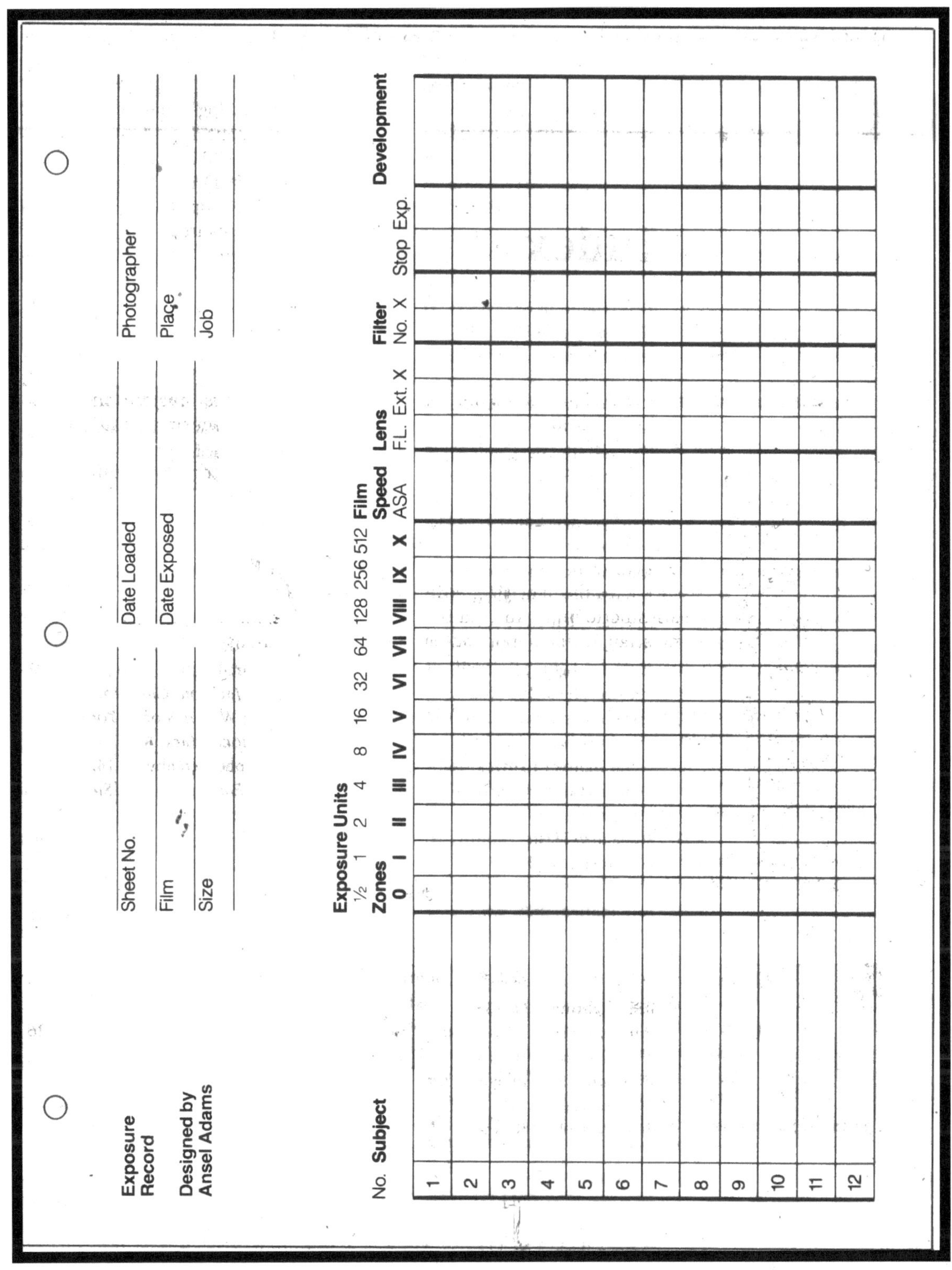

Exposure Record

Designed by Ansel Adams

Sheet No.

Film

Size

Date Loaded

Date Exposed

Photographer

Place

Job

No.	**Subject**	**Exposure Units** ½	1	2	4	8	16	32	64	128	256	512	**Film Speed**	**Lens**			**Filter**				**Development**
		Zones 0	**I**	**II**	**III**	**IV**	**V**	**VI**	**VII**	**VIII**	**IX**	**X**	ASA	F.L.	Ext.	X	No.	X	Stop	Exp.	
1																					
2																					
3																					
4																					
5																					
6																					
7																					
8																					
9																					
10																					
11																					
12																					

Appendix C - Illustrations

Illustrations			
Chapter	**Illustration**	**Description**	**Attribution**
Introduction	Figure I.1	Komics Kid	Manzanita Photography
One	Figure 1.1	Gordon Moore	Emelio Segr Visual Archives
One	Figure 1.2	William Shockley John Bardeen Walter Brattain	Emelio Segr Visual Archives
One	Figure 1.3	Jack Kilby	Courtesy of Texas Instruments
One	Figure 1.4	Robert Noyce Gordon Moore	Wikimedia Commons
One	Figure 1.5	David Coons	Wikimedia Commons
One	Figure 1.6	George E. Smith	Wikimedia Commons
One	Figure 1.7	Willard Boyle	Wikimedia Commons
One	Figure 1.8	Casio QV-10	Courtesy of Rodger Carter
One	Figure 1.9	John Knoll	Courtesy of Jeff Schewe
One	Figure 1.10	Thomas Knoll	Courtesy of Jeff Schewe
One	Figure 1.11	Jon Cone	Courtesy of Jon Cone
One	Figure 1.12	Graham Nash R. Mac Holbert	Courtesy of R. Mac Holbert
Two	Figure 2.1	Thomas Aquinas	Bridgeman Art Resource
Two	Figure 2.2	James Joyce	University of Buffalo Library
Two	Figure 2.3	Edward Weston	Bridgeman Art Resource
Two	Figure 2.4	Ansel Adams	Bridgeman Art Resource
Three	Figure 3.1	Joseph Campbell	The Joseph Campbell Foundation
Three	Figure 3.2	The Electromagnetic Spectrum	Courtesy of Cyberphysics.co.uk
Three	Figure 3.3	Color Temperature	Manzanita Press
Three	Figure 3.4	Wave Diffraction Patterns	Courtesy of Dicklyon at en.wikipedia [Public domain], from Wikimedia Commons
Three	Figure 3.5	Refraction	Alamy
Three	Figure 3.6	James Clerk Maxwell	Emelio Segr Visual Archives
Three	Figure 3.7	Richard Feynman	Emelio Segr Visual Archives

Illustrations			
Chapter	**Illustration**	**Description**	**Attribution**
Four	Figure 4.1	Grayscale	Manzanita Press
Four	Figure 4.2	Grayscale Zones	Manzanita Press
Four	Figure 4.3	Color Wheel	Wikimedia Commons
Four	Figure 4.4	HSB Color Model	Wikimedia Commons
Four	Figure 4.5	Paint Color Space	Alamy
Four	Figure 4.6	Lab Color Space	Wikimedia Commons
Four	Figure 4.7	RGB Color Space	Wikimedia Commons
Four	Figure 4.8	CMYK Color Space	Wikimedia Commons
Four	Figure 4.9	Autumn Leaves	Manzanita Photography
Five	Figure 5.1	Standard Exposure Model	Manzanita Press
Five	Figure 5.2	Focal Length	Manzanita Press
Five	Figure 5.3	The Characteristic Curve	Sprwals Educational Foundation
Five	Figure 5.4	Solarization (Man Ray)	Art Resource
Five	Figure 5.5	Emulsion	Courtesy of William Schneider http://www.ohio.edu/PEOPLE/schneidw/index.html
Five	Firure 5.6 (Left)	Film Grain	Harman technology Limited
	Figure 5.6 (Right)	Film Grain	Wikimedia Commons
Five	Figure 5.7	The Bayer Filter	Wikimedia Commons
Five	Figure 5.8	Yankee Harbour	Manzanita Photography
Six	Figure 6.1	Lower Yellowstone Falls	Manzanita Photography
Six	Figure 6.2	Polarized Light	Manzanita Photography
Six	Figure 6.3	Yellow Mountain W.H.S.	Manzanita Photography

Illustrations			
Chapter	**Illustration**	**Description**	**Attribution**
Seven	Figure 7.1	Venus and the Waning Moon	Manzanita Photography
Seven	Figure 7.2	Pleiades Star Cluster	Manzanita Photography
Seven	Figure 7.3	Grand Canyon N. P.	Manzanita Photography
Seven	Figure 7.4	Phillip Burton Wilderness	Manzanita Photography
Seven	Figure 7.5	King George Island	Manzanita Photography
Seven	Figure 7.6	Lassen N. P.	Manzanita Photography
Seven	Figure 7.7	Lassen N. P.	Manzanita Photography
Seven	Figure 7.8	Cape Mendocino	Manzanita Photography
Seven	Figure 7.9	Mendocino Coast	Manzanita Photography
Seven	Figure 7.10	Ansel Adams W. A.	Manzanita Photography
Seven	Figure 7.11	Ishi W. A.	Manzanita Photography
Seven	Figure 7.12	Channel Islands N. P.	Manzanita Photography
Seven	Figure 7.13	Three Sisters W. A.	Manzanita Photography
Seven	Figure 7.14	The Limb Effect	Manzanita Photography
Seven	Figure 7.15	Rockefeller Grove	Manzanita Photography
Eight	Figure 8.1	Diane Arbus	Getty Images
Eight	Figure 8.2	Anna May Wong/E. Steichen	Conde Nast
Eight	Figure 8.3	Apples/Apple Pie	Scott Bauer - Wikimedia Commons
Eight	Figure 8.4	Lighting Diagram	Manzanita Press
Nine	Figure 9.1	Paul Strand	Art Resource
Nine	Figure 9.2	Pablo Picasso	Bridgeman/Getty
Nine	Figure 9.3	Russian Gulch	Manzanita Photography
Nine	Figure 9.4	Grand Canyon	Manzanita Photography
Nine	Figure 9.5	Rule of Thirds	Manzanita Press
Nine	Figure 9.6	Hyper-Focal Distance	Manzanita Photography
Nine	Figure 9.7	Pantanal National Park	Manzanita Photography

Bibliography

Internet References

http://en.wikipedia.org

www.calumet.com

www.bhphotovideo.com

http://www.photo.net/history/timeline#

Literary References

A History of Photography
The Musee d'Orsay Collection 1939-1925
Edited by Francoise Heilbrun
Editions Skira Flammarion
Paris, France

Adams, Ansel,
Examples: The Making of 40 Photographs
Little, Brown and Company
Boston

———,
The Camera
A New York Graphic Society Book
Little, Brown and Company
Boston

———,
The Negative
A New York Graphic Society Book
Little, Brown and Company
Boston

———,
The Print
A New York Graphic Society Book
Little, Brown and Company
Boston

Adobe Photoshop CS
User Guide
Adobe Systems Incorporated

Adobe Photoshop CS2
User Guide
Adobe Systems Incorporated

Baierlein, Ralph,
Newton to Einstein
Trail of Light
Cambridge University Press

Brayer, Elizabeth,
George Eastman – A Biography
The Johns Hopkins University Press
Baltimore and London

Campbell, Joseph,
Myths of Light
New World Library
Novato, California

———,
The Mythic Image
Princeton University Press
Princeton, New Jersey

_____,
Thou Art That
Transforming Religious Metaphor
New World Library
Novato, California

Coomaraswamy, Ananda K.,
Christian & Oriental Philosophy of Art
Dover Publications, Inc.
New York

_____,
The Door in the Sky
Princeton University Press
Princeton, New Jersey

Dykinga, Jack
Large Format Nature Photography
Amphoto
An Imprint of Watson-Guptill Publications
New York

Eismann, Katrin, and Duggan, Sean,
The Creative Digital Darkroom
O'Reilly
Beijing, Cambridge, Farnham, Koln, Paris, Sebastopol, Taipei, Tokyo

Fraser, Bruce
Camera Raw with Adobe Photoshop CS2
Peachpit Press
1249 Eighth Street
Berkeley, Ca 94710

_____, and Blatner, David
Real World Photoshop CS2
Peachpit Press
Berkeley, CA

Greene, Brian,
The Elegant Universe
W. W. Norton
New York, London

———,
The Fabric of the Cosmos
Vintage Books
New York

Grey, Tim,
Photoshop **CS2 Workflow**
Sybex Publishing
1151 Marina Village Parkway
Alameda, Ca 94510

Gustavson, Todd,
Camera
A History of Photography from Daguerreotype to Digital
Sterling Innovation
An imprint of Sterling Publishing Co.
New York and London

Haynes, Barry, and Crumpler, Wendy, and Duggan, Sean,
Photoshop Artistry
New Riders
Berkeley, CA

Isaacson, Walter,
The Innovators: How a Group of Hackers, Geniuses, and Geeks Created the Digital Revolution
Simon & Schuster
New York, New York

Jeffrey, Ian,
How to Read a Photograph
Harry N. Abrams, Inc.
New York, New York

———,
Photography a Concise History
Thames and Hudson
London and New York

Johnson, Chris,
The Practical Zone System for Film and Digital Photography
Focal Press
Boston, New York, San Francisco

Johnson, Harald
Mastering Digital Printing
Thomson Course Technology
25 Thomson Place
Boston, MA 02210

Johnson, Stephen,
On Digital Photography
O'Reilly
Beijing, Cambridge, Farnham, Koln, Paris, Sebastopol, Taipei, Tokyo

Jung, Carl
Mysterium Coniunctionis
Bollingen Series
Princeton University Press

Joyce, James,
A Portrait of the Artist as a Young Man
Bantam Books
New York, Toronto, London, Sydney, Auckland

King, Julie,
Everyday Photoshop for Photographers
McGraw-Hill/Osborne
2100 Powell Street, 10th Floor
Emeryville, California 94608

Mahon, Basil,
The Man Who Changed Everything
The Life of James Clerk Maxwell
Wiley

Moore, Robert, and Gillete, Douglas,
King Warrior Magician Lover
Rediscovering the Archetypes of the Mature Masculine
Harper SanFrancisco
A Division of Harper Collins Publishers

Newhall, Beaumont,
The History of Photography
The Museum of Modern Art
Distributed by Bulfinch Press
Little, Brown and Company

Newton, Sir Isaac,
Optics
Great Books of the Western World
Encyclopedia Britanica
Chicago

Peterson, Bryan,
Learning to See Creatively
Amphoto Books

Rosenblum, Naomi,
A World History of Photography
Abbeville Press Publishers
New York and London

Shopenhauer, Arthur
On Vision and Colors
Berg Publishers
Oxford, England
Providence, RI

Strobel, Leslie, and Compton, John, and Current, Ira, and Zakia, Richard,
Basic Photographic Materials and Processes
Focal Press
Boston, Oxford, Auckland, Johannesburg, Melbourne, New Delhi

Stroebel, Leslie,
View Camera Technique
Focal Press
Boston, Oxford, Auckland, Johannesburg, Melbourne, New Delhi

von Goethe, Johann Wolfgang
Theory of Colours
The MIT Press
Cambridge, Mass.

White, Minor, and Zakia, Richard, and Lorenz, Peter,
The New Zone System Manual
Morgan & Morgan, Inc.
Dobbs Ferry, New York

Index

C

D

E

F

M

N

O

P

Q

R

S

T

U

V

W

X

Z

www.ingramcontent.com/pod-product-compliance
Lightning Source LLC
LaVergne TN
LVHW070117110826
845147LV00002B/138

* 9 7 8 0 9 9 0 7 4 7 4 0 6 *